FREE WILL BAPTIST HISTORY

Exploring Our Origins & Identity

ROBERT E. PICIRILLI

© 2019 by Robert E. Picirilli

Published by Randall House Publications
114 Bush Road
Nashville, TN 37217

All rights reserved. No part of this publication may be reproduced, stored in a retrieval system, or transmitted in any form or by any means—electronic, mechanical, photocopy, recording, or any other means—except for brief quotation in critical reviews, without the prior permission of the publisher.

Printed in the United States of America

13-ISBN 9781614841081

Table of Contents

Preface v

Chapter 1 1
"We Give Ourselves to One Another": The Story of the Free Will Baptist Church Covenant

Chapter 2 35
The Spread of Free Will Baptists From North Carolina to South Carolina: Redding Moore and the First Churches and Preachers, 1816-1849

Chapter 3 55
United Baptist Origins of Free Will Baptists in Georgia—and in Southeast Alabama and West Florida

Chapter 4 109
The Founding of the Free Will Baptist Work in Texas: The Story of A. M. Stewart From Georgia

Chapter 5 131
Free Will Baptist Participation in Unity Movements in the South, 1870 to 1910

Chapter 6 179
The Free Will Baptist School in Unicoi, Tennessee: A Story of J. W. Lucas and Free Will Baptists of the South and North, 1890-1910

Chapter 7 233
The Christian Workers Institutes, 1941-52

Appendix 269
An addition and correction to chapter five of the volume, *Little Known Chapters in Free Will Baptist History*

Preface

There is more than one theory of Free Will Baptist history among those of us who do research and writing on the subject. Perhaps the reader will find it interesting to know something about the different points of view.

One view is what I call purist. Those who take this approach seem to think that our history is simply a fairly well-defined lineage from the English General Baptists through Paul Palmer in North Carolina and on from there. Anything else is relatively incidental and hasn't contributed much to who or what we are. The important thing, for this approach, is to uncover how the movement spread from North Carolina southward and westward, with its theology and practice defining the denomination.

At the opposite extreme is a view that Free Will Baptists are a hodge-podge of different movements, melded together in a kettle of origins relatively independent of each other. We're a "duke's mixture," they say, and there's not much of a tie that binds us.

Yet another approach to Free Will Baptist history is to focus on the heroes of the Free Will Baptists of the North, starting with Benjamin Randall. They were the greatest Free Will Baptists, it seems, and we can delight in their stories and measure ourselves in the light of the movement they shaped.

I would contend that none of the views is entirely wrong or basically right. There are some truths in each of them, to be sure, but the best understanding of Free Will Baptist history, as I see it, takes another approach. To use the metaphor of a stream of water, like a river, there is in our history a "mainstream." That stream is the movement that began in North Carolina in 1727 with Paul Palmer. Its influence moved southward and westward and continues to flow to this day. But as this mainstream has developed, it has been fed by various tributaries that were at first independent of it and have made their own contributions to the story.

One of the more important tributaries is to be found in the remnants of the Randall movement that did not go with the main body of the Free Will Baptist denomination into the Northern (now American) Baptists. In recognizing this, we need to avoid errors on both sides. On one side, we need to understand that *their history is not our history, as such*. They were not the Free Will Baptist denomination we know. The Randall movement was a different Free Will Baptist denomination, and it went out of existence of its own accord. But on the other side, we need to avoid thinking that they were unimportant for us. Their history *is* part of the history of some of us. Indeed, there is a significant segment of *our* Free Will Baptist denomination that rightly understands itself—in part, not in whole—in light of the Randall movement. This segment probably includes some of the present-day Free Will Baptists of West Virginia, Kentucky, Ohio, Illinois, Missouri, and Texas, at the least—and perhaps others. Even so, this is not the mainstream. It is one of the tributaries.

Another tributary, not as large but nonetheless significant, is to be found in the movement known historically as Separate Baptists. I have shown, in a previous volume entitled *Little Known Chapters in Free Will Baptist History*, that the Free Will Baptists of the Cumberland Association in Middle Tennessee originated in this movement. Although this may be a smaller tributary, it is not an insignificant one. Furthermore, I strongly suspect that the Separate Baptists contributed more to us than just the Cumberland Association; but this remains conjecture at the present. Even so, one of the chapters in this volume, devoted to Free Will Baptist origins in Georgia, will show an ideological connection with Separate Baptists.

The problem is we have not researched our history well enough at this point to be able to trace all the tributaries that have fed into the mainstream of Free Will Baptist history. Another tributary we know something about, for certain, was also in Tennessee. These were our fellow free-willers of the Stone Association. We may not know all we wish we did about the origin of that group, but we know enough to say it did not grow out of the Palmer movement or the Randall movement. For another example, Paul Woolsey was sure the origins of the Toe River Association, originally composed of churches in North Carolina and Tennessee, and from which have come the Union Association and others in Appalachia, were completely independent of Free Will Baptists anywhere else. See my booklet, *History of Tennessee Free Will Baptists*, for an introduction to these two groups. It is not unreasonable to believe some similar tributaries might be found in other states.

Yet another significant tributary to the mainstream is the Chattahoochee Association in Georgia, originally known as the Chattahoochee Association of United Baptists (this name holding a clue to its origin). The ministers and laity of this association went on to carry the Free Will Baptist banner into other places, like Alabama and West Florida, for example. This interesting and significant story makes up one of the chapters in the present volume. And yet another story in this volume is about A. M. Stewart, who left the Chattahoochee, settled in Texas, and apparently organized the first Anglo Free Will Baptist church in that state.

There are other stories out there, waiting to be discovered. We need to dig them out, and to approach the work willing to go where the facts lead. We don't need to confuse the tributaries with the mainstream. Neither do we need to ignore them.

What does all this have to do with this volume? If nothing else, the reader should know how I'm approaching Free Will Baptist history, and the stories I tell can be read in that light. I delight in telling stories, and in telling them in the full detail that comes from researching them carefully, providing much collateral information that can help other researchers. I realize some readers may find the detail boring at times; if so, they can skim the material. But there are intriguing insights in the details. Mainly, I desire that everyone interested in our history will realize that only by careful research can we ever hope to uncover all the connections in our big story—our "narrative," as some use the word.

Indeed, there are "connections." I find it interesting how often elements of these stories meet together. A. M. Stewart, founder of the work in Texas, also shows up in the chapter on unity movements and had strong ties to the Chattahoochee in still another chapter. So does D. J. Apperson, in the same chapters. J. W. Lucas, head of the school at Unicoi, likewise shows up in the chapter on unity movements. I really believe, after a hundred stories like these have been fully expounded in great detail, we may obtain a fresher and clearer picture of the rich history of Free Will Baptists.

The reader won't miss the fact that a couple of the stories in this volume involve another author, Robert L. Vaughn, a Texan, and a Baptist preacher. Although not a Free Will Baptist, he is very interested in all aspects of Baptist history. He is a gifted researcher and has added much to our knowledge of several of the stories in this volume. Yet another chapter has Joe McKnight, of South Carolina, as a co-author. Joe has done more research on our history in that state than anyone I know, and his contributions are essential to the chapter on South Carolina beginnings.

And I must say a word, again, on behalf of our Free Will Baptist Historical Collection, maintained (along with the website fwbhistory.com) by the Free Will Baptist Historical Commission. Without the resources of the Collection, I would not be able to produce such a volume as this. I hope to see the day when, throughout our denomination, there is an appreciation for the importance of this resource that leads to *action*. There are many things "out there" among us that need to be gathered and placed in the Collection. We have a long way to go in understanding our history, and we need to preserve the records that will contribute to that understanding.

I am grateful for the reception that our people gave to *Little Known Chapters in Free Will Baptist History*. I would like to call attention to the appendix in this volume that adds an important correction to what was stated there about the triennial General Conference led by Thomas Peden. I am likewise grateful to Randall House for giving me the opportunity to provide another volume of stories that explore our origins and identity.

Robert E. Picirilli

1

"We Give Ourselves to One Another"
The Story of the Free Will Baptist Church Covenant

Free Will Baptists are familiar with a church covenant published for churches of the denomination by the National Association of Free Will Baptists (hereafter NAFWB). It has had essentially the same content and form since the NAFWB came into existence in 1935.

My purpose, in this chapter, is to trace the history of this church covenant, telling a story that is generally unknown and somewhat complex. With few exceptions, I will treat this history *only* through 1935, when the NAFWB was organized. While some associations continued to publish a different covenant after that date, we can assume that the official covenant has been the same for all Free Will Baptists who are part of the NAFWB since it was organized. It is *not* my purpose to provide commentary on the *meaning* of the covenant; I have done that elsewhere.[1] As we know it now, the covenant adopted in 1935 is familiar in its division into seven paragraphs. It remains our "official" covenant, even though there have been minor differences, at times, in punctuation, paragraphing, or wording.

---

[1] Robert E. Picirilli, *Your Church and You* (Nashville, TN: Randall House Publications, 1978). See also Roy Thomas, *Studies on the Free Will Baptist Church Covenant* (Nashville, TN: Free Will Baptist Home Missions Department, n.d.).

I. The Origin of Our Covenant in the Randall Movement

Where did this form of the covenant come from, and how did it come to be the form adopted by the NAFWB in 1935? The answer, at least on the surface, is easy to obtain. Within the (Eastern) General Conference (formed in 1921) and the (Western) Cooperative General Association (formed in 1916), there arose interest in uniting the two regional bodies in one national organization. At the 1926 session of the General Conference, John L. Welch was chosen to represent at the next session of the Cooperative General Association.[2] Soon, committees from both organizations were meeting jointly and working toward union, and in 1933 the General Conference, meeting at the East Nashville church, adopted the report of the joint committee, which included this:

> We agree to accept the Articles of Faith of the 1901 Treatise, also the Church Covenant contained in the same Treatise, together with all the forms and usages set forth in same, with such amendments as may be made and approved by the body when perfected into one organization.
>
> We heartily agree to the merging of the General Conference and Cooperative General Association into one body, and we urge that steps be taken immediately for the final consumation [sic] of such a union.[3]

By "the 1901 Treatise," they meant the treatise published by the Randall movement, the Free Will Baptists of the North who merged with the Northern Baptists in 1910-11.[4]

In fact, the covenant published in 1901, which the new NAFWB adopted, had been the covenant of the Randall General Conference since 1892. Furthermore, it was the *fourth* different covenant that had been *officially* published in the treatises of the Free Will Baptists of the North.

Indeed, the use of church covenants within the Randall movement goes as far back as the original church in New England, planted by Benjamin Randall himself in New Durham, New Hampshire, in 1780. Randall wrote a covenant

---

[2] Minutes, General Conference of Free Will Baptists, 1926, 9.
[3] Minutes, General Conference of Free Will Baptists, 1933, 12.
[4] At this writing we do not have a copy of the 1901 Randall treatise for confirmation; however, there is no reason to doubt that it contained the covenant in essentially the form adopted by the NAFWB.

for his forming church, dated June 30, 1780. It immediately followed their Articles of Faith and read as follows:

> Believing the above Articles to be according to Scripture, and necessary for the visible government of the church of Christ, we, whose names are here underwritten, do freely covenant together to walk according to them.
>
> Therefore we do now declare that we have given ourselves to God, and do now agree and give ourselves to one another in love and fellowship; and do agree to take the scriptures of truth for our rule of faith and practice, respecting our duty toward God, our neighbors and ourselves.
>
> We do promise to practice all the commands of and ordinances of the New Testament of our Lord and Saviour Jesus Christ, so far as they are or shall be made known unto us by the light of the Holy Spirit of truth, without which, we are sensible, we cannot attain to the true knowledge thereof.
>
> And do promise to bear one another's burdens and so fulfill the law of love which is the law of Christ.
>
> And we do agree to give liberty for the improvement of the gifts of the brethren.
>
> And to keep up the public worship of God amongst ourselves and not to forsake the assembling ourselves together as the manner of some is.
>
> And also agree not to receive any person into fellowship except they give a satisfactory evidence of a change of life and heart.
>
> And also they shall promise to submit to the order and discipline as above.
>
> May God enable us to keep this covenant. Amen.[5]

This covenant was originally signed by Randall, Robert Boody, Nathaniel Buzzell, Joseph Boody, Judith Chartel, Margery Boody, and Mary Buzzell. It contains very little that was carried over into later versions, but the early commitments to give ourselves both to God and to one another, and to the Scripture as the rule of faith and practice, continued to be prominent.

Randall's original covenant was probably used not only by the congregation in New Durham but also by some of the early congregations that grew out of

---

[5] All but the preamble copied from Roy Thomas, ed., *The Journal of Benjamin Randall and the First Free Will Baptist Church New Durham, New Hampshire* (Nashville, TN: The Home Missions Department of the National Association of Free Will Baptists, 1993), 31—except that in paragraph four the word is *bare* instead of *bear*. (The journal represented in this volume was not Randall's personal journal; instead it was the church record, some of it written by Randall as clerk.) The preamble (and the correction to *bear*) is copied from I. D. Stewart, *The History of the Freewill Baptists for Half a Century: Volume I. From the Year 1780 to 1830* (Dover, NH: Free Will Baptist Printing Establishment, 1862), 54—where the entire covenant also appears with slightly different wording. (No volume II of this history was ever published.)

that one. At first, anyway, the other meetings were regarded as arms of the New Durham church. But as the young denomination grew and developed organizationally, other influences contributed to an evolving expression of the covenant used by the Free Will Baptist churches of the North.

The General Conference of the Randall Free Will Baptists was organized in 1827. They published many editions of their treatise of faith and practices. The first two editions (1834, 1839) did not contain a church covenant. Apparently there had been some difference of opinion about the use of a written covenant, as indicated in the minutes of the General Conference for 1847:

> 3. Whereas there exists in the denomination a difference of opinion, in relation to the propriety of using written covenants in our churches …
> *Resolved*, that such a difference of opinion ought not to create a breach of Christian or church fellowship, but [those involved] should exercise mutual forbearance and endeavor to express their views with candor, Christian kindness and courtesy.[6]

The third edition of the treatise, apparently reflecting this ambivalence, was published in 1841. It included this explanation:

> By request of some of our brethren, we insert the following as a suitable form for a church covenant, for the benefit of our brethren in the ministry, who may be called to assist in the organization of new churches, and of those churches which have not already adopted a covenant.[7]

And then they offered not one but *two* possible covenants for consideration, one lengthy and one much shorter. Both forms are very different from the more "official" forms that appeared in all editions of the treatise from then on.

The first of the two printed in 1841 is lengthy, with a preamble, nine numbered paragraphs, and a conclusion. The seventh paragraph is notable for its detailed statement about total abstinence:

---

[6] *Minutes of the General Conference of the Freewill Baptist Connection [etc.]*, 1827-1856 (Dover, NH: Freewill Baptist Printing Establishment, 1859), 282.

[7] *A Treatise of the Faith of the Freewill Baptists: with an Appendix, containing a summary of their usages in church government, written under the direction of their General Conference*, Third Edition (Dover, NH: Trustees of the Freewill Baptist Connection, 1841), 153.

> 7. We will not use intoxicating drinks ourselves, nor allow them to be used in our families, nor furnish them for persons in our employment, except in either case, they are cautiously used for medicinal or mechanical purposes. We will not be guilty of buying or selling these deadly articles, and will use our influence to discountenance the use, purchase and sale of them in the community, except for the above named purposes.[8]

Also of interest is paragraph nine, which contains a promise that when new members are accepted into the church the covenant will be read to them and they must "assent to its principles." Furthermore, "Any members violating it shall be considered subjects of labor by the church."[9]

The other form included in the 1841 treatise is deliberately identified as shorter—"which some churches may prefer." It too is very different from any of the official forms that appeared in subsequent editions. The entire commitment to total abstinence, for example, is worded thus: "Finally, we agree to neither make, sell, or use intoxicating drinks, as beverage, and that we will disapprove of these things in others."[10]

In the various editions after 1841, the covenant took four different forms, each of them appearing first, respectively, in 1848, 1869 (again in 1886), 1871, and 1892 (the same as in 1901). Here follow some brief observations comparing these four forms.[11]

The 1848 form is much lengthier, with 572 words, while the others run between 360 and 390. The paragraph divisions vary, ranging from three to seven.

Each has a "preamble" that expresses a basis for the covenant. For the early forms, this basis is "the duty of all who love our God and Saviour to unite with the visible church of Christ" (1848) or the fact that "the union of Christians in a visible church" is Scriptural (1869). The later forms cite, instead, that we have given ourselves to God and to one another (1871, 1892). Some also cite

---

[8] Ibid., 155.
[9] Ibid., 156.
[10] Ibid., 157.
[11] In the rest of this chapter, I will make many references to covenants published in either an association's treatises or its minutes, as the case may be. To avoid so many footnotes, in the text I will give the dates of the various editions of the treatises or minutes. It should then be easy enough for the reader to find the material cited in the respective publications.

commitment to the articles of faith that appear in the treatise just before the covenant (1848, 1871). This citation was ultimately replaced by "having adopted the Word of God as our rule of faith and practice" (1892).

Among the key elements of all four forms, but with various wordings, are the following.

Commitment to the spiritual welfare of one another. One promises "fervent prayer, faithful admonitions, and affectionate rebukes, if necessary" (1848). The ideas in 1 Thessalonians 5:13-14, clearly expressed as seeking to "strengthen the weak, encourage the afflicted, admonish the erring" (1892), start showing up early (1869, 1871). So does the admonition of Ephesians 4:3 to "keep the unity of the Spirit in the bond of peace" (all but 1848).

Commitment to church services and meetings. One even requires regular reporting to the monthly church conference (1871). In the early years, a Randall church had a monthly conference, typically on a Saturday (sometimes called a "covenant meeting"), that was deliberately intended to evaluate members' faithfulness to the covenant. Other clauses include being "careful of each other's reputation and usefulness" (1869), a promise to "watch over each other in love" (1871) and to "cheerfully submit to such regulations as the majority may approve" (1869)—which is especially interesting for its open-ended possibilities.

Responsibility to support financially the church, the ministry, and other enterprises. One expression of this is "for the support of a faithful ministry among us, and for all other necessary means of grace" (1848). This responsibility includes support for the needy, "especially the poor of our own church" (1848). And it includes "other benevolent enterprises": namely, "Missions, Sabbath Schools, Moral Reform, Anti-Slavery, [and] Education" (1848). Later, these become "Home-culture, Temperance, Sabbath-schools, Education and Missions" (1869). Finally, they are more general (1892). Mention of responsibility to the *denomination* does not show up until 1871.

Negative: practices that will be avoided. All the forms have some expression of this, although they differ widely. At first, these are named: "vain extravagance and sinful conformity to the world," "all sinful amusements, as theatres, dances, gambling, and … all vain festivals," "all unchaste and profane conversation," and "the reading of wicked and corrupting publications" (1848). Then the statement becomes more general: "those worldly indulgences and amusements which tend to lessen true piety in ourselves or weaken Christian influence over others" (1869). Finally: "all vain amusements and sinful (later, "unholy") conformity to the world" (1871).

All four forms include a promise to avoid all "sanction" (support, approval) of the use and sale of intoxicating beverages. One specifically commits not to "furnish to others" (1871).

Finally, each form ends with a prayerful benediction. The earliest of these cites Paul's prayer for final sanctification in 1 Thessalonians 5:23 and links to it the blessing expressed in Revelation 5:13b (1848). After a weaker conclusion in 1869, this one returns in 1871, finally replaced by the prayer of 1 Thessalonians 5:23 alone (1892).

As noted, the 1892 Church Covenant was almost in its final form in the Randall movement, being essentially the same as in 1901 and thus in the form adopted by the NAFWB.[12] The biggest differences were in paragraphing and in the final paragraph: "Sabbath schools" became "Sunday schools"; and "evangelistic efforts for the salvation of souls and the conversion of the world" became "evangelistic efforts for the salvation of the world."

Later in this chapter, I will reproduce only the last three of the Randall covenants—1869/1886, 1871, and 1892—since these are the only ones that were used in more than one association or geographical area among the churches that eventually formed the NAFWB.

II. A Survey, State by State, of Covenants Used in the South[13]

As noted, the NAFWB was formed in 1935. It included some former Randall movement churches that would have used one or more of the covenants found in the treatises of their General Conference. The greater part, however,

---

[12] *A Treatise on the Faith and Practice of the Freewill Baptists* (Boston, MA: F. B. Printing Establishment, 1894), 63-65.

[13] I am using "the South" loosely, to cover Free Will Baptists anywhere who were not part of the Randall movement at the time the NAFWB was formed. They included Free Will Baptists in West Virginia, Kentucky, Southern Illinois, and other areas not typically thought of as in "the South."

were churches of the South and Southwest that were not part of the Randall movement, at least not when the NAFWB was formed.

The story of our church covenant within the denomination represented by the NAFWB is therefore much more complex. This movement—originating with Paul Palmer in North Carolina and contributed to by some other groups—was not nearly so unified and centralized, and the variety shows up in the fact that several different covenants were in use here and there.

Typically, one may find "official" church covenants published either in the minutes of an association or in any treatise[14] of faith and practices used by an association. I have examined all the treatises and minutes published by any associations of churches, before 1936, among the Free Will Baptists who formed the NAFWB—including non-affiliated associations. Of course, I have examined these only *insofar as they are available* in the Free Will Baptist Historical Collection; there are many early minutes that we do not have.

This section presents the results of my survey, briefly, state by state. In each listing, I will indicate the earliest date when the covenant referred to appeared. The reader should understand that in many of these cases the covenant might well have been used earlier, which could be determined if we had all the minutes. In a few instances, I give a date later than 1935 because it seems likely that a covenant was in use earlier, but we do not have the earlier minutes to confirm this usage.[15]

Important: any of these covenants that were used more broadly than by one association or in one geographical area will be reproduced in full and commented on in more detail in the next section of this chapter.

North Carolina

The denomination in the South, in its mainstream, traces its origin to Paul Palmer in Eastern North Carolina in 1727, well before the beginning of the Free Will Baptist denomination in the North in 1780. The chief influence in

---

[14] I will frequently use *treatise* not as a title but in a generic sense to refer to any published treatment or setting forth of doctrine and polity, regardless of the actual name of the publication.

[15] This prompts me to say that the FWB Historical Collection desperately needs more minutes from almost every one of our associations in existence. I urge all Free Will Baptists to help us with this.

the Palmer movement, for doctrine and polity, was apparently from the English General Baptists. The development of church covenants in the Tar Heel state is therefore the place to begin the story in the South.

We have no information about the use of a covenant by Palmer himself, or among the early churches that followed his doctrine. As for organizational structure, we know that early in the nineteenth century (at least as early as 1827 when Jesse Heath wrote to *The Morning Star*)[16] there was an Annual Conference of Free Will Baptists of North Carolina, and that in 1830 this body subdivided into the Bethel and Shiloh conferences for a time and then reunited, at least by 1845, into a General Conference. This organization ultimately divided into the Central, Eastern, and Western conferences, and these three, joining together with the Cape Fear Conference, ultimately formed the North Carolina State Convention (which succeeded the Union Conference).

Not surprisingly, there are almost no covenants to be found in the minutes of most of the major associations in the eastern part of North Carolina. The probable reason for this is that they all subscribed to the same treatise of faith and practices.

Early, that treatise—known as *An Abstract of the Former Articles of Faith* (etc.)—did not include a church covenant. This was true at least through the edition published in 1895. Ultimately, *four* different covenants appeared in North Carolina before 1935, as follows.

1. The earliest covenant I found dates to 1883, in a separate treatise published by the Cape Fear Conference. It subsequently became the form most often used among the traditional Free Will Baptists in the eastern part of the state, appearing in the North Carolina treatise first in 1916 and from then through 1944.[17] It also appears in an undated treatise published by the French Broad Association (Form 4 in the next section).

---

[16] See Robert E. Picirilli, *Little Known Chapters in Free Will Baptist History* (Nashville, TN: Randall House, 2015), 75-77.

[17] Ultimately, the NAFWB form prevailed in the official state treatise, at least by the 1949 edition. This continued to be the case even after the convention separated from the NAFWB in 1962, with some minor modifications. A 1976 edition of the North Carolina treatise added "the abuse of drugs" to the clause promising abstention from the use and sale of intoxicating beverages; it also made some relatively minor changes to the paragraph promising "We will everywhere hold Christian principle sacred."

2. Almost as old as this covenant is one found in a 1905 treatise published by the Free Will Baptist Press in Ayden for the triennial General Conference (1895-1910) led by Thomas Peden.[18] The covenant included there is the same as the one used in the Randall movement in 1869/1886 (Form 2 in the next section).

3. The minutes of the North Carolina State Convention, in 1918 and 1919, printed the 1892 Randall form that became the NAFWB covenant. This covenant is also in a 1929 treatise published by the Toe River Association (Form 1 in the next section).

4. An entirely different covenant appeared in the minutes of associations in the western part of the state: Jack's Creek 1905, French Broad 1921, Western[19] 1924, and Toe River[20] 1928. Free Will Baptist associations in this part of the state were not so tightly bound to the older associations in the eastern part (Form 5 in the next section).

South Carolina

The situation in South Carolina closely parallels that in North Carolina, which is not surprising. The associations in the eastern part of South Carolina were closely tied to the older associations in eastern North Carolina. Redding Moore, apparently the founder of the first Free Will Baptist churches in South Carolina, went there from North Carolina in about 1816. The Annual Conference in North Carolina, in 1831, dismissed him and his churches to have their own completely independent conference in South Carolina.[21]

Two forms of the covenant were used in South Carolina before 1935, although the first is not published in any official documents there.

1. Apparently the South Carolina Conference, along with the Central Conference that grew out of it, used the treatise that was published in North Carolina—which I remember being referred to commonly, in my youth, as "the old blue-back discipline." It is not surprising, then, that these conferences did not

---

[18] For the story of this conference, see Picirilli, 151-180.
[19] Not to be confused with the Western Conference in the eastern part of the state.
[20] This association includes churches in North Carolina and Tennessee.
[21] The story of Moore and the South Carolina Conference is told in another chapter in this volume.

publish their own church covenant in their minutes. They used the same forms, if they used any covenant at all, as their brethren who used the North Carolina treatises (Form 4 in the next section).

2. In the western part of the state, however, the Beaver Creek Association, at least as early as 1925, used the very same form as was used in the Jack's Creek, French Broad, Western, and Toe River associations in western North Carolina (Form 5 in the next section).

Virginia

Except for a couple of associations in the western part of the state, the Virginia associations did not exist before 1935. I found two covenants that were older than that.

1. The John Wheeler association is broader than Virginia, having churches in other states as well. Although it dates back just prior to 1880, the oldest minutes we have are for 1949. In them appears a covenant that, not surprisingly, is the same as the one used by associations in the western part of North and South Carolina (Form 5 in the next section).

2. The John Thomas Association used a different covenant, first appearing in its minutes for 1923, and being the same as that which appeared in the North Carolina treatise from 1916-44 (Form 4 in the next section).

Georgia

The origins of most of the associations in Georgia were with a group of people, more or less indigenous to the state, known as United Baptists. The first such association was the United Baptist Association, and we have some minutes from 1840 to 1854, with no church covenants included. Otherwise, I found four different covenants in use in Georgia, apparently before 1935.

1. The oldest association still existing is the Chattahoochee, which changed its name from United Baptist to United Free Will Baptist during the years between 1854 and 1874 (for which we have no minutes). The only minutes before 1935 to include a covenant were for 1894, essentially the same as the 1848 Randall Covenant. Furthermore, this particular covenant does not appear in any of the minutes of any other associations in the South or Southwest that I could

examine, including the associations (in Georgia, Southeast Alabama, or West Florida) that trace their origins to the Chattahoochee. Since it is unique to the Chattahoochee, I will not provide further discussion of this covenant in the next section of this chapter but will make a few observations here.

This Chattahoochee covenant is interesting for the changes it made in the 1848 Randall covenant. Instead of the verb *covenant*, it uses *agree to*. And where the 1848 Randall covenant committed to support *anti-slavery*, the Chattahoochee omitted that promise. Unintentionally, I assume, the final paragraph said, "May the God of peace sanctify us … to the *erring* (instead of *coming*) of our Lord Jesus Christ"!

2. The oldest covenant used in Georgia in minutes available to us was essentially the same as the 1871 Randall covenant: in the Liberty 1893, Georgia Union 1900, South Georgia 1909, and Benjamin Randall 1927. There are a few minor differences in wording. The Benjamin Randall, for example, in addition to other adjustments, adds a short paragraph at the end: "If I fail to keep this covenant, I hereby agree that I shall be justly dealt with by the church" (Form 3 in the following section).

3. A few associations that were part of the United Free Will Baptists used a form of the covenant that has its own unique wording, in eight paragraphs, structured much like other covenants: South Georgia 1907, Union 1926, and Little River 1936. (We do not have any earlier minutes for this last association, organized about 1906; they probably used this covenant before 1935.)

Since this covenant was used only in this relatively small area, I will not include it in the following section. Among its more unique wordings are these: in paragraph 5, "We agree to neglect our secular or worldly avocation to attend the stated meetings of the church"; in paragraph 6, "We believe that all Christians are endowed with certain talents and influences, for the improvement of which they will be accountable to the Great Head of the church"; and in paragraph 7, "We believe the worldly dance and drinking ardent spirits with the co-mingling with drunkards are sins." Finally, paragraph 8 reads, "It shall be the duty of all pastors to read or have read this Covenant and to explain every part and clause thereof to the church quarterly."

4. The Benjamin Randall minutes for 1938 print an entirely different form, a shorter version that is the same as that found in the North Carolina treatise from 1916 to 1944—except that the final, benedictory paragraph is omitted, perhaps unintentionally. Since we do not have the minutes of this association between 1933 and 1938, this covenant might have been used in Georgia before 1935. Furthermore, several associations existing before 1935—Martin and Midway, for examples—did not print any covenant in their minutes; they probably used the covenant, if any at all, in the treatise they used, which might well have been the one published in North Carolina (Form 4 in the following section).

One interesting thing about the use of covenants in Georgia is that there are instances of covenants *for associations* rather than for churches. The Georgia State Convention minutes for 1918 contain a Convention Covenant; and the minutes for 1922 contain a Covenant of the Ministerial Association.[22] Associational covenants also appear in minutes for the Martin Association 1887, Liberty 1893, and Union 1914.

Florida

The only Florida associations old enough to have significance for this study are those in the West Florida panhandle, to which the movement spread from Southwest Georgia and Southeast Alabama: the North Florida, West Florida Liberty, and Salem associations. The Alabama-Florida State Line Association also included some Florida churches but published no covenant in its minutes. Among these, I found only two associations publishing a covenant. The West Florida Liberty Association[23] contained no printed covenant.

The two associations publishing a covenant in their minutes were the Salem in 1935 and the North Florida in 1940. Their 1926 and 1927 minutes, respectively, did not include a covenant, but we have no minutes between then and the 1935 and 1940 minutes. Apparently then, and probably before 1935, both of them began using this covenant, which was the same as appeared in the Ben-

---

[22] This was an older Georgia state organization; the present one began in 1938.
[23] Originally the West Florida and South East Alabama Liberty Association.

jamin Randall minutes, in Georgia, between 1933 and 1938. It was the covenant used in the North Carolina treatise from 1916 to 1944 (Form 4 in the following section).

Alabama

I found four different church covenants in use in Alabama before 1935.

1. The oldest appears in the 1912 minutes of the Mount Moriah Association, and in the 1913 minutes (and on through 1935) of the Cahaba River Association. It is the 1892 Randall/NAFWB form. This same form also appears in the minutes of the Liberty No. 2 Association[24] for 1936, in the 1930 minutes of the Muscle Shoals State Line Association, and in the 1939 minutes of the Alabama-Mississippi State Line Association. Furthermore, there is a strangely abbreviated version of the NAFWB form that appears in the minutes of the Flint River Association for 1937 and 1940 (Form 1 in the following section).

2. Next oldest to this is a covenant that appears in the 1916 and 1920 minutes of the Liberty No. 1 Association, in the 1925 minutes of the other Liberty No. 2 Association,[25] and in the minutes of the Southern Union Association from 1931 to 1938. This covenant is unique in its brevity, having a total of just 65 words. Since I will not deal with this form again in the following section, I include the entire covenant here.

> In order to have more perfect and free Christian love and fellowship for each other, and to advance the cause of our Lord and Master, we do hereby agree and covenant by the help of God our Father, and aided by the Holy Spirit, to keep the ordinances, precepts and examples as laid down in the New Testament of our Lord and Savior Jesus Christ.

3. Especially interesting is a covenant unlike any seen thus far, appearing in several Alabama associations (and, as we will see, in other places farther west): the Morning Star in 1917, the Southeastern in 1926, and the Bear Creek in 1933 (Form 6 in the following section).

---

[24] There were apparently two different "Liberty No. 2" associations in Alabama; this one was in the central part of the state, while an earlier one (we have only the 1925 minutes) was in the southern part.
[25] See the preceding note.

4. The Progressive Association—organized shortly before the NAFWB, in 1933—in its minutes for 1933-37 print the same covenant as in the North Carolina treatise from 1916 to 1944 (Form 4 in the following section).

Several of the older associations in the state, including Mount Moriah, Vernon, and Jasper in the western part of the state (sharing the same origins), published no church covenant in their minutes (except for the 1912 minutes of the Mount Moriah mentioned above). It is not clear, then, what covenant they used, if any: probably the same as whatever treatise they used, which is uncertain, especially in the earliest years of their existence from about 1850.

As in Georgia, there was an "Associational Covenant" that appeared in the 1902 minutes of the Alabama-Florida State Line Association, but not before or after that year. This affinity is not surprising since the southeastern Alabama churches originally resulted from the growth of the United Free Will Baptists in Georgia.

Mississippi

Two covenants appear in the minutes of associations in this state.

1. The earliest I found is in the 1925 through 1931 minutes of the Water Valley Association, an obvious adaptation of the Randall movement covenant of 1869 and 1886. Most of the wording is the same, but some changes appear, including the omission of the commitment to abstinence from intoxicating beverages (Form 2 in the following section).

2. The Zion Rest Association[26] minutes did not include a church covenant in 1905, but the 1940 minutes include one that was certainly earlier than 1935. Indeed, this form of the covenant is well known among Baptist churches in America and is known as the New Hampshire Covenant. It was first published, apparently, in 1832 by the New Hampshire Baptist Convention and later, in 1853, in *The Baptist Church Manual* published by the American Baptist Publication Society. This form is widely used by many Baptist churches in this country.[27]

---

[26] This later became the South Mississippi Association.
[27] Champlin Burrage, *The Church Covenant Idea: Its Origin and Its Development* (Philadelphia, PA: American Baptist Publication Society, 1904), 201-02.

Most of the paragraphs begin by saying, "We engage to ..." Among the things to be avoided are "all tattling, back-biting and excessive anger," as well as "the sale and use of intoxicating drinks as a beverage." The concluding paragraph promises that the member, upon removing from this place, will soon unite with another church, "where we can carry out the spirit of this Covenant." Since this covenant is unique to the Zion Rest Association among Free Will Baptists, I will not treat it again in the following section.

Tennessee

There were also four different forms of the church covenant in use among Tennessee Free Will Baptists before 1935. A couple of old associations, the Stone and Bethlehem, did not publish a covenant in their minutes. Given their relative independence from other Free Will Baptists in the state, they might not have used any of the covenants I have found.

1. The earliest I found was in the 1884 minutes of the Union Association in East Tennessee. This association did not, before or after this, make a practice of printing a covenant in its minutes, but in 1884 a committee on the state of the denomination (within the association) recommended several steps to strengthen the association and the churches. One of these was the adoption of a covenant, apparently written by the committee—which consisted of A. Burgess, W. A. Headrick, and W. B. Woolsey. This covenant consists of one lengthy paragraph that includes a preamble and ten covenant agreements. Although these are worded uniquely, the promises are typical of other church covenants. Among the more interesting items are the third, "We covenant to give our attention to the reading of the Bible rather than to any work of man," and the ninth, "We covenant to maintain a Christian fellowship with all other Christian denominations, as far as practicable, and also to patronize them as far as it is in our power, not forgetting, however, that our own church has the highest claims upon us." Given the uniqueness of this covenant to this association, I will not deal with it in the following section.

2. The Cumberland Association also did not print a covenant in its minutes, at least not from 1876 on, but the treatise it published in 1902 includes a covenant, essentially the same as the 1892 Randall/NAFWB form. The Cumberland

had exposed itself to the influence of the General Conference in the North, and this is not surprising.

The Tennessee River Association, beginning with its minutes for 1924, also printed the NAFWB form of the covenant. So did the Toe River, in its 1929 treatise; this association had churches in Tennessee and North Carolina (Form 1 in the following section).

3. The Toe River Association also published, in its minutes in 1928, 1929, and 1933, the same covenant that was used in other associations in western North Carolina (Form 5 in the following section).

4. The Clinch Valley Association, in its 1935 minutes, printed the same covenant that appeared in the North Carolina treatise from 1916 to 1944—minus the final, benedictory paragraph (Form 4 in the following section).

Arkansas

There are a number of associations in Arkansas that began earlier than 1900, but most of them did not publish a covenant in their minutes. These include the Antioch, Arkansas (District), Carroll County, Hamburgh, New Hope, New Mt. Zion, Old Mt. Zion, Polk Bayou, Saline, Union Band, and Western Arkansas associations. If they used a covenant at all, it was probably the covenant published in whatever treatise they used; but I have no record as to what this was. Otherwise, I found three covenants in the minutes of associations in this state.

1. The Arkansas State Association, in the minutes for 1901, printed a covenant in the 1892 Randall/NAFWB form. The Little Missouri River, in the 1925 minutes, printed this same covenant (although in 1891 they provided no covenant). This was also true for the Social Band, which in 1911 printed no covenant; in 1933 they printed the 1892 Randall/NAFWB form (Form 1 in the following section).

2. In 1903, however, the Arkansas State Association printed a different one, essentially the same as the one used by the Morning Star, Southeastern, and Bear Creek associations in Alabama. The main difference is a different seventh paragraph. Instead of promising not to neglect secret and public prayer, as in the Alabama version, this one promises to "shun all appearance of evil, and all

amusements that do not tend to the glory of God" (Form 6 in the following section).

3. The Big Spring Association[28] minutes, from 1921 to 1934, printed a covenant that is essentially the same as the Randall movement covenant of 1871 (Form 3 in the following section).

Missouri

I found only one covenant published in the minutes of associations in Missouri, although more than one was probably used there. I say this because some of the churches and associations in the state were part of the Randall movement in the North. At least some of these probably used Randall General Conference treatises older than the one published in 1892 and so might have used covenants contained in those older treatises.

The only covenant I found printed in minutes of associations in Missouri, however, was the 1892 Randall/NAFWB form (Form 1 in the following section). It appeared in several different associations, as follows, with the dates indicating the earliest minutes in which this covenant appeared[29]: Cave Springs 1914, Central Western Missouri 1914, Missouri State 1915, Union 1922, and Indian Creek 1932. There were a few other associations that were older than 1935, but we have no printed minutes for them before that date.

Oklahoma

The story in this state is varied. I found three different covenants in use in Oklahoma before 1935.

1. A number of the oldest associations were organized in the 1890s, and several of these used the very same covenant as in the Morning Star, Southeastern Alabama, and Bear Creek associations in Alabama. These were the Territorial Association 1899, Grand River 1910, Eureka 1914, Eureka and Roberts-McGee 1918, and Gaines Creek 1934 (Form 6 in the following section).

---

[28] In early years, this is "Big Spring"; more recently it is "Big Springs."
[29] I repeat that this depends on the minutes available in the Collection. If we had all the minutes, these dates would no doubt be earlier.

Interestingly, this form of the covenant is one of the few that did not include a commitment regarding the use of alcoholic beverages. But when the Eureka and Roberts-McGee associations went back into their separate organizations,[30] the *constitution* of the Roberts-McGee Association included Article VIII, which read:

> It shall be distinctly understood that the use of intoxicating liquors as a beverage is expressly in violation of the Constitution and rules of this Association, and any church member violating the same shall be dealt with by the church of which he is a member and any minister being found guilty of the same shall first make acknowledgment to the church of which he is a member and must also make acknowledgment to the Association, or be expelled therefrom.

2. Yet another group of associations, including two that also began before or shortly after 1900, used an entirely different form of the covenant: namely, the same as the Randall movement covenant of 1869/1886 but omitting the promise of total abstinence (Form 2 in the following section). The Hopewell Association, in its 1903 minutes, printed this covenant with minor changes.[31] The Southern Oklahoma in 1916 and Eastern Oklahoma in 1930 used essentially the same covenant form, with some unique wording. (Perhaps all three of these shared similar influences in their origins, but I do not have information about this.)

3. In some of the Oklahoma associations, the 1892 Randall/NAFWB form was used. These include the State Association 1923, Canadian 1921, First Mission 1928, First Oklahoma 1931, Center 1917, Dibble 1927, and the Southern and Grand River (both changing to this form in 1927). The Hopewell also changed to this form in 1931 (Form 1 in the following section).

Texas

As in Oklahoma, the older associations in this state were formed in the late nineteenth century or shortly after the turn of the century. Only two covenants show up before 1935, in the minutes available, in the state.

---

[30] They had combined in 1918.
[31] The 1922 Hopewell minutes show a more extensive revision of this same form, one that apparently includes a number of promises that were originated by the association.

1. The oldest of these dates to 1910, at least, in the only minutes we possess for the West Texas Association. This covenant is the same as the one in the 1903 minutes of the Hopewell Association in Oklahoma, which was in turn based on the Randall movement covenant of 1869/1886, also used by the Southern Oklahoma and Eastern Oklahoma associations. (I do not know whether there was a connection between the Hopewell and the West Texas associations.)

The Woodlawn Association (dating to about 1900) also used this covenant at least as early as 1940 (Form 2 in the following section).

2. The other covenant in use in Texas was the 1892 Randall/NAFWB form. It appears in the 1917 minutes of the Northeast Texas Association, as well as in the minutes of the Central Texas and West Fork associations in 1932 and 1935, respectively (Form 1 in the following section).

The Rest of the Country

The states just surveyed include all the southeastern states from North Carolina and Virginia, moving southward and westward through Georgia, Florida, Alabama, Tennessee, Mississippi, Arkansas, Missouri, Oklahoma, and Texas. There were no Free Will Baptist associations (other than in the Randall movement) west of these before 1935.

Along the northern border of this section of the country there were also some Free Will Baptist associations that would become part of the NAFWB: specifically, in West Virginia, Ohio, Kentucky, Indiana, and Illinois—and extending into Kansas and Nebraska on the West and Michigan in the North.

Some of these associations were formed after 1935. Some of the ones formed earlier were part of the Randall movement; if they used a covenant at all, they probably used the form that was published in the Randall movement treatise, and beginning in 1892 that would have been the NAFWB form that was adopted when the NAFWB was formed in 1935 (Form 1 in the following section).

I examined the minutes we have of all of these associations and found just one covenant in use other than the NAFWB form. This appeared in the 1948 minutes of the Mt. Olive Association in Kentucky, the oldest minutes we have for an organization formed about 1934. It is the same as the covenant published in the North Carolina treatise from 1916-44, except that it lacks the concluding, short, benedictory paragraph (Form 4 in the following section).

III. The Big Picture: Patterns of Usage

As I examined the treatises and minutes published among the Free Will Baptists of the NAFWB (and unaffiliated), primarily before 1935 when the NAFWB was formed, I found that there were almost a dozen different forms of a church covenant in use at different times and places. Of these, not counting the ones used by just one association or in a limited area, six different forms were especially prominent and more widely used. My purpose, here, is to indicate what those forms were and where they were used. It seems possible that some patterns emerge that suggest a kinship of sorts among associations in different places. My purpose, however, does not go beyond a few suggestions about such kinship possibilities.

Form 1: Randall 1892/NAFWB

This covenant first appeared in the Randall movement in 1892. The picture nearby is a promotional poster (on card stock) issued by Hillsdale College in Michigan, date unknown, entitled "A Free Baptist Church Covenant." This is, of course, the official covenant of the NAFWB, as I have indicated already. Even before 1935, when the NAFWB was formed, this was perhaps the most widely used covenant in the denomination in the South and Southwest.

> Having given ourselves to God, by faith in Christ, and adopted the Word of God as our rule of faith and practice, we now give ourselves to one another by the will of God in this solemn covenant.
>
> We promise by His grace to love and obey Him in all things, to avoid all appearance of evil, to abstain from all sinful amusements and unholy conformity to the world, from all sanction of the use and sale of intoxicating beverages, and to "provide things honest in the sight of all men."

We agree faithfully to discharge our obligations in reference to the study of the Scriptures, secret prayer, family devotions, and social worship; and by self-denial, faith, and good works endeavor to "grow in grace and the knowledge of our Lord and Savior Jesus Christ."

We will not forget the assembling of ourselves together for church conferences, public worship, and the observance of the ordinances of the Gospel, nor fail to pay according to our ability for the support of the church, of its poor, and all its benevolent work.

We agree to accept Christian admonition and reproof with meekness, and to watch over one another in love, endeavoring to "keep the unity of the Spirit" in the bonds of peace, to be careful of one another's happiness and reputation, and seek to strengthen the weak, encourage the afflicted, admonish the erring, and as far as we are able, promote the success of the church and of the Gospel.

We will everywhere hold Christian principle sacred and Christian obligations and enterprises supreme; counting it our chief business in life to extend the influence of Christ in society; constantly praying and toiling that the kingdom of God may come, and His will be done on earth as it is in heaven.

To this end we agree to labor for the promotion of educational and denominational enterprises, the support of missions, the success of Sunday schools, and evangelistic efforts for the salvation of the world. And may the God of peace sanctify us wholly, and preserve us blameless unto the coming of our Lord Jesus Christ.[32]

This covenant appears in the Arkansas State minutes for 1901, the Cumberland (TN) treatise for 1902, the Mount Moriah (AL) minutes for 1912, the Cahaba River (AL) minutes for 1913, the minutes of three associations in Missouri (Cave Springs, Central Western Missouri, and Missouri State) in 1914-15, the Northwest Texas minutes for 1917, and the North Carolina State minutes for 1918-19.[33] All these were before 1920, and the geographical width demonstrates how broadly this covenant was used, well before the NAFWB was formed.

Indeed, before the NAFWB was formed, this covenant was used in other associations in North Carolina, Tennessee, Alabama, Arkansas, Missouri, Oklahoma, and Texas—not to mention other states where the Free Will Baptist

---

[32] *A Treatise of the Faith and Practices of the Free Will Baptist* [sic] (Purdy, MO: Free Will Baptist Gem Print, 1936), 68-70.

[33] The reason for the last seems, surely, to be that the North Carolina State Convention joined the Cooperative General Association in 1916 and remained in it until 1919. That broader association had officially adopted the 1892 Randall/NAFWB covenant.

work was aligned with the Randall movement, like West Virginia, Ohio, Kentucky, and Illinois.

Nor is this difficult to understand. Two factors were no doubt involved. (1) Throughout the denomination, including the Deep South, the existence of the Randall Free Will Baptists in the North was well known, and many obtained literature from New England, including the treatises published there. (2) Furthermore, this form was adopted by the Cooperative General Association when it was organized in 1916. That organization soon came to include the Nebraska Yearly Meeting, the Northern Kansas Yearly Meeting, at least five associations in Missouri, two in Texas, the North Carolina State Convention, several associations in Oklahoma, one in Illinois, and a tri-state association in Ohio, Kentucky, and West Virginia.

Looking back, one can understand why those who formed the NAFWB decided to adopt this form of the church covenant.

Form 2: Randall 1869/1886

This form of the church covenant, appearing first in 1869 and then again in 1886, was the last, in the Randall movement, before its final 1892 form. This covenant read as follows.

> Believing that the union of Christians in a visible church is sanctioned by the teachings of Christ and the practice of his apostles, that it is adapted to promote piety and increase Christian influence, we do now heartily enter into covenant before God and with each other.
>
> We will constantly strive to maintain true piety in our own hearts, to keep ourselves in vital communion with God, and commend religion to others, not only in words, but by means of a devout spirit and a holy example, always careful of each other's reputation and usefulness.
>
> We will watch over each other in the spirit of true charity—seeking to bear each other's burdens, assist the needy, strengthen the weak, encourage the despondent, sympathize with the sorrowful, reprove the erring, win back the straying to duty, aid in maintaining wholesome discipline, receive Christian admonition and reproof in meekness, keep the unity of the spirit in the bond of peace, and cheerfully submit to such regulations as the majority may approve. We will contribute, according to our ability, for the support of a faithful ministry, maintain secret and family prayer, and aid, by our presence and otherwise, in sustaining public and social worship, and in giving success to the various means of grace.

We will give an active and consistent support to the great causes that aim to promote morality and Christian progress, such as Home-culture, Temperance, Sabbath-schools, Education and Missions. We will refuse all sanction to the sale and use of intoxicating liquors as a beverage, and to those worldly indulgences and amusements which tend to lessen true piety in ourselves or weaken Christian influence over others, so that the cause of religion be not reproached on our account.

We will everywhere hold Christian principle sacred and Christian objects supreme, counting it our chief business in life to spread Christian knowledge and diffuse the Christian spirit in society and among all the nations of the earth, constantly praying and toiling that the kingdom of God may come, and his will be done on earth as it is done in Heaven.

May He who has promised his help, enable us to keep this covenant, grant us grace to be faithful in all things, until He shall gather us to himself, and crown us with final victory. Amen.[34]

This form of the covenant also appeared among Free Will Baptists who are part of the history of the denomination outside the Randall movement: in the minutes of the Hopewell Association (OK) in 1903 and the West Texas Association in 1910, and (in somewhat modified form) in other associations in these two states: the Southern Oklahoma (1916) and Eastern Oklahoma (1930); it also appeared in the Woodlawn (TX) minutes for 1940 and might well have been much earlier than that.

But this form also appeared in places other than Oklahoma and Texas. The minutes of the Water Valley Association in Mississippi printed it in 1928-31. It also appeared in what we might call a "special edition" of the treatise published by the Free Will Baptist Press in North Carolina in 1905 for use by the triennial General Conference led by Thomas E. Peden. At the time, Peden was leading the Free Will Baptist Seminary in Ayden, North Carolina, and he was trying to convince the courts in Ohio that the General Conference he led was the true General Conference of the Randall movement before they changed their name to Free Baptists.[35] Then perhaps we should not think that the North Carolina Free Will Baptists were officially using this treatise or this covenant. Neverthe-

---

[34] *A Treatise on the Faith and Practice of the Freewill Baptists, Written under the direction of their General Conference*, 9th ed. (Dover, NH: Free Will Baptist Printing Establishment, 1869), 35-36.

[35] For the story of Peden and this General Conference, which met triennially from 1895 to 1910, see Picirilli, 151-180.

less, they probably would not have published it had they not thought it represented them accurately; and it apparently saw some distribution.

As for these associations in Oklahoma and Texas, it may be that there were some shared influences in their origins. It seems a stretch, however, to assume that any kinship extended back to the Water Valley Association in Mississippi—although that is possible. In the end, the use of this covenant, anywhere, could be simply explained by the ready availability of treatises from the North that found their way outside the Randall General Conference.

Form 3: Randall 1871

Between the 1869 and 1886 printing of the covenant above (Form 2) in the Randall movement's General Conference treatise, a different one was published in the 1871 treatise, and it too was used by some associations in the South. This treatise read as follows.

> Having given ourselves to God through Jesus Christ, and adopted the foregoing articles as our confession of faith, we now give ourselves to each other by the will of God, and agree to the following Church Covenant:
>
> 1. We solemnly covenant before God, that we will strive by his assisting grace to exemplify our profession by a corresponding practice. We covenant and agree as members of the church and as Christians, to watch over each other in love for mutual upbuilding in gospel faith, endeavoring to keep the unity of the Spirit in the bond of peace, to be careful of each other's reputations, to confess our faults one to another, to strengthen the feeble, and kindly admonish the erring, and to labor together for the building up of the church and the denomination, and the salvation of sinners.
>
> 2. We promise that we will faithfully and constantly maintain secret and family prayer, and religiously instruct those under our care.
>
> 3. We covenant and agree to use our influence to sustain the regular public worship of God, contributing according to our ability and circumstances for the support of the ministry and other church expenses among us; that we will be benevolent to the needy, and especially to the poor of our own church.
>
> 4. We also promise, that, so far as we shall be able, we will attend upon public worship, the social meetings of the church, and report ourselves regularly at the monthly conferences; and that we will walk in all the ordinances of the Lord's house.
>
> 5. We covenant and agree that we will abstain from all vain amusements and sinful conformity to the world; that we will not traffic in, use, nor furnish to others, intoxicating drinks as a beverage; and that we will sustain the benev-

olent enterprises of our denomination and the church—as Missions, Education, Sabbath Schools, Moral Reform, and all others which tend to the glory of God and the welfare of men.

And may the God of peace sanctify us wholly, and preserve us blameless unto the coming of our Lord Jesus Christ; that we may join the glorified around the throne of God in ascribing blessing and honor and glory and power to him that sitteth on the throne and unto the Lamb forever. Amen.[36]

This covenant was apparently not as widely used as the others that were "borrowed" from the Randall movement treatises, but it did appear in some associations in Georgia and one in Arkansas, all before 1935. Among these, the earliest minutes (among those available) to print this covenant were: Liberty (GA), 1893; Georgia Union, 1900; South Georgia, 1909; Benjamin Randall (GA), 1927; and Big Spring (AR), 1921.

This raises the possibility, although it does not prove, that there were some common influences among these. This is certainly the case for the Georgia associations, with their United Baptist background, but whether there was any connection between them and the Big Spring in Arkansas I do not know. Again, however, treatises published by the Randall Free Will Baptists were often found in the South, and that fact alone could account for these associations' use of this one.

Form 4: North Carolina 1883, 1916-44

A very different form of the covenant appeared in the minutes of the Cape Fear Conference in North Carolina in 1883. Then, with minor changes, it was published in the 1916 edition of the North Carolina treatise, where it read as follows:

> Having been brought, as we believe by the divine grace to accept the Lord Jesus Christ as our Savior and Preserver, we do now solemnly and joyfully covenant and agree, by God's help, to walk together in brotherly love.
>
> We, therefore, enter into covenant as members of this Church and as Christians, that we will watch over each other in love, sharing together each other's joys and sorrows; that we will not forsake the assembling of ourselves

---

[36] *Treatise on the Faith and Practice of the Freewill Baptists, Written under the direction of their General Conference* (Dover, NH: Freewill Baptist Printing Establishment, 1871), 35-36.

together, nor omit the great duty of prayer for ourselves and others; that by divine assistance we will endeavor to bring up those under our care in the nurture and admonition of the Lord; that in all things we will strive to exemplify our profession by a corresponding practice, to abstain from all sinful conformity to the world, to be just in our dealings, faithful in our engagements, and exemplary in all our deportment; that we will abstain from the sale and use of intoxicating liquors as a beverage; that we will sustain the worship, ordinances, discipline, and doctrines of this church; that we will contribute cheerfully, according to our ability, to the support of the ministry, the expense of the church, the relief of the poor, and general spread of the gospel.

In keeping this solemn Covenant may we ever enjoy the blessings and presence of the great Head of the Church.[37]

Sometimes this was with or without the final benedictory paragraph. The 1916 and 1921 editions, for example, included the paragraph, but in 1922 it was published without it and this continued through 1944.

This form of the covenant became widely influential among Free Will Baptists before 1935, probably rivaling the influence of the Randall 1892/NAFWB form discussed above as Form 1. Consequently, wherever the North Carolina treatise was used, this form of the covenant also was probably used. This would have been true in many places in the South and westward, since the literature published in Ayden was widely known and used. No doubt there were associations that used this treatise and its covenant even though their minutes print no covenant, and so we lack direct evidence for that usage. This leaves us unsure just how many associations made use of this covenant.

Even so, there are some associations, widely scattered, that printed this form of the covenant in their minutes, thus giving direct evidence for its broader use. I found it in these: Benjamin Randall (GA) 1938, Progressive (AL) 1933, Salem (FL) 1935, North Florida 1940, John Thomas (VA) 1923, Clinch Valley (TN/VA) 1935, and Mt. Olive (KY) 1948.[38] It also appeared in an undated treatise published by the French Broad Association (NC), even though their minutes printed the one I will describe next.

---

[37] Minutes, Cape Fear FWB Conference, 1883, 24-25.
[38] For those in this list with the minutes identified as later than 1935, we do not have minutes earlier than the years indicated, but the associations themselves date to before 1935 and they probably used this form earlier than the date shown.

Form 5: Appalachia 1905

Interestingly, yet another form of the covenant arose in the mountains of western North Carolina shortly after the turn of the century. The earliest appearance, in the minutes we have, was in the 1905 minutes of the Jack's Creek Association, and it reads thus:

> I. Having given ourselves to the Lord through Jesus Christ, we agree to adopt the Freewill Baptist Faith. We now give ourselves to each other by the help of God.
>
> II. We solemnly covenant before God that we will carefully observe the commandments implied in a Confession of Faith, and in the spirit of meekness rebuke and admonish those who have gone astray, and watch over each other, being careful of each other's reputation, and use our influence to the upbuilding of the church and for the advancement of the cause of Christ, endeavoring to seek the unity of the spirit in the bonds of peace, and to confess our faults one to another, and to strengthen those that are weak.
>
> III. We promise that by the help of God that we will faithfully practice family and secret prayer, and strive to cultivate the doctrine of God's revealed word in the minds of those under our care.
>
> IV. We also agree to use our influence for the support of the Gospel and to contribute liberally to aid the ministry according to our several abilities. Also we agree to be liberal with those that are afflicted and needy, and especially those of our own denomination.
>
> V. We also agree to attend the monthly meetings regularly if not providentially hindered, and submit to all ordinances implied in a Profession of Faith.
>
> VI. We also agree to abstain from all sinful and vain amusements.
>
> VII. We also agree to abstain from all intoxicating liquors, and not to use it as a beverage, nor to aid or assist in the manufacture of such nor furnish it to others.
>
> VIII. We also agree to encourage Home and Foreign Missions, Education, Sabbath-schools, good morals, and everything that is to the glory of God and to the welfare of men. And may the God of peace sanctify us wholly and preserve us blameless until the coming of our Lord Jesus Christ, that we may be happily admitted into the kingdom of God, where we may ascribe honor unto the Lamb forever. Amen.[39]

Comparing this covenant with the 1871 Randall covenant (Form 3, above) will show that there are several common words and phrases; it seems likely,

---

[39] Minutes, Jack's Creek FWB Association, 1905, 13.

therefore, that whoever developed this covenant was aware of that covenant from the Free Will Baptists of the North.

At any rate, this covenant appeared not only in the minutes of the Jack's Creek Association but also in the minutes of some other western North Carolina associations: French Broad 1921, Western North Carolina 1924, and Toe River (with churches in North Carolina and Tennessee) 1928. It also appeared in neighboring western South Carolina in the minutes of the Beaver Creek Association in 1925, as well as in the John Wheeler minutes for 1949. This last association included churches in Virginia and other states; although it was organized before 1900, our earlies minutes are for 1949.

Among these associations there are some variations on this form, but it is clear that all of them were using it. Perhaps it represents some local rewriting of the 1871 Randall form. Some of these associations, including the oldest among them—the Toe River—definitely were in communication with the General Conference of the North.

Form 6: Alabama—Oklahoma Early

One more church covenant was used, before 1935, by a group of associations: three in Alabama, the Arkansas State Association, and five associations in Oklahoma. Its earliest appearance, in the minutes we have, is in the Territorial Association (OK) for 1899; the following version appears in the minutes of the Morning Star Association in Alabama in 1917:

> Having been brought as we humbly trust by divine grace to embrace the Lord Jesus Christ as our Savior, and having obtained justification by faith in His name, we as members of the Free Will Baptist church at _____ agree.
>
> 1. To watch over each other in love, to pray for each other as members of a common faith, ever striving to keep the unity of the spirit in the bonds of peace.
>
> 2. We will not speak evil of one another nor will we persecute or expose the faults of the weak members of our church; but will endeavor to be governed by Paul's instruction to Timothy; That we will reprove, rebuke and exhort each other as members of a common brotherhood.
>
> 3. We are commanded to do good unto all men, especially to those who are of the household of faith, but we should remember that our relations to each other are closer and the obligations more binding than that of a common

bond of Christian charity. In adopting this covenant we become a family, and assume in a Christian sense, the care and responsibility that the members of a family should feel for each other.

4. We will attend the stated meetings of the church unless we are providentially hindered or uncontrollable circumstances prevent us. And we will contribute of our means as the Lord has prospered us for the support of our pastor and other necessary expenses of our church, and we will prefer the services of our own church to that of any other, and will pray for our pastor while he is preaching the Word to us.

5. We will not injure our influence in the house of the Lord by occupying seats with the ungodly and sinners, but will occupy seats near the pulpit, and use the natural powers which God has given us to praise His holy name. We will sing with those who sing and pray with those who pray.

6. We will not be guilty of the sin of Sabbath-breaking by making Sunday visits to our neighbors, which is a double sin against the law of God, for in so doing we fail to attend the house of the Lord and hinder others who might wish to do so. Let us remember the law of Moses which condemns Sabbath breaking and the word of the inspired Apostle which says, "Forsake not the assembling of yourselves together as the manner of some is." [Note: the Arkansas State version reads, *"We will not be guilty of Sabbath-breaking, that is, we will not push the ox in the ditch to get to pull him out on the Sabbath, nor by doing any work therein, for the Lord said, "Keep the Sabbath day holy."*]

7. We will not neglect the secret and public prayers and those of us who are heads of families will strive to dedicate our household to the service of God by teaching our children the great necessity of the Christian religion as the only hope of happiness after death. We will adopt the covenant of Joshua, the servant of the Lord, and say, "But as for me and my house we will serve the Lord." [Note: the Arkansas State version reads, *"We will shun all appearances of evil, and all amusements that do not tend to the glory of God. We will adopt the covenant of Joshua, the servant of the Lord."*][40]

Our minutes for these associations, as for nearly all associations, are not complete, so we cannot be sure where this covenant *first* appeared. In the minutes we have, it appears thus: in Alabama, in the Morning Star 1917, Southeastern Alabama 1926, and Bear Creek 1933; in the Arkansas State minutes for 1903; and in Oklahoma in the Territorial 1899, Grand River 1910, Eureka 1914, Eureka and Roberts-McGee (combined) 1918, and Gaines Creek 1934.

---

[40] Minutes, Morning Star FWB Association, 1917, 5, 2 (pages unnumbered, printed out of order).

This particular pattern may be suggestive, especially since this covenant apparently originated neither in the Randall movement nor anywhere else in the southern movement. Perhaps among the earliest Free Will Baptists in Oklahoma were some who came from Alabama and brought with them a covenant that had originated there. In both states, the associations sharing this covenant might have shared similar influences. The singular appearance of it in Arkansas in 1903 might be explained in more than one way; perhaps someone from Alabama was involved. Without other kinds of evidence, however, such discussions are speculative.

There is another interesting thing about this covenant. The same form (without the seventh paragraph) appeared in the *Baptist Review* issue for January 30, 1905.[41] This paper was published by B. W. Nash, a leader among a small group, known originally as Union Baptists, in North Carolina. Nash promoted the union of all Baptists in the South holding to free agency and free communion, and in this effort he led in the formation of a Southern Baptist Association[42] in which a number of Free Will Baptists participated. Whether this was the covenant of that association or of the Union Baptists is not clear, but it is possible that it came to Free Will Baptists from Nash, or that Nash got it from Free Will Baptists. Interestingly, the 1896 minutes of the Territorial Association in Oklahoma, one of the associations using this covenant, recorded the adoption of the *Baptist Review* as "our organ or church paper" and "a faithful advocate of our doctrine." Much more information would be required to establish the origin of this covenant.

IV: Some Concluding Observations About Church Covenants

I have traced this history of our Free Will Baptist Church Covenant, through 1935, for two reasons. One is for the sake of the information itself, as I have

---

[41] Thanks to Gary Barefoot, Curator of the Free Will Baptist Historical Collection at the University of Mount Olive in North Carolina, for sending scans of this issue of the *Baptist Review*, which may be the only issue in existence.

[42] Not to be confused with the Southern Baptist Convention. The story of FWB participation in this and other unity movements in the South is told in another chapter in this volume.

presented it. I trust it will prove interesting and helpful to those studying the history of our movement.

My other reason, however, cannot be hidden: it gives me the opportunity to say some things, though briefly, about the importance and nature of a church covenant. The idea of a church covenant is very old, perhaps as old as the church itself. Burrage has noted that the seed of the idea can be found as early as the end of the first century, when Pliny the Younger wrote to the Roman emperor Trajan (probably in about A.D. 112) that the Christians "bound themselves by an oath at their meetings not to be guilty of theft, or robbery, or adultery, or the violation of their word or pledge."[43]

Why have a church covenant?

To answer simply, because a local church exists in a covenant relationship. I say "local church" because that is where the basis for a church covenant lies.

Covenant relationships are the most important ones we have. Marriage, for example, is a covenant relationship, in which two persons express and define their permanent commitments to each other.

A local church is a covenant relationship—whether anyone writes a formal covenant or not. Because of that, it is far better to have one written, else those in the relationship may not understand what they are committed to or what is expected of them.

Every time a member joins a church, the written covenant ought to be featured and committed to again, by both the one joining and those already in.

I've mentioned in this chapter that the early Randall churches had "covenant meetings" once a month. That wasn't a bad idea. I'm not saying we need to re-institute that practice, but I am saying that our covenant commitments ought to be publicly highlighted within the church on a regular basis.

And when the covenant commitments are broken, church discipline ought to follow.

---

[43] Burrage, x.

Does every Free Will Baptist church have to use the NAFWB covenant?

I have mixed feelings about answering this. If I say yes, I'll be wrong. If I say no, I'll be misunderstood.

The truth is, the commitment of members to live in a covenant relationship is a local church commitment. Consequently, it is ultimately up to the local church—when it is being formed and thereafter—to determine what those commitments are.

At the same time, the NAFWB covenant is a good one, having stood the test of time in broad geographical and cultural diversity. But if a local church is going to use it, that church ought to give it serious consideration and adopt it, making sure it meets its own needs. In other words, a local church must not count on the fact that the denomination has an "official" covenant.

And it wouldn't be the end of the world if any given local Free Will Baptist church adapted the NAFWB form, or even wrote its own covenant from scratch. (I hope that's not regarded as heresy!) Of course, in the latter case, there would have to be no principles of doctrine or conduct that contradicted Free Will Baptist essentials. But at least the church would have to face deciding what is essential to its life. And that's a good thing.

What must a good covenant include?

To put this one way, a church covenant needs to include everything, at least in principle, that the people of that church feel is absolutely essential to the identity and life of that church.

The six covenants reproduced in the preceding section of this chapter provide good examples of the sort of things that should be expressed. A preamble should state the basis for the covenant. The covenant itself should identify the basic commitments required. These will include commitments to each other, to the church as a body (attendance, financial support, etc.), and to the behavior that is expected of all members of the church if they are going to be in good standing in the church and represent it accurately to the world that watches.

I would urge that most of these commitments should be expressed in terms of *principles* rather than for specific behaviors, primarily because this is the way we obey the Bible itself. Our God commands some specific behaviors, both negative and positive, of course; but for the most part He gives us principles that we have to apply in making specific decisions. And as long as we are both sincere and understanding in applying the principles, God is pleased.

A church *could*, of course, insist that all its members contribute a certain amount (or percentage) for its support, or attend a certain number (or percentage) of its services. It *could* forbid not only any use of intoxicating beverages or illicit drugs but also the movies, use of tobacco, and so on. I'd be the first to say that *whatever* a given *congregation* (not just its pastor), prayerfully and carefully considered, feels is absolutely essential for it to be the church it intends to be, might be included, regardless how specific. Nearly all our historic covenants forbid any use of alcoholic beverages, for example—and there's probably no way of arriving at this practice without specifically requiring it.

Even so, it would be very easy for a church covenant to become cultic if it undertook to define an exhaustive list of specific behaviors prohibited or required. *Principles* are the way to go, but those principles must be clear enough to be understood by the congregation as a whole and by the members who make up that congregation.

Why am I making a big deal out of this?

I do it because there are far too many members of our churches whose lives do not even match basic Biblical Christianity.

I do it because emphasizing the importance of covenant commitments will help resolve that problem.

Let's bring back our church covenant and put it to work.[44]

---

[44] I have also discussed these matters in *Discipleship: The Expression of Saving Faith* (Nashville, TN: Randall House, 2013), 195-198.

2

The Spread of Free Will Baptists From North Carolina to South Carolina

Redding Moore and the First Churches and Preachers, 1816-1849

By W. J. McKnight and Robert E. Picirilli

The original Free Will Baptists in the United States began in 1727, in North Carolina, led by Paul Palmer. The rest of that century was a struggle for the movement, and there is no evidence that it spread beyond the Tar Heel State until after 1800. As indicated in a previous volume, as late as 1807, when Jesse Heath entered the Free Will Baptist ministry in North Carolina, there were but five churches in the denomination.[1] By the time Heath wrote this information, in 1827, however, there had been revival and the movement was growing and spreading.

The first and most natural place for the Free Will Baptists to spread to, beyond the state of their origin, was South Carolina.[2] And the story of that outreach primarily grows out of the story of one preacher named Redding Moore.[3] Our purpose in this chapter is to tell that story in as much detail as possible;

---

[1] Robert E. Picirilli, *Little Known Chapters in Free Will Baptist History* (Nashville, TN: Randall House, 2015), 77-78. This information was in a letter Heath wrote to *The Morning Star* in 1827.

[2] After all, eastern South Carolina was nearer to them than much of their own state.

[3] His first name is variously spelled Reading, Redden, Reddin, or in other ways.

however, not a great deal of information has survived. In spite of much research, there are gaps in what we know.

Meet Redding Moore (c.1780-1849)

Probably the best introduction to Moore is in a note written in 1901 by his grandson, J. B. (John Beaty) Moore, also a Free Will Baptist preacher in South Carolina. At the time the grandson penned this information, he was apparently serving as pastor at Old Bethel FWB Church, as it has come to be known. The church needed a new record book, purchased one, and the grandson wrote a short preface in the front. Here is what he wrote, transcribed with original spelling:

> PREFACE OF THE RECORDS OF BEATHEL CHURCH
>
> Be it known unto all who it may consiern that the original record of the above name Bethel Church has bin disstoyed as this being the third book that has bin purchushed for this church the former has bin so kept that the deffinet time and date of the orgernizeation of the church cannot be obtained. Therefore we can safley say that the Bethel Church was orgernized by Eld. Redding Moore, between the dates of <u>1820</u> and <u>1830</u>. Elder Redding Moore, who was onced a citircern of Green County North Carolina, and came to South Carolina in the year 1816. Who was then a member of Grimsley church in Green County North Carolina and at that time was a Licenuate Preacher and in the fall of 1816 he Redding Moore went back to North Carolina at the setting of the Eastern Conference, and was ordained to the Minestrey then return home to South Carolina. Commencing to orgernizing churchis in the State of the Faith once deliverd unto the Saints known as the Original Free Will Baptist Church of South Carolina and in the date of <u>1818</u> he orgernized the South Carolina Conference with the three name churches <u>Mother</u> <u>Little Sister</u> and <u>Pine Grove</u> <u>Church's</u>.[4]
> Elder J. B. Moore / Hyman S. C. / this July 14, 1901

We do not know much about Moore before 1816. Even the exact year of his birth is uncertain: sometime near 1780 in North Carolina—in Greene County, according to the work of genealogist Winston McElveen on the Moores and others.[5] Three other sources give different dates. One is in the Mortality Schedule attached to the 1850 U. S. Census, reporting deaths during the previous year. That schedule appears to show that "Reddin" Moore died at age 72

---

[4] From a photocopy in the FWB Historical Collection.
[5] Winston H. McElveen, *William Ezekiel McElveen: Ancestry and Descendants* (Hartsville, SC: AMG, Inc./Jiffy Print, 1984), 72.

in September 1849, which would put his birth back to about 1778. But the age number is difficult to read; it could be 76,[6] and it appears that someone drew a line though the last digit. If he was 76, that would mean he was born in about 1774. Another source is an undated, handwritten notation in the back of the record book (1858-1929) of the South Carolina FWB Conference, recording basic information about the founding elders. For "Redden" Moore it says, "age 68 years, 2 months, 11 days, died 1849. He was a preacher of righteousness 32 years."[7] This information is stated very precisely and would date his birth to 1781. Harrison and Barfield also say 1781 and agree that he was "born and raised" in Greene County, North Carolina, and was a member at the Grimsley FWB Church.[8] One wonders whether Moore himself knew the year of his birth.

The McElveen book also says that Redding Moore and family appear in the 1790 census in North Carolina, and, indeed, the 1790 U. S. Census lists "Reading Moore" on a line in North Carolina. But this is not our Redding Moore, since he would have been a minor at the time, and the censuses of that period only named heads of household. McElveen suggests that the one in the census might have been the father of our Redding Moore.[9] While that seems a good possibility, we have no confirmation.

There is a possible reference to Moore in a North Carolina newspaper in 1812. In an announcement by the Grand Jury of Greene County, "Reading Moore" is listed as one of the jurors.[10] This could be our Redding Moore, who would have been about 32 years old at the time; and this was before he relocated to South Carolina.

---

[6] Whoever transcribed this for Ancestry.com took it to be 76.

[7] *Minutes of the South Carolina Conference of Free Will Baptists 1858-1930*, transcribed by Clara L. and Robert E. Picirilli (Nashville, TN: printed by Randall House Publications for Robert E. Picirilli, 2009), vi.

[8] T. F. Harrison and J. M. Barfield, *History of the Free Will Baptists of North Carolina* (Ayden, NC: W. E. Moye, 1897), 402.

[9] McElveen, 72.

[10] *The* (Raleigh) *North-Carolina Star*, Apr. 17, 1812. Clipping sent by Benoit Hancock, who also sent one from *The Raleigh* (NC) *Register*, Jan. 2, 1846, with an announcement listing "Reading Moore" as one of the delegates from Pitt County to the State Whig Convention. It seems unlikely that our Redding Moore would be active in a political convention back in N. C. this long after he had settled in South Carolina. Consequently, this also raises some doubt about the identity of the person in the 1812 clipping.

Relocation From North Carolina to South Carolina

The first thing we know for certain about Moore is that he moved to South Carolina in 1816, as his grandson indicated in the Bethel record book.[11] The fact that he was a member of the Grimsley FWB Church in Greene County, North Carolina, is interesting, in that Jesse Heath was from that same church. It seems likely that they knew one another. At the time, apparently, Moore was licensed to preach but had not yet been ordained.

Another line of evidence tends to confirm the year 1816. Elias Hutchins, an itinerant evangelist from the Free Will Baptists of the North, visited the work in North and South Carolina in the winter of 1829-30 and his visit included some time in Redding Moore's home late in 1829—apparently for five days beginning on December 16. Hutchins reported on this visit in a letter to *The Morning Star*, dated in January, 1830, and written from North Carolina:

> Wednesday, 16th, we arrived at Eld. Redding Moore's, in Marion district, where we were kindly received. He moved from his brethren in this State, and took up his abode among strangers, that knew nothing of the Free-Will Baptists, and began to preach *free salvation* in South Carolina, about 13 years ago. It has been his lot to encounter considerable opposition, and pass through many discouragements; but the Lord has been his support. The church of which he is pastor now consists of about fifty members; and, to encourage his heart, after toiling alone for years in his Master's vineyard, two preachers have lately been raised up to assist him in this glorious work in his declining years.
>
> As Eld. M. lives about 30 miles from the church just mentioned, I was denied the pleasure of visiting it: I, however, attended several meetings with him in his own neighborhood, which were generally interesting, and in some, signs of a revival were visible.[12]

This also points to 1816 and seems trustworthy in light of the fact that Hutchins was obtaining his information directly from Moore.

His relocation to South Carolina apparently coincided with his purchase of a tract of land. The deed, to Moore from William Alsobrook, was dated "this fifth day of March in the year of our Lord one thousand eight hundred and sixteen

---

[11] Harrison and Barfield, 402, agree.
[12] *The Morning Star*, Feb. 17, 1830, as cited in Picirilli, 92. We will make some comments about other implications of this quotation, especially for the church and ministers involved, below.

and in the fortieth year of Independence of America": March 5, 1816, in other words. The purchase price was $550, for a "tract of land lying on the North side of Jeffreys Creek containing three hundred & fifty acres more or less." This description fails to pinpoint the precise location, given that Jeffries Creek begins just south of Hartsville, South Carolina, and meanders southeastward through Darlington and (the present) Florence counties into the Pee Dee River. At the time, this was in Marion District, where the deed was formally attested on June 1.[13] According to the deed, "the waters of the Mill Pond does drown or may drown one part" of the land. (Yet another deed, for Redding's son Calvin, shows this to be "McIvers Mill Pond," but we cannot identify that.[14])

This purchase was just the beginning of Redding Moore's acquisition of land. A few years later he was in possession of another large tract in Darlington District. We do not know when he purchased it, but he sold 335 acres to Stephen Reavell in 1827. In 1834 he purchased 394 acres from Alexander Cunningham for $294.50. This tract was "on the S W side of Peedee River Marion District," apparently near or adjoining the land purchased in 1816.[15] He sold 160 acres of this land, in two tracts, in 1846 and 1848. The first, 60 acres, was to Barney Wallace, and the second, of 100 acres, to John B. Smith.[16]

Redding Moore: Family and Census Information

Redding Moore was married twice—his first wife died—and had children by both. To the first, named Ann, were born Samuel (1807), Calvin (c. 1810), William James (c. 1824), and Elizabeth (c. 1825). To the second, Nancy (Jones), were born Nancy Frances (c. 1834), Blaney Johnson (c. 1838), and Joseph Jolly (c. 1842). The first two were born in North Carolina, the others in South Carolina.[17]

---

[13] Marion County Deed-book I, 109-110.
[14] Lee Barrow, in an email to Sherwood Lee dated Oct. 30, 2014, referring to Marion County Deed Book R, 114.
[15] Marion County Deed-books O and P, 150-152.
[16] Marion County Deed-books U and V, 95-96, 274.
[17] One of the writers of this chapter, Robert Picirilli, has a personal interest in Redding Moore: "He was my 3rd great-grandfather on my grandmother's side. His daughter (by Nancy), Nancy Frances, married Andrew J. Kennedy; their son William James Kennedy was the father of Dilly Kennedy, my grandmother (on my mother's side). Apparently he was also my 2nd great-grandfather on my grandfather's side. Redding's son (also by Nancy), Joseph Jolly (according to the story handed down in my family), fathered a

Of interest for our story is the fact that some later FWB ministers in South Carolina were descendants of Redding. His firstborn, Samuel (1807-1880), followed in his father's footsteps as a FWB preacher. So did a grandson, one of Calvin's sons named John Beaty Moore (1847-1925), who wrote the note cited above from the Bethel Church record book. There were probably others. By the way, Samuel had a son named Redding, and Calvin a son named Redden.

In the 1820, 1830, and 1840 censuses, Moore appears in Marion District in South Carolina. In the household in 1820, besides Redding and his wife, were 4 white persons less than 16 years of age and 2 slaves. The 1830 census shows 7 other white persons and 1 slave. In 1840 there were 6 white persons under 20 and no slaves.[18] As already noted, Redding Moore's name appears, in the 1850 census, only in the attached Mortality Schedule, since he had died in September 1849.

Redding Moore appears in some other records of less consequence. In September 1841, he and Stephen Smith were listed in a deed as "chalk carriers" in a land survey. In December 1841, he was witness to a deed. In September 1842 he, along with three of his Smith neighbors, signed a petition asking for the formation of a new county.[19]

Early Ministerial Work and First Churches

It is clear, both from Hutchins's letter and from J. B. Moore's note in the Bethel record book, that Redding Moore began immediately to preach the gospel and to gather churches. Apparently he did not feel authorized to do this in an official capacity, so—according to J. B. Moore—he returned to the Eastern FWB Conference of North Carolina, where he had been licensed, in the fall of 1816 and was ordained.[20]

---

son named Robert by his wife's sister, Nancy Harrell, who was living with them. Robert, who wore his mother's last name, married Dilly Kennedy (his first cousin, once removed), the parents of my mother, Lena Harrell. Furthermore, my wife, Clara Lee, was the daughter of Allene Carraway Lee, who in turn was the great granddaughter of Redding Moore through his daughter Elizabeth. We did not know this when we married."

[18] As seen in the transcribed summaries.
[19] Notes in an email from Lee Barrow to Sherwood Lee dated Oct. 30, 2014.
[20] Harrison and Barfield, 402, agree with the year of his ordination.

This report is certainly incorrect in at least one detail. Although the Eastern Conference existed in North Carolina in 1901 when J. B. Moore wrote, it did not exist in 1816 when Redding Moore was ordained. The conference by that name began after the Annual Conference of North Carolina divided in about 1890.[21] But even if Moore were anachronistically using "Eastern Conference" because the churches that ordained Redding Moore in 1816 were subsequently in that conference, that provides no help in seeking confirmation of J. B. Moore's report. In fact, we have no information at all about *any* conference of FWB churches in North Carolina in 1816. Even so, it is very likely that what J. B. Moore reported is accurate, in that Redding Moore returned to North Carolina for formal ordination.

After ordination, on his return to the place we may call his "mission field," Moore began to organize churches. According to J. B. Moore he formed Mother, Little Sister, and Pine Grove FWB churches, all three apparently by 1818 when they organized a conference of their own. One source says he organized the three churches in 1817.[22] The tradition in South Carolina is that these were the first three churches of the denomination in the state and that they organized the South Carolina Conference of Free Will Baptists. It is possible that J. B. Moore's note intended to name them in the order of their founding, but that is more than we can be sure about.

Mother FWB Church was in Clarendon County, just over the Williamsburg County line. Given the name chosen, it might have been the first of the three churches organized by Redding Moore. It was active in the South Carolina Conference for many years and was a leader in terms of attendance, activity, and influence. Beginning about 1878, however, Mother Church began to be less consistent in representing at the annual sessions, and the Conference acted to look into the situation. Ultimately, the Conference placed the church under its

---

[21] The earliest NC conference for which any record exists was apparently called the Annual Conference, and the earliest record, found in Harrison and Barfield, 197-202, is for 1829. In 1830, this conference divided "for convenience" into the Eastern and Western divisions, with the Western including the South Carolina churches and being known as the Bethel Conference (which might have been the name of the annual conference already), and the Eastern being named the Shiloh Conference. See Harrison and Barfield, 202-205.

[22] Harrison and Barfield, 402, agree that the conference was formed in 1818. (The date there, for the organization of the churches, is 1827, but the context makes clear that this was a misprint for 1817.)

watch-care, and by the 1920s spent some of its missions money on behalf of the church, helping it to reorganize in 1921. In the 1930s, Mother Church became one of several FWB churches in the South Carolina Conference to identify with the Pentecostal movement that was strong at the time. The property, located at 10327 Salem
Rd, New Zion, South Carolina—near the intersection of Salem Road and McIntosh Road—is now home to New Hope Christian Church. The old cemetery, adjoining the church, is accessible. The photograph nearby shows the entrance to the cemetery as it is today; the engraved plaque on the right says, "Old Mother Church Cemetery / Founded 1877."

Piney Grove—often Pine Grove—*FWB Church* was in Williamsburg County, about ten miles from Mother Church. Its "first regular minister" was apparently Samuel McKenzie.[23] It was faithful in reporting to the South Carolina Conference until nearly the end of the 19th century. In 1883, a group of members left the church and founded New Town FWB Church, located less than five miles away. After this, Piney Grove's participation in the South Carolina Conference was sporadic, and by 1924 it was no longer listed in the Conference minutes. By the 1930s, the church had identified with the Pentecostal Free Will Baptists in the area. In 1938, a group of members left and founded the Floyd Chapel Pentecostal Church, which was erected next to the Piney Grove property, where services had ceased by the 1950s. In 1970, the New Piney Grove Free Will Baptist Church of the Pentecostal Faith was built not far from the old location. The cemetery at the original location is still accessible.[24] (The photograph nearby shows the cemetery, with the present Pentecostal FWB Church in the left background.)

---

[23] William Willis Boddie, *History of Williamsburg: Something About the People of Williamsburg County, South Carolina, From the First Settlement by Europeans About 1705 Until 1923* (Columbia, SC: State Company, 1923), 194.

[24] The church and cemetery are located between Lake City and Turbeville off U. S. Highway 378. About six miles from Lake City, Springs Road leads south about a mile to Piney Grove Road, where the cemetery is.

Little Sister (Camp Branch) FWB Church is in Williamsburg County. This church has been active in and reported faithfully to the South Carolina Conference until the present day. The 1883 and 1884 minutes of the Conference record that one of five quarterly meeting groups was called the Little Sister Quarterly Conference. In 1910 the church changed its name to Camp Branch FWB Church, adopting the name of the community where it is located. This is therefore the oldest continuously operating Free Will Baptist Church in South Carolina, and it is located at 192 N. Bethel Road, Scranton, South Carolina.

We may add to these three the church named by J. B. Moore as having been formed by Redding Moore between 1820 and 1830: *Bethel FWB Church* (now known as "Old Bethel").[25] That church is situated between the Pee Dee River and Jeffries Creek, in what was originally Marion District, so it seems possible that it was on or near land that belonged to Moore. Harrell family tradition claims that Robert Harrell, the illegitimate son of Redding Moore's son, Joseph Jolly Moore, donated the land for the Bethel cemetery across the road from the Bethel church building, and it would also be possible that Harrell's land was originally part of or near Redding Moore's property. At present these possibilities cannot be confirmed.

If we had records of the annual conference in North Carolina during the period 1816-1829, we might well be able to name other churches in South Carolina under the influence of Redding Moore. As it is, the earliest information in existence is in the form of excerpts from the minutes found in Harrison and

---

[25] An early survey map, obtained by W. J. McKnight, shows a church at the apparent location of Bethel Church but names it "Moore's Church," which may indicate that it was called that in the community.

Barfield's history of NC Free Will Baptists, beginning in 1829. That year, the only church in South Carolina listed as a member of the conference was Indian Spring in Wayne County in Sumter District. We have no information about that church. The excerpts for 1830 and 1831 do not include lists of the churches.

Perhaps we should also mention *Bethany FWB Church* as one of those in whose founding Redding Moore might have played a part. The church community has nurtured, for many years, the tradition that this was so. And it is certainly possible, especially in light of the fact that one of Redding's parcels of land—the tract in Darlington County of which he sold part, at least, in 1827—was not far from the Pine Log FWB Church, as it was originally known. Benoit Hancock has done more research into Bethany's history than anyone else we know, and he concluded that "Pine Log Meeting House" was built in 1818, but that this was the typical Meeting House of those days, built either by a community or an individual for multi-use purposes, often for more than one congregation. Hancock says that Bethany was not officially organized as a FWB church until 1848.[26] Even at that date, Moore might have played a part.

There were probably other churches organized by Redding Moore, but we have no clear evidence.

Organizing the South Carolina Conference

As already indicated, J. B. Moore's note in the Bethel record book says that Redding Moore and the first three churches—"of the faith once delivered unto the saints"—organized the South Carolina Conference of Free Will Baptists in 1818. This may be correct, but a different line of evidence must also be considered. It is clear that the South Carolina churches under Moore's influence continued to be regarded, until 1831, as belonging to the Bethel FWB Conference that was made up primarily of North Carolina churches; the only other association of Palmer movement Free Will Baptist churches in existence at the time was the Shiloh Conference, which had amiably separated from the Bethel Conference the previous year. The minutes of the Bethel Conference in North

---

[26] Raymond Benoit Hancock, *A Brief History of Pine Log/Bethany Original Free Will Baptist Church 1818-2018* (Moncks Corner, SC: Raymond B. Hancock, 2018), 12. This was printed for the church's two hundredth anniversary celebration.

Carolina for 1831, held at Probability Church in Duplin County, include this: "On motion, by Eld. Redding Moore, the Free Will Baptist churches in South Carolina, in connection with himself, were dismissed, and authorized to organize an Annual Conference in their own section of country."[27]

Indeed, the earliest reference to Redding Moore in Free Will Baptist records is in a letter dated May 28, 1827 (referenced above), from Jesse Heath, of North Carolina, to *The Morning Star*, a weekly newspaper published in Maine by the Randall movement Free Will Baptists. This was Heath's second letter to publisher John Buzzell and included answers to some of Buzzell's questions, one of them to give him "the names of a few of our most useful ministers." In reply, Heath identified eleven as "the most useful ministers" (among the Palmer Free Will Baptists in the Carolinas at the time), one of them being "Reading Moore."

That Moore continued to identify with the body of Free Will Baptists based in North Carolina, and to visit there, is confirmed in a measure by the minutes of a local FWB church in Hookerton, North Carolina, for November 20, 1830. After the record of the business session during the day on Saturday, this note appears:

> On the evening the brethren met to commemorate the Lord's death. Elder Readding Moore administered the sacrament—the meeting solemn and interesting. A door again being opened for the reception of members, one came forward for fellowship and confessed her faith in the Redeemer and accordingly received the right hand of fellowship in order to baptism.
>
> On Sunday morning the brethren retired to water; there five candidates followed the dear Redeemer into the watery grave. The ordinance was administered by elder Readding Moore.[28]

Which is it, then? Was the South Carolina Conference organized in 1818, as J. B. Moore wrote? Or was it organized in 1831 as would be deduced from the minutes of the Annual Conference in North Carolina? Perhaps both were true. It seems highly likely that the small number of churches in South Carolina would have organized for fellowship and mutual watch-care in 1818, even while

---

[27] Harrison and Barfield, 212. This is the only source of the minutes of that session.
[28] Minutes, Hookerton FWB Church, 5 (Nov. 30, 1930). The Hookerton Church began as an arm of the Grimsley Church, and Jesse Heath assisted in constituting the church.

they continued to be a part of the larger, more distant conference in North Carolina until 1831. Perhaps they regarded themselves as something like a "quarterly conference" or "union meeting" of the larger conference. Harrison and Barfield say that in 1818 Moore "organized those three churches into a Yearly Meeting, or Conference."[29] These two historians apparently did not see any contradiction between this and their own report of the 1831 dismissal of Moore and his churches to organize their own annual conference.

The old, handwritten record book for the South Carolina Conference identifies the 1897 session as its 79th. That would seem to put the organization back to 1817 or 1818. But those who met in 1897 and identified their session as the 79th apparently had no direct evidence in their records of the date of the founding of the conference. This record book covers the period 1858 to 1929, with a few gaps. But the 1897 minutes are the first ones to assign a certain number to the session. This arouses the suspicion that someone among them, perhaps J. B. Moore himself, had done some research and decided that the conference had been organized in 1818. Then again, that might have been what J. B. Moore had heard directly from his grandfather.

Early Ministers Working With Moore

The 1830 letter from Elias Hutchins to *The Morning Star*, quoted above, said, reporting on his visit with Redding Moore, that "to encourage his heart, after toiling alone for years in his Master's vineyard, two preachers have lately been raised up to assist him in this glorious work in his declining years." The question is, who were those two preachers?

There is not a long list of possible answers to this question. Among them, the two most likely seem to be Samuel McKenzie and Moab Hewitt. One reason for saying this is the fact, already mentioned, that in the back of the handwritten record book of the South Carolina Conference (1858-1929, with gaps) the following appears:

> South Carolina, Williams Burg District
> To the brethren and friends of the Free Will Baptist churches:

---

[29] Harrison and Barfield, 402.

> The death and memory of the beloved Elders who lived in the service of the Lord for years past and gone. They took the Bible for their instruction and when became to die they departed this life in the strongest triumph of a gospel faith.
>
> Redden Moore: age 68 years, 2 months, 11 days, died 1849. He was a preacher of righteousness 32 years.
>
> Moab Hewitt:
>
> Samuel McKenzie: died Dec. 24, 1864, a preacher of righteousness 26 years and then died.

The person who entered this obviously did not have information about Hewitt. There are no others listed.

Samuel McKenzie was born about 1790, according to a source which also reports that (1) he was probably the second son of Daniel and Rebecca McKenzie; (2) his wife's name was Margaret (perhaps a McElveen) and that the McKenzies and McElveens settled that area along the Williamsburg and Sumter District line; (3) the Piney Grove FWB Church was built on land he owned; (4) he died December 24, 1854 [should be 1864]; and (5) he and his wife were "most likely" buried in the Piney Grove cemetery in unmarked graves.[30]

This unknown source depended mostly on William Boddie's history of Williamsburg County. That volume confirms that Samuel was Daniel McKinzie's son.[31] More important, it informs us that Samuel was one of "a handful of Free Will Baptists" who built Piney Grove FWB Church, and that he was the church's "first regular minister."[32] It seems very likely, then, that McKenzie was among those who worked with Redding Moore in gathering this church.

At the fall term, 1833, of the Williamsburg District Court, the Grand Jury made the following presentation: "We ... present as a grievous evil in our land the intemperate use of ardent spirits ... [and] ... recommend to the Legislature to grant all the aid and facilities which in their wisdom may be proper for them to grant in restraint of this great evil." Samuel McKenzie was one of the jurors who signed this.[33]

---

[30] "Samuel McKenzie, s/o Daniel," sheet in the FWB Historical Collection, source not identified.
[31] Boddie, 241.
[32] Boddie, 194.
[33] Boddie, 312-13.

We do not have much more information about McKenzie. He was still active when the existing (handwritten) record book of the South Carolina Conference took up in 1858. In those minutes, his name appears several times to pray, make motions, and to preach. This pattern continues, more or less, in the minutes from 1859 through 1861. After that, his name appears only in the list of preachers in the Conference. Strangely, this is still true in the 1864 minutes, when the session convened in early October after McKenzie died about two weeks earlier, in September. Perhaps those at the session had not received word, or perhaps they wished to honor his name one final time.

Moab Hewitt. His Find-A-Grave memorial provides only a little information: (1) that his dates of birth and death were about 1795 to 1863; (2) his wife's name was Sarah; and (3) he was a Free Will Baptist minister.[34] We also have record of his purchase of a tract of land—87.5 acres—for $110, from the estate of Benjamin Smith, in Sumter District, in 1851.[35] While we do not know when he was ordained, it was at least by 1837 when he filed an affidavit as "Rev. Moab Hewitt," and newspapers in the 1840s show him as officiating at marriage ceremonies; the 1860 census lists him as "FWB Clergyman."[36]

Like McKenzie, Hewitt was still active when the old record book took up in 1858. In that session, the minutes show that he preached the introductory sermon and was elected moderator. During the years immediately following, he continued to be actively involved in the sessions. His name appears in the minutes as late as 1861, but not thereafter. In that year, the name of William M. Hewitt begins to appear as a minister in the Conference; we know that Moab Hewitt had a son by that name and assume this was that son.

---

[34] Find-A-Grave memorial #53656070. Winnie Yandell (wvy) has attached a note to this record that he was the "first" moderator of the South Carolina Conference in 1858; but the Conference is much older than that, as indicated in this chapter. Lee Barrow, creator of this memorial, indicated via email that a Marion District deed (Book Z, p. 421), dated in March 1863, refers to adjacent landowner Mrs. Sarah Hewitt; he infers, reasonably, that Moab must have been dead by that time else the property would have been listed in *his* name. Given the lack of reference to him in Conference minutes after 1861, he might have died at any time from then until March 1863. Barrow notes that Hewitt's surviving family, on Jan. 1, 1864, filed "to sell the real estate of Moab Hewitt dec'd."

[35] Interestingly, the negro slave in the estate was sold for $550, five times as much.

[36] Lee Barrow, in an email to W. J. McKnight dated August 12, 2005.

The account by Harrison and Barfield names Redding Moore's "companions in the ministry" as John Wilson, Samuel Moore, Wright Wilson, Moab Hewitt, and Nathan Hall,[37] thus providing us with other contemporaries that we may regard as among the pillars of the South Carolina Free Will Baptists in the early years. It seems doubtful that Nathan Hall[38] labored alongside Moore, however, given that his name does not appear in the South Carolina Conference minutes before 1864.

John T. Wilson (1789-1869), like many of those involved in our account, came with his family to South Carolina from North Carolina. He was about 18, then, when the family settled in Sumter District (now part of Williamsburg County). He married Ruth Ellis in 1812, relocated to Darlington District in 1830, and bought 490 acres there in 1831, subsequently receiving (from the state) a grant of an additional 657 acres in 1837. The 1850 census confirms his presence there and is the source of information about the dates of his and his wife's births in North Carolina.[39] The photograph nearby, from the Darlington County Historical Society, is said to be that of Wilson.[40]

We have essentially no information about his conversion or ordination, and very little about his ministry, especially before 1858, when the South Carolina record book takes up. Uncorroborated local tradition said he, on horseback, swam across Lynches River once each month to preach at Piney Grove Church, but no dates are attached to this bit of information. The annual Conference minutes from 1858 to 1867 show him to be active there, making motions, praying, preaching, and being listed as one of the ministers. In 1861, he preached the

---

[37] Harrison and Barfield, 402.
[38] Find-A-Grave memorial #41494417.
[39] Information in this paragraph is from sources gathered by W. J. McKnight, including his "History of Free Will Baptists in South Carolina" columns in *The Informer* for Sep.-Oct. 2001, 5; Nov.-Dec, 2001, 5; and Jan.-Feb., 2002, 5.
[40] We wonder about the triangular "medal" he was wearing. If any reader recognizes it, please inform one of us.

introductory sermon and was elected moderator. The minutes do not usually name the churches' pastors, but in 1863 he was listed as pastor at Mother, Sand Hill, and Crossroads churches.[41] This last church was apparently gathered by him and built on land he owned at Wilson's Crossroads in Darlington District (between Darlington and Timmonsville), and one court witness testified that Wilson "preached many times from his pulpit at Wilsons Crossroads" even after he became infirm and his son Thomas had him declared a lunatic.[42] Thomas Wilson followed in his father's footsteps as a minister in the South Carolina FWB Conference.

Samuel Moore (1807-1880) was Redding's oldest son, born in North Carolina.[43] When the South Carolina Conference was organized in 1818, he would have been about twenty-five years old. Consequently, he might have worked with his father from the beginning in South Carolina or soon thereafter, but we do not know when he was ordained. He married Judith Hicks, also born in North Carolina, in 1826. In 1864, his address was Effingham, in Marion County, but in 1878 it was Effingham, in Williamsburg County.[44] By this time he had obviously settled away from the area of his father's residence near Mars Bluff in Marion (now Florence) County.[45]

When the old record book of the South Carolina Conference takes up in 1858, Samuel Moore figured prominently in its activities, alongside McKenzie, Hewitt, and the two Wilsons. The minutes from 1858 to 1880 record his name in various capacities, although after 1873 he was not always present. He served as moderator at least twice, in 1860 and again in 1878. In 1863 and 1864, he is listed as pastor at Bethel.[46] The minutes for 1881 contain this: "On motion,

---

[41] *Minutes of the South Carolina Conference of Free Will Baptists, 1858-1930*, 2-23.

[42] Letter from Eleanor W. Bradley to H. F. Rudisill, Oct. 10, 1963, copy in possession of W. J. McKnight.

[43] Boddie, 328, lists him as one of the "Tar Heels" who came to Williamsburg, SC.

[44] Effingham had not changed counties and was in Marion County (now Florence County). Either the clerk erred in 1878 or Moore had moved across Lynches River into Williamsburg County but still received his mail in Effingham, which was not far away.

[45] The Cape Fear FWB Conference minutes for its organizational session in 1855, include a motion that "Bro. Moore from South Carolina be invited to a seat with us." This was thought by some, including Herbert Carter of the Pentecostal FWBs in North Carolina, to be a reference to Redding Moore, but he had died in 1849. This is therefore probably Samuel Moore, Redding's son. See W. J. McKnight, "The Cape Fear Mystery," revised (unpublished), in the Historical Collection.

[46] *Minutes of the South Carolina Conference of Free Will Baptists, 1858-1930*, 2-43.

agreed that the names of Elder Samuel Moore, Elder Wright Wilson and Brother John Matthews, deceased, be enrolled on this conference ledger."[47]

Wright Wilson (1804-1881),[48] whose death was noted in the South Carolina Conference minutes along with that of Samuel Moore (above), though considerably younger, was apparently active in the ministry before Redding Moore's passing from the scene in 1849. Whether he was related to John T. Wilson is not clear, but according to his Find-A-Grave information one of his sons was also apparently named John T. Wilson. We have no information, however, about Wright Wilson's ministry during those early years. He is said to be the founder of the Horse Branch FWB Church.[49]

The old record book of the Conference, which takes up in 1858, mentions him frequently, at least through 1868. In 1859, and again in 1862 and 1868, he preached the introductory sermon and was elected moderator, and he was moderator in 1867. He must have been one of the more popular preachers, given that he preached often at other times during the annual sessions. In 1863, he was listed as pastor at Providence and Antioch churches, both in Williamsburg District, and only at Antioch in 1864. In 1865, he was named to be an itinerant preacher throughout the conference, at a salary of $100. After 1868, we do not find his name in the minutes (but we do not have minutes for 1869-1872) until the notice of his death in 1881, already mentioned. He is said to be buried in Wilson Cemetery near Andrews, South Carolina.

The Death of Redding Moore

As already noted, the Mortality Schedule attached to the 1850 Census indicates that Redding Moore died in September 1849, of consumption. His will was attested on September 19.[50] The contents do not reveal any significant information about him or his ministry, except for the fact that he was a man of some means. He bequeathed to his two daughters, Elizabeth (Smith) and Nancy

---

[47] *Minutes of the South Carolina Conference of Free Will Baptists, 1858-1930*, 45.
[48] Find-A-Grave memorial #75383243.
[49] Cassie Nicholes, *Historical Sketches of Sumter County: Its Birth and Growth*, vol. 1 (Columbia, SC: R. L. Bryan Co., 1975), 123.
[50] The Marion County, South Carolina, Genealogy & History website includes a transcribed copy of Redding Moore's will; we also possess a photocopy of the original. It was recorded in Will Book 2, page 125.

Frances (Kennedy) thirty acres each; to his son William James the rest of that tract (acreage not indicated); to a grandson Stephen a tract of land; to grandson Redding (son of Samuel) twenty-five dollars; to sons Calvin and Samuel one dollar each.

To his wife Nancy he bequeathed the rest of his land, together with all the household and kitchen furniture, the stock of all description, and the crop growing on the farm at the time of his death. These resources were to be used for the rearing of the two youngest sons, Blaney Johnson and Joseph Jolly (who were about eleven and seven in 1849); when Nancy died or remarried what remained of her inheritance was to be divided between these two sons.

According to John Kennedy, a genealogist descended from Moore through Blaney Johnson, Redding and his wife Nancy were buried in "the cemetery at Moore's Crossroad." But the location of a cemetery at "Moore's Crossroads" is uncertain. Another of Redding's descendants, Bliss Sports, insists that the cemetery in Lynches River Park, which was originally linked to Sand Hill Free Will Baptist Church, was previously known as "Moore's Cemetery" and is where Redding was buried. But if so, his grave is unmarked. It seems likely that we will not be able to locate the place of his burial.

Concluding Observations

There had been some earlier general atonement Baptists in South Carolina. Indeed, Paul Palmer himself had visited one in Charleston in 1735.[51] Some account of these early "free willers" has been given us by other FWB historians, including Davidson.[52] But they did not survive for long. The Free Will Baptists described in this chapter, of whom Redding Moore was first, were the ones who established churches that are directly linked to the Free Will Baptists in South Carolina today.

It is often the case that a movement derives its impetus from the labors of a man committed to a cause. Redding Moore was apparently such a man.

---

[51] See George Stevenson, "Paul Palmer," in *Dictionary of North Carolina Biography*, vol. 5, ed. William S. Powell (Chapel Hill, NC: University of North Carolina Press, 1994), 12.
[52] William F. Davidson, *The Free Will Baptists in History* (Nashville, TN: Randall House, 2001), 22-24.

Out of the South Carolina Conference have come other conferences in the eastern part of the state, still waving the banner of our denomination today: namely, the Eastern Conference, which was amiably divided from the South Carolina Conference in 1916[53]; and the Central Conferences, which was created in 1946. In the western part of the state, the Beaver Creek Association, organized in 1924, more likely had its origins in the movement of Free Will Baptists from the western part of North Carolina. That story remains to be told—and needs to be.

---

[53] *Minutes of the South Carolina Conference of Free Will Baptists, 1858-1930*, 124-25.

3

United Baptist Origins of Free Will Baptists in Georgia—and in Southeast Alabama and West Florida

There have been different accounts of the beginning of the Free Will Baptist (often hereafter FWB) movement in Georgia. So far, at least three of our historians have published on the subject: Damon Dodd,[1] William Davidson,[2] and Daniel Williams.[3] In the following paragraph, I will summarize briefly the earlier view of Dodd. Davidson and Williams, more recently and in contrast to Dodd, have reached conclusions that I think should now be regarded as settled: namely, that Free Will Baptists in the Peach State, in large part, developed from an earlier movement known as United Baptists. I am convinced by their research, and my account will build on theirs. With the help of skilled researcher Robert Vaughn, I can provide much additional information about these United Baptist forebears of our denomination in Georgia.[4] The story, fleshed out, is interesting and helpful, much of it previously unknown to us.

---

[1] Damon C. Dodd, *Marching through Georgia: A History of the Free Will Baptists in Georgia* (n.p., self-published, 1977.
[2] William F. Davidson, *The Free Will Baptists in History* (Nashville, TN: Randall House, 2001), 196-202.
[3] Daniel Williams, *Origins of Free Will Baptists in Georgia* (Georgia Free Will Baptist Historical Society, 2010). The article in this booklet was also published in at least two other formats. This was originally written by Williams as a senior at Mercer University, under the guidance of the able Georgia Baptist historian Robert G. Gardner. Williams is now on staff at the Baptist archives at Mercer.
[4] Items provided by Vaughn are greatly appreciated and are identified in the footnotes by (RLV).

Dodd, based primarily on a family Bible and weak anecdotal evidence passed down within the Brodnax family,[5] concluded that one John T. Brodnax,[6] from South Carolina, settled in Columbus, Georgia. He preached free will doctrine and established Providence Free Will Baptist Church there, sometime between 1793 and 1795, and donated land for the Church building. Furthermore, he influenced Cyrus White toward free will beliefs.[7]

Subsequent research has shown that Dodd's view is untenable, and both Davidson and Williams have pointed out its problems.[8] John T. Brodnax was not a preacher. The family Bible referred to belonged to his son, James E. Brodnax, who donated the land for the Providence Church, which was begun much later than the date Dodd gave. We must look elsewhere for the origins of Free Will Baptists in the state.[9]

Background: Earlier Arminian Baptists in Georgia

Although this goes beyond my primary purpose, I will briefly describe a movement of Baptists, in Georgia, that was probably the earliest to hold "free will" sentiments. For additional detail, I recommend the account by Williams.[10]

Jeremiah Walker, a Virginia Separate Baptist minister, was the leader of this movement. He relocated to Georgia in the mid-1780s, became pastor of Hebron Baptist Church in Elbert County in 1786, and was elected clerk of the Georgia Baptist Association in 1788. In September of that year, he preached a sermon that he subsequently published as *The Fourfold Foundation of Calvinism Examined and Shaken.*

---

[5] The family name is often spelled Broadnax and sometimes appears as Bradnax.
[6] Find-A-Grave record 28264911: https://www.findagrave.com/memorial/28264911?search=true.
[7] See Dodd, 31-33, for his account. He also published this view in "Free Will Baptists in Georgia," *Viewpoints: Georgia Baptist History* 6 (1978), 55-62.
[8] Davidson, 199-200; Williams, 1, 25 (note 2).
[9] James E. Brodnax (1822-1885; Find-A-Grave memorial #28264965), son of John Travis Brodnax, was a minister in the Chattahoochee, appearing in their minutes first in 1879; he might have been ordained well before then. His obituary appears in the Chattahoochee minutes for 1885, 11-12, written by James M. Bray.
[10] Williams, 4-6. See also Davidson, 196. A more detailed, helpful account appears in Robert G. Gardner, "The Forgotten General Baptist Association in the South," *The Quarterly Review*, vol. 39, no. 1 (Oct-Dec, 1978), 63-72. See also John S. Moore, "Jeremiah Walker in Virginia," and Robert G. Gardner, "Jeremiah Walker: Georgia General Baptist," both in *Virginia Baptist Register*, 1976, 719-30 and 731-44 respectively.

Since the Georgia Baptist Association was dominantly Calvinistic at the time, Walker's views created a stir, resulting in division. Walker was joined by three other ministers: David Tinsley, Matthew Talbot, and Nathaniel Hall—all three also originally from Virginia. The Association adopted articles of faith and rules of decorum, apparently aimed at excluding Walker and his associates. The four men and their churches (mostly formed with groups coming out of the churches they had served[11]) decided to organize a separate association. There is very little record of this body, and John Asplund's *Register* is a primary source of information[12]:

> These three ministers in Georgia, with Nathaniel Hall in South Carolina, got separated from the Association and their Churches, on the account of sentiments, viz. holding Universal Provision and finally falling from grace, got forty members to join them, and in October, 1790, set up their own association, called general Baptists.[13]

This association was small and struggled. Walker died in 1792. Apparently the association existed for no more than five or six years. The subsequent history of the four churches is only partly known[14]; in some cases the members reconciled with their original Georgia Baptist Association churches. If they continued in the views of Walker, perhaps—as Williams suggests—they "kept their Arminian beliefs to themselves."[15]

I have mentioned this early movement both because of their views and because some FWB historians have tended to suggest they were Free Will Baptists. Apparently they held our doctrines, but they did not wear our name and, so far as anyone can tell, had no connection with any of the people that became Free Will Baptists in the state.

---

[11] This was true for the three Georgia churches, but the South Carolina church came as a whole.

[12] Another source is Jesse Mercer, *A History of the Georgia Baptist Association* (Washington, GA: n.p., 1838); Mercer's father, Silas Mercer, was involved in the dealings with Walker's group.

[13] John Asplund, *The Annual Register of the Baptist Denomination in North America*, 1st ed. (Richmond, VA: Dixon, Nicholson & Davis, April 1792), 67, as cited by Williams, 5. This does not necessarily mean that "General Baptists" was an official title; in the absence of minutes, any title they assumed is not known.

[14] Gardner, *Quarterly Review*, 70-71, provides some information about them.

[15] Williams, 6.

Did these folks skip some stones into the Baptist pool, creating ripples that would afterward influence the United Baptists? Perhaps. Davidson, after mentioning that they disbanded, observes that "the ground had been cultivated for the coming of other Arminian enterprises in days to come."[16] But "cultivated ground" is not quite a connection. Even so, the possibility of some influence is removed from the realm of the far-fetched by the fact that Walker's funeral was conducted by Abraham Marshall,[17] son of Separate Baptist Daniel Marshall and a friend of Jesse Mercer, who said Abraham Marshall was "never considered a predestinarian preacher. To use his own figure; he used to say, 'he was short-legged and could not wade in such deep water.' He, with several others, was considered sound in the faith, though low Calvinists."[18]

Background: The United Baptists

Entirely apart from the activity in Georgia, Baptists by the name of "United Baptists" were a well-known historical phenomenon in post-colonial America. In short, this was the name chosen when the Separate Baptists and the Regular Baptists in Virginia merged in 1787. I will not take time for details about this important event, but a few observations seem necessary.[19]

The Regular Baptists represented the earlier Baptist tradition in the colonies as it was influenced by the Particular Baptists who came from England. This tradition, usually following the Philadelphia Baptist Confession, was thoroughly Calvinistic. The Separate Baptists represented an indigenous American movement, highly influenced by the evangelistic momentum that came about from the preaching of George Whitfield and others. Led by Shubal Stearns and Daniel Marshall, a group of these "New Lights" migrated from Connecticut to North Carolina, where they settled at Sandy Creek in 1755.

These Separate Baptists were more moderate in their Calvinism and apparently were tolerant of those with Arminian leanings. Indeed, historian William

---

[16] Davidson, 196.
[17] David Benedict, *A General History of the Baptist Denomination in America*, vol. 2 (Boston, MA: Lincoln & Edmands, 1813), 392. (RLV)
[18] C. D. Mallary, *Memoirs of Elder Jesse Mercer* (New York, NY: John Gray, 1844), 201. (RLV)
[19] I have given a little more information in Robert E. Picirilli, *Little Known Chapters in Free Will Baptist History* (Nashville, TN: Randall House, 2015), 40-43.

L. Lumpkin makes clear that there were often tensions among the Separates over the differences between Calvinistic and Arminian views of salvation, especially as to universal provision and individual responsibility[20]—but not always involving the possibility of apostasy.

In 1787, then, the Separates and Regulars in Virginia merged and took the name United Baptists. This name then began to spread in the states on the Eastern seaboard and in the early Western frontier areas like Kentucky and Tennessee. One should consider that the settlers in different areas were not completely isolated. There was frequent travel from one cluster of settlements to another, and news of events like the 1787 merger would soon spread. There was a broad Baptist milieu in the country, and when groups of Baptists formed organizations they did not simply make up names from thin air; the names they chose usually had significance already.

Apparently, the Regulars and Separates in Georgia had already reached a similar understanding in 1786. In May of that year, Jeremiah Walker, as clerk of the Georgia Baptist Association, wrote a letter in which he said, "We rejoice at length that 'the two sticks are made one,' by abolishing the nominal distinctions, *regular* and *separate*, which have long unhappily divided the Baptists Churches."[21] Robert Gardner said, regarding this: "Unlike Virginia Baptists, who issued a formal statement of reconciliation in 1787, Georgia Baptists quietly produced the same results in the late 1780s."[22]

It seems certain, then, that the first United Baptists in Georgia, who apparently organized the United Baptist Association in 1831, were aware of the significance of that name when they adopted it. I will return to this history shortly. At this point, however, I cite the minutes of the Chattahoochee United Baptist Association,[23] for the year 1850, to show such awareness among the United Baptists at an early date. The minutes include a "Circular Letter," a common

---

[20] William L. Lumpkin, *Baptist Foundations in the South: Tracing Through the Separates the Influence of the Great Awakening, 1754-1787* (Nashville, TN: Broadman, 1961), 148.
[21] Mercer, 139-40. (RLV)
[22] Robert G. Gardner, et al., *A History of the Georgia Baptist Association, 1784-1984*, 2nd ed. (Atlanta, GA: Georgia Baptist Historical Society, 1996), 16. (RLV)
[23] The Chattahoochee story will be related below; they were organized out of the United Baptist Association in 1835 or 1836 and the two were considered "sister associations."

practice in those days. The letter rehearses some of the background history, including tensions between Arminian and Calvinistic Baptists in Virginia, dating back to 1775 when some understanding of mutual tolerance had been reached. Jeremiah Walker, by the way, was actively involved in that meeting on the Arminian side.

The Circular Letter then states the following about the 1787 meeting of the Regulars and Separates:

> It appears that both parties entertained fears until the year 1787, when it was settled to the satisfaction of all. The terms of union were entered on the minutes. ... After considerable debate as to the propriety of having any Confession of Faith at all, the report of the Committee was received, with the following explanations: "To prevent the Confession of Faith from usurping a tyrannical power over the conscience of any, we do not mean that every person is bound to the strict observance of every thing therein contained. Yet it holds forth the essential truths of the Gospel, and that the doctrine of salvation by Christ, and the unmerited grace alone ought to be believed by every christian, and maintained by every minister of the Gospel. Upon these terms we are united, and hereafter desire the names of Regular and Separate be buried in oblivion, and that from henceforth we shall be known as the United Baptist Churches of Christ, in Virginia."[24]

This shows two things. First, the United Baptists in Georgia understood the historical background of that name and adopted it conscious of that significance. Second, they understood that the accord reached in Virginia afforded tolerance for Arminians (at least insofar as universal provision is concerned) and considered themselves in that camp. Indeed, as the Circular Letter goes on to indicate (see below), they linked themselves—at least in spirit—to the original Separate Baptists who participated in the 1787 merger in Virginia.

Cyrus White and the Beginning of the United Baptists in Georgia

When Georgians flipped their calendars to the new year of 1829, it might have appeared to some that the Baptist house was in harmonious order. Before the year was out, however, it would become clear that the peace was seriously disturbed. Most of the Baptists—perhaps all of them—were part of the Georgia

---

[24] Minutes of the Chattahoochee United Baptist Association, 1850, 5.

Baptist Convention. Indeed, Cyrus White had represented the Ocmulgee Association when the Georgia Baptist Convention was organized in 1822, with only two associations—Ocmulgee and Georgia Baptist—participating.[25]

But all was not well. The most serious issue was that which has come to be known as the missionary versus anti-missionary tension. All of the Baptists, insofar as public expressions are concerned, were probably Calvinistic in their theology. But some were more rigid in this than others. The most thoroughgoing (some would say "extreme") Calvinists were against organized missions programs. The more moderate Calvinists, influenced perhaps by the Second Great Awakening, were more evangelistic and committed to the missionary endeavor. This led—ultimately, in 1837—to the division between the Primitive (or Hardshell) Baptists and the Missionary Baptists.[26]

More important for our purposes, the question of a universal atonement arose. The precise reason for this is not clear, but there is a strong tendency for those who aggressively pursue the conversion of others to regard the atonement as making it possible for anyone who may be a target of evangelism to be saved.[27] Whether that played a part or not, in the Ocmulgee Baptist Association, which was part of the Georgia Baptist Convention, the question of the extent of the atonement arose in 1829. At the annual session, the Walnut Creek Church lodged this query: "Did Jesus Christ suffer, bleed and die, on the Cross, for all mankind? Or only, for as many as the Divine Father gave Him in Covenant of Grace?"[28]

To this question the Association responded, (1) by recommending that "the churches and members search the Scriptures for their own satisfaction," and (2) by reprinting its constitution, where Article Four spoke directly to the question at issue:

---

[25] A. A. Marshall, "Georgia's Religious Denominations: Sketch of the Baptist Church from the Time of Its Organization Down to the Present," *The* (Atlanta, GA) *Constitution*, Feb. 11, 1900, 20. (RLV)

[26] Marshall, 20.

[27] Williams, 9, quotes Anthony Chute to say that for White "the doctrine of limited atonement was unscriptural and a deterrent to evangelism." See Anthony L. Chute, *A Piety Above the Common Standard* (Macon, GA: Mercer University Press, 2004), 83.

[28] Minutes of the Ocmulgee Baptist Association, 1829, 2, as cited by Williams, 7.

> We believe in the everlasting love of God to his people, and the eternal election of a definite number of the human race, to grace and glory; and that there was a covenant of grace or redemption, made between the Father and the Son, before the world began, in which their salvation is secure, and that they in particular are redeemed."[29]

This was a fairly standard Calvinistic expression, and its full implications conceived a limited atonement, grounding both election and redemption in an eternal covenant between the Father and Son to save the elect only and unconditionally. I assume that all the parties involved understood this, even if some might have thought there was some wiggle room on the answer to the question about the extent of the atonement.

Regardless, some did not agree that the atonement provided only for the elect. Among them was an influential minister named Cyrus White, pastor of Bethlehem Church in the Ocmulgee. In December of 1829, he published a pamphlet entitled *A Scriptural View of the Atonement*. In it, he argued at length for universal atonement. He said, for example, that the parable of the marriage supper in Luke 14 showed that those invited included many who did not come and yet for whom there was provision.

A good possibility is that the preaching of White, or of some others who agreed with him, had led to the question being raised in the Ocmulgee. It also seems likely that White's publication was deliberately aimed at Article Four as cited above, or at least at the interpretation that the majority of those in the Georgia Convention placed on it.

It is possible, of course, that White had been influenced—directly or indirectly—by Jeremiah Walker's published sermon, as mentioned above, or by some of those who had been part of the little association of general Baptists, of Georgia and South Carolina, that had ceased to exist some thirty years earlier in about 1795. But so far, no connection between White and Walker or that group has been shown.

After White's pamphlet was circulated, a heated controversy erupted within the Ocmulgee and the larger Baptist community in the state. I recommend Wil-

---

[29] Minutes of the Ocmulgee Baptist Association, 1829, 2-3, as cited by Williams, 7.

liams's treatment for details, and I will only summarize the highlights, drawing on his account.[30] The first major shots in response were fired in 1830 by Jesse Mercer, in the form of ten letters addressed to White and published in Mercer's newspaper, *The Christian Index*, defending limited atonement.[31]

At its annual session in October 1830, the Ocmulgee charged the Bethlehem church with having departed from the faith expressed in the Association's constitution and withdrew from the church and its two ordained members, White and John Holmes. The next year's minutes show that there were three other churches' names missing; they joined with Bethlehem in forming the United Baptist Association in 1831—to which I will return below.

The controversy was not contained within the Ocmulgee but also enveloped the Flint River Association to the west. Its 1829 minutes include a lengthy resolution against the teaching "that Christ atoned equally for the whole human family or that he died for, and bought many souls now in hell." It went on to recommend that a church expel any member or minister holding such a doctrine, and that any church, or part of a church, with this view be excluded from the Association.

At the same 1829 meeting, the Association began to deal with the report of a committee that had been constituted to investigate a Sharon church in Henry County. This church had applied for membership, having been dismissed (in good standing, apparently) from the Yellow River Association in 1828. Some charged the church with having departed from the Abstract of Principles of the association, and this involved the Sharon pastor B. H. Wilson, closely associated with White, accused of having preached White's views and having persuaded the majority of the church. The committee had therefore recognized a minority of the church as the true Sharon church. Apparently the matter was continued until 1830, when the Flint River also dealt with division within the Teman

---

[30] Williams, 7-10.

[31] They were subsequently published together, in booklet form, as *Ten Letters Addressed to the Rev. Cyrus White in Reference to His Scriptural View of the Atonement* (Washington, GA: The News Office, 1830). Summaries of both White and Mercer can be found in Williams, 8-9, and in the blogs (Ministry and Music – Seeking the Old Paths) of Robert L. Vaughn for Aug. 28, 2017: "Scriptural View of the Atonement: a Review of Sorts" (http://baptistsearch.blogspot.com/2017/08/scriptural-view-of-atonement-review-of.html) and "Mercer responds to White" (http://baptistsearch.blogspot.com/2017/08/jesse-mercer-responded-to-cyrus-white.html). Mercer University in Georgia was named for Jesse Mercer.

church, also in Henry County. Barnabas Strickland, apparently the pastor, and Ephraim Strickland, a licensed minister, were found to hold White's doctrine of the atonement.[32] Again, the association recognized the minority as the true church.[33]

A sidelight of the controversy is that the Georgia Baptist Association expressed some misgivings about how the Flint River had handled the affair and lodged some complaints along those lines. Subsequently, the United Baptist Association, as shown in the minutes of its meeting at Bethlehem Church in December, 1831, sent six of its men to the next session of the Georgia Baptist Association. They were B. H. Wilson, Barnabas Strickland, J. Reeves (probably John), Cyrus White, J. Travis, and J. Wilson, and they bore a letter asking for opportunity to provide a correct view of their case and expressing hope that errors, on either side, could be corrected. This did not prove to be a solution to the problem, but the Georgia and Flint River Associations soon came to a somewhat hesitant agreement and produced a short "Adjustment of the Differences."[34]

The division within the Sharon and Teman churches, then, involved the controversy about the atonement and election. In December 1830, there was a convention at the Sharon church, which, with Teman, had withdrawn from the Flint River. No organization resulted from this meeting, but the convention adopted a statement that became known as the Sharon Confession of Faith. The fifth article of that confession is significant and expresses a somewhat different view of election:

---

[32] Both Stricklands are named in the 1840 minutes of the United Baptist Association. J. H. Campbell, *Georgia Baptists: Historical and Biographical* (Richmond, VA: H. K Ellyson, 1847), 111, says Barnabas was moderator of the United Baptist Association for the first three years of its existence.

[33] For an extensive report of the controversy from the Flint River perspective, see "Report. The Committee appointed to draw up an Answer to a publication by those churches that have seceded from the Flint River Association, which appeared in the Christian Index of 1831." This report was sent to *The Primitive Baptist* (Tarborough, NC) by William Moseley, where it appeared in the issue for June 25, 1835 (1:12). (Available at www.hathitrust.org.) (RLV) For another report representing a somewhat different perspective, see the minutes of the Chattahoochee United Baptist Association, 1848, 4-7; this "Report of Select Committee" includes the efforts of the Georgia Baptist Association, which had criticized the Flint River, to effect reconciliation with the Flint River.

[34] This paragraph reflects the "Report of Select Committee" referenced in the preceding note.

> We believe in a Covenant between the Father and Son at which all Grace is treasured up, and in the doctrine of Election according to the foreknowledge of God through Sanctification of the Spirit, and belief of the truth according to 1st Peter, 1st chap. 2nd verse, and 2nd Thess. 2nd chap. 13th verse: "God hath from the beginning chosen you to salvation, through sanctification of the Spirit and belief of the truth;" but that Election should not be so construed as to make God the author of sin either directly or indirectly, nor on the other hand do we believe the creature can do any thing meritorious in his salvation.[35]

It seems obvious that this article was intended to present the subject of Article Four of the confession of the Georgia Baptists (above) in a subtly but clearly different light, preserving the so-called eternal Covenant of Grace between the Father and the Son but representing election as conditional—"according to foreknowledge" and "through belief of the truth." (Arminius often said similar things.)

Did those at this convention regard themselves as *Arminian*? The *Free Baptist Cyclopaedia* said they were Arminian.[36] But perhaps they would not have thought so, at least not with the meaning that many today would attach to that name. Indeed, the Sharon Confession makes no direct statement about the extent of the atonement, although its Article 13 (to be quoted below) seems clearly to *assume* universal provision.

Williams reports that Jesse Campbell, writing just seventeen years later in 1847, said that Sharon and Teman were "not ready to join with Cyrus White and company, whom they 'believed to be *Arminian* in their sentiments'."[37] Perhaps, but one should remember that Jesse Campbell was not sympathetic to White, so his estimate of the attitude of the Sharon and Teman churches may be biased. Indeed, in 1831, Sharon and Teman *did* join with the churches that had left Ocmulgee to form the United Baptist Association, which was the mother association—though, as we will see, not the most influential or lasting association—of United Baptists in Georgia.

---

[35] Minutes of the United Baptist Association, 1846, 3, as cited by Williams, 13.
[36] *The Free Baptist Cyclopaedia*, G. A. Burgess and J. T. Ward, eds. (Chicago, IL: Free Baptist Cyclopaedia Co., 1889), 227.
[37] J. Campbell, 267, as cited by Williams, 12 (page 110 in the 1874 edition published in Macon by W. Burke & Co.)

The United Baptist Association, 1831—?

Information about the formation of this organization is sparse and the only minutes that we know to exist are for seven years: 1840, 1842, 1846, 1849, 1851, 1853, and 1854. The 1849 minutes refer back to a convention at Bethlehem Church (where Cyrus White was pastor) in 1831, apparently when the association was organized—although Jesse Campbell said it was organized in 1832 at Teman church.[38]

The information available seems to mean that 1831 was the year. The churches that met and organized were, at least primarily, those that had left the Ocmulgee Association and the Sharon and Teman churches that had come out of the Flint River Association. Perhaps the thing they shared most in common was the treatment they had received in their associations. But it seems certain they also shared misgivings about limited atonement and unconditional election.

My reason for saying this is found, again, in the Circular Letter attached to the minutes of the Chattahoochee Association of United Baptists in 1850. As noted, this letter recited some of the historical background of the United Baptists, including the meeting in 1787 in Virginia when Regular and Separate Baptists merged and took the name United Baptists. That Circular Letter then went on in the following way:

> This union [in 1787] continued for upwards of forty years, when Cyrus White, and other ministers, became convinced of the justness of their principles, went on to preach the same doctrine that had been proclaimed by the Separate Baptists as far back as 1714, when they were called Newlights. By referring back to the year 1829 or '30, you will discover that some disposition was manifested by the Regular Baptists, to make binding their Articles of Faith on all Baptists, when it became the duty of the Separate Baptists to set forth their principles again.
>
> "To our brethren abroad, greeting: We, the United Baptist Association of Georgia, are fully convinced from recent developments, that a short summary of our principles of Theology is imperiously demanded, at the present important crisis; And, whereas, at a Ministers' meeting held not long since at Forsyth, Monroe county, embracing talent of no ordinary character, a precedent was established at war with the sacred and inalienable right of private judgment,

---

[38] J. Campbell, 267, as cited by Williams, 14 (page 110 in the 1874 edition). But the "Report..." cited earlier refers to the minutes taken at Bethlehem in 1831, which, I think, settles the matter.

and which in legitimate tendency, supersedes the authority of Christ, as the only King of Zion, by making it obligatory on all who wish to be considered strenuously orthodox, to subscribe to the tradition of forefathers, as embraced and set forth in the Georgia, Oakmuga [sic], Yellow River and Flint River Associations, which embrace the doctrine of eternal, unconditional and personal election, namely, that there was an eternal, personal Covenant entered into between the Father and the Son. The conditions of said covenant are such as to exclude from eternal life, all those not included therein; and that those whose names are included in said covenant shall be inevitably drawn by the spirit, and brought to a knowledge of that high relation which they have had the honor of sustaining to the Lord Jesus Christ, from eternity; from which sentiment they say we dissent, which we readily acknowledge. But notwithstanding we have been represented as discarding the doctrine of the Covenant, and consequently the doctrine of election, yet it has been our highest felicity to advocate the Covenant, and also election, as exhibited in the Bible … [quoting Isaiah 42:6; Zechariah 9:11, and 2 Timothy 1:9] … And as to the doctrine of election, we believe it as it is revealed to us in the Scriptures by our Lord Jesus Christ and his holy Apostles. But it is to be lamented that so many of the ministry of modern times so mistify [sic] election, as to exclude moral agency and man's accountability. We believe that God, in the economy of his grace has made ample provision for the salvation of the world, through repentance and faith in our Lord Jesus Christ. For God so loved the world that he gave his only begotten Son, that whosoever believeth in him shall not perish, but have everlasting life; and, upon the broad base of Revelation, faith and practice, we solicit a correspondence with brethren of a kindred spirit throughout the Union."[39]

I have quoted this lengthy portion of the 1850 Circular Letter because of its significance for the doctrine of the United Baptist Association at its founding. The 1836 ministers' meeting referred to, at Forsyth, was "for the purpose of endeavoring to heal the unhappy difficulties which have existed for some years in the denomination." Andrew Cumbie, Ephraim Strickland, John Reeves, and William Byars represented the United Baptists and communicated the fact that they had no quarrel with the traditional Articles of Faith "except a part of the fourth Article, and some connexion with it in the sixth."[40]

---

[39] Minutes of the Chattahoochee United Baptist Association, 1850, 5-6.
[40] *History of the Baptist Denomination in Georgia*, compiled for The Christian Index (Atlanta, GA: J. P. Harrison & Co.), 188. (RLV) This source, 185-196, contains a detailed account of the Forsyth meeting, at which J. Campbell, 111, said "some of the ministers of this [United Baptist] Association would not unite … in subscribing to the old confession." Andrew Cumbie (1802?-1875) appears again in the 1842 minutes of the Chattahoochee where he served on a committee with White (see below) and preached. According to

From the circular letter quoted above, a number of things are clear:

(1) They (the Chattahoochee) were referring back to the original controversy that began in the Ocmulgee Association in 1829-30. They attributed to Cyrus White and others the preaching that ignited that controversy. And in referring to forty years after 1787 they indicated that such preaching had begun at least two years before 1829.

(2) Interestingly, they identified themselves, in spirit, with the original Separate Baptists who had participated in forming the United Baptists in Virginia. I assume they were thinking primarily of the liberty of those Separate Baptists, in that merger, to preach universal atonement.

(3) In the last, long paragraph in quotation marks, they were quoting an earlier document of the United Baptist Association. It seems clear that the document was prepared in connection with the same events just referred to, and in that case it went back to the 1836 meeting in Forsyth that came about as a result of the founding of the United Baptist Association in 1831. The reference to the Yellow River, Georgia, Ocmulgee, and Flint River associations confirms that the document was written in response to the original controversy.

(4) Consequently, the United Baptist Association held free will views from the beginning: namely, they objected to unconditional election and upheld universal provision and responsibility. At the same time they upheld the doctrine of the eternal covenant of grace between the Father and the Son *as they interpreted it*. In this regard, and in rejecting unconditional election, they were saying the same thing as in the Sharon Confession, quoted above.

The Sharon church did not continue with the United Baptist Association for long. According to Williams, it joined the Central Baptist Association in 1834. No doubt some of the other churches returned to the traditional associations. The Teman church, however, continued its affiliation and hosted the United Baptist Association in 1840.[41]

---

his obituary (*The Christian Index*, Dec. 23, 1875, 6) (RLV), while his "first labors as a preacher" were with the United Baptists, he "united with the regular Missionary [Baptists] about the year 1845." He thus serves as an example of several United Baptist ministers who "returned" to the regular Baptist fold, typically joining those who were missionary-minded. John Reeves is listed in the 1842 Chattahoochee minutes as a minister representing the Republican Church in Muscogee County; he was moderator in 1847.

[41] Williams, 14.

It is not clear how long the United Baptist Association continued to exist. As indicated, the latest minutes we have were for 1854. The Chattahoochee United Baptist Association corresponded regularly with the United Baptist Association, but there are no minutes for the Chattahoochee between 1854 and 1879. In 1854 this correspondence was active, but in 1879 and thereafter there is no reference to it. I assume, then, that the United Baptist Association had ceased to exist at some time between 1854 and 1879. David Benedict, writing in 1848, expressed his personal opinion that "they are gradually becoming assimilated in all respects to the old body, and will soon again be wholly absorbed in their ranks."[42] Given the mildness of the Arminianism of the United Baptists, and the tendencies of the broader Baptist movement in that same direction, this would not be a surprising outcome. But there are other possibilities, one being that the churches ultimately united with other United Baptist Associations as the United Baptist movement expanded. It is clear that this was the case for some of them.

The Doctrine of the Early United Baptists

I am interrupting my account of events to focus, in this section, on the doctrine of the United Baptists during their first twenty-five years or so. This includes both the United Baptist Association and the Chattahoochee United Baptist Association, which was formed out of the first in about 1835 and maintained sister association relations with it at least through 1854, the year of our latest minutes of the two associations until 1879.[43] (I will return to the Chattahoochee story below.)

It appears that the United Baptists came to be regarded in a less heretical light by the regular Baptists, or at least by some of them. Perhaps this was after the first heat of the controversy had waned, perhaps even after Cyrus White was off the scene. At any rate, in September 1842 *The Christian Index* had this to say, in an article headed "United Baptist Association":

---

[42] David Benedict, *A General History of the Baptist Denomination in America and Other Parts of the World* (New York, NY: Lewis Colby and Co., 1848), 744, as cited by Williams, 16.

[43] Beginning in that year we have minutes only for the Chattahoochee.

> We have been more than once solicited to give our views in relation to persons belonging to this body, whether or not it would be proper to receive them into the regular churches without re-baptism, re-ordination, &c. In a late number of the Index we stated that we thought it would be altogether proper to receive them without such baptisms or ordinations. ... Not to pursue this course would argue a scrupulousness, in our judgment, not consistent with the spirit of our discipline.[44]

The editor went on to say, perhaps revealing the reason for his gracious attitude, "These Churches ought to come back again to the old Associations."

In March 1843, *The Christian Index* made further observations about the United Baptist Association:

> This Association is in favor of education and missionary operations. On a hasty view of their confession of faith, we find nothing worthy of a serious objection. If they do not go as far as some of us do, they go far enough, it appears to us, for all practical purposes. While we believe, as conscientiously and as firmly as any one does, in the doctrine of particular election, limited atonement, &c., we are decidedly opposed to making any brother an offender for a word. Unless there is something in these brethren more objectionable than we can discover in the minutes before us, we should think that the wall of separation between us has existed sufficiently long, and long enough separated between those who love and serve our Saviour."[45]

Indeed, in October, when the statistics of Georgia Baptists were given in the pages of *The Christian Index*, both the United Baptist Association and the Chattahoochee United Baptist Association were included.[46]

The doctrine of the United Baptists, at this time in their history, is relatively easy to identify, even though for a while they apparently did not publish a confession or articles of faith of their own construction.[47] They had rejected limited atonement and unconditional election and upheld the freedom of human beings to accept or reject the gospel. In 1840, the United Baptist Association considered the possibility of writing "a treatise on doctrine and discipline," and they

---

[44] *The Christian Index*, Sep. 23, 1842, 601-02.
[45] *The Christian Index*, Mar. 17, 1843, 169-70.
[46] *The Christian Index*, Oct. 4, 1843, 493. (RLV)
[47] I say "apparently" because there are many gaps in the minutes we have of both associations during this period.

appointed a committee to work with the Chattahoochee in such a venture if it were deemed appropriate.[48] Nothing came of this, as far as we can tell.

In 1843, however, the United Baptists—from both associations, it seems clear—finally wrote a document of their own. The occasion was a ministers' meeting at Corinth Church in Marion County (a church of the Chattahoochee), July 28-31. They prepared a Constitution, Covenant, Government and Ordinances, Articles of Fundamental Doctrine, and Declarative and Explanatory Views. And they "unanimously agreed" to publish all of it in *The Christian Index*, where it appeared in full in the issue for August 25, 1843.[49] Then, apparently, at the fall meetings of the two associations the documents were presented and recommended for action. The associations, if approving, would then recommend the document to the churches for adoption. We do not possess the minutes of either association for 1843, but a report in *The Christian Index* indicates that at the October meeting of the United Baptist Association the delegates

> Agreed that we recommend to the churches of the body for their consideration, and if they think proper the adoption of the constitution and doctrinal views set forth by the Ministers' and Deacons' meeting, held at Corinth, Marion county, Ga., in July last, and published in the Christian Index, vol. 11, No. 34, for August 25, 1843.[50]

The doctrinal views ("Articles of Fundamental Doctrine") were few and short: seven, in fact, that spoke of God, Jesus Christ, the sinfulness of humanity, justification by faith alone, the necessity of obedience to the revealed will of God, regeneration as the work of the Holy Spirit essential to salvation, and a general resurrection and judgment. None of these articles spoke to any of the issues between the United Baptists and other Baptists. The only reference to the atonement says, simply, that Jesus "died to make atonement for our sins."

Following these doctrinal views was a set of "Declarative and Explanatory Views," and it is difficult to know what to make of them. Immediately after them, this appears:

---

[48] Minutes of the United Baptist Association, 1840, 4.
[49] *The Christian Index*, August 25, 1843, 537-540.
[50] *The Christian Index*, Dec. 1, 1843, 782.

The reader is requested to take notice, that the above declarative views were not set forth by the Ministers' Meeting. The copy which the committee intended to report with the constitution was mislaid. With this explanation, however, they are forwarded for publication, that churches adopting the constitution may spread these views upon their church books, by which means uniformity will be promoted in the connection.

What are we to understand from this? Indeed, it is in these "Declarative and Explanatory Views" that doctrines are covered more extensively, *but they make few if any commitments about the doctrines that had been at issue.* Item 43 says that "the blessings of salvation are made free to all by the gospel, that it is the immediate duty of all to accept them by a cordial and obedient faith, and that nothing prevents the salvation of the greatest sinner on earth but his own voluntary refusal to submit to the Lord Jesus Christ." But nothing affirms universal atonement *as such*, although this statement might have been intended to imply it. Election is described in item 45, and the only thing said that might reflect the controversy is that it is "perfectly consistent with the free agency of man."

It is true that these articles do not affirm the particular and unconditional election and limited atonement that were affirmed by the Georgia Baptist Convention, as already noted; and the idea of an eternal Covenant of Grace between the Father and Son is not present. Even so, there is also no definitive commitment to universal atonement or to conditional election. The freedom of the will and the possibility of salvation for all are only mildly stated, and mostly by implication. Perhaps that was thought to be "Arminian" enough!

I am left to wonder if these articles were deliberately designed to avoid offending Calvinists, or perhaps to make room for people who preferred a middle ground. Now *add* to this a most interesting, and somewhat puzzling, twist. Later that same year, *The Christian Index* made reference to what had been published in August and added a note that two of the "Regular Calvinistic" associations of Baptists, in good standing with the other Baptists of the State Convention, *had adopted the articles of faith proposed by the United Baptists!*[51] The *Index* editor then raised the question what they all must do if the two United Baptist associations

---

[51] I *assume* this refers to the short "Articles of Fundamental Doctrine" and not to the "Declarative and Explanatory Views," but this is not clear and might not have been the case.

decided to adopt those articles of faith. His answer: to be consistent, they would have to receive them as being of the same faith and order.[52]

The question, then, was whether the United Baptists, in the two associations, would indeed adopt this new 1843 document which had been recommended to the churches for their consideration. The churches would have the final say; indeed, the document itself reaffirmed that associations do not bind the churches. I am inclined to doubt that this document was adopted by the churches. It does not appear in any of the years of minutes we have—admittedly few—of either of the two associations, following 1843.[53] But after our long gap in minutes between 1854 and 1879, *the "Doctrinal Views" in the 1879 minutes are essentially the same as these 1843 "Declarative and Explanatory Views."*[54]

What *did* happen, in the 1840s, was that they printed again the Sharon Confession of Faith.[55] In 1840, the United Baptist Association had asked the churches to indicate whether they wanted the Sharon Confession reprinted, and in 1846 and 1849, at least, they printed that confession in the minutes, as did the Chattahoochee in 1848 and 1850. In 1846, it was prefaced with a strong statement that it was not meant to be a creed or test of fellowship, since they took "the word of God as the only infallible rule of faith and practice"[56]—a

---

[52] *The Christian Index*, Dec. 1, 1843, 782.
[53] I am tempted to wonder other things. Did the positive reaction of *The Christian Index* contribute to the rejection of the articles of faith, if in fact they were rejected? Even more deeply, did the 1843 document itself result from some behind-the-scenes agreement between leaders of the regular Baptists and the United Baptists, hoping for reunification? There had been some sort of proposal for union, as indicated in what *The Christian Index* reported, in the same December 1843 issue: namely, that the United Baptist Association had also adopted the following: "We notice with regret the terms of union proposed by the Flint River Association through their committee to the United Baptists, and settle the question thus: 'That we are not willing to rescind our principles, which we think we have deduced from the Scriptures, to be united with any body of people. ... We are willing to reunite on the basis of the New Testament."
[54] The 1879 "Doctrinal Views" include all nine of the 1843 "Declarative and Explanatory Views," with minor changes, plus five new ones. The 1879 minutes, page 2, say, "Articles of faith to be published as in the Minutes of the Ninth Annual Association of this body." The ninth session would apparently have been 1844, whose minutes we do not have. Consequently, it is very likely that the articles published in 1844 were the same (with perhaps some editing) as those published in *The Christian Index* in 1843.
[55] Williams, 15, 19, wonders why they went back to the Sharon Confession—a good question—and considers the possibility that doing so represented a temporary trend back to Calvinism. To me, the Sharon Confession is more clearly Arminian than the 1843 document. I am guessing that the 1843 document was never adopted. I wish we had all the minutes so we could be sure.
Minutes of the United Baptist Association, 1846, 3. See also 1849, 4. (All quotations from this confession are from this source.)

qualification repeated frequently. This insistence, of course, was in keeping with their tradition. The 1851 minutes reprinted their original constitution and expressed strongly this same concept: namely, that the association did not have the authority to bind the churches and that the Old and New Testaments serve as the only authoritative rule of faith and practice.[57] In this stance, they were following the tradition held dear by the Separate Baptists with whom they identified themselves in spirit.

I take it, then, that during the first twenty-five years of the United Baptists, the Sharon Confession was a fairly accurate expression of their beliefs. It was a relatively standard expression of sound, Christian doctrine. Article 12 expressed a forthright view of total depravity and its effects: "We believe that men by nature are so morally depraved that they will not come to God for life and salvation, and but for the influence of the Holy Spirit none would ever come to Him." That is precisely what I teach about depravity.

I have already cited Article 5, which affirmed both the eternal Covenant of Grace between the Father and the Son and conditional election. I find nothing objectionable in this, although I acknowledge that the idea for such a covenant between the First and Second Persons of the Trinity seems to have a Calvinistic origin. The Sharon Confession affirmed it but did not give it the full meaning of the Calvinists.

Article 13 was apparently intended to express both a strong missionary obligation and (in combination with Article 5) universal atonement:

> We hold that it is the command of God to his people to publish His word and promulgate the Gospel of Christ to all nations, making known to the human family the plan of Redemption through the Atonement of Christ, and we believe it is the duty of every rational descendant of Adam to whom the message of reconciliation is addressed, to exercise repentance toward God and faith in our Lord Jesus Christ."

---

[57] Minutes of the United Baptist Association, 1851, 2-3. Essentially the same constitution appears in the minutes of the Chattahoochee Association for 1851, 5-6. That the Chattahoochee considered themselves one with the United Baptist Association is clearly implied by the fact that the tables of statistics in the 1848 through 1854 minutes add the statistics of the United Baptist Association to their own and give the totals of the two associations combined.

This seems intended to say that "every rational descendant of Adam" could possibly be saved through the atonement of Christ.

Article 9 of the Sharon Confession said, "We believe that Saints will persevere in Grace to the end of their lives." Obviously, then, they did not officially believe in the possibility of apostasy.

Furthermore, the 1851 minutes of the United Baptist Association contain the following item: "Refused to correspond with the Salem United Association in consequence of their open communion principle and practice." There was no article in the Sharon Confession on this subject. The 1843 document said that "none are entitled to partake ... but orderly members of a gospel church, who have been received into the church in the divinely appointed way, even by baptism"[58]—which might be interpreted for closed or open communion. The *Free Baptist Cyclopaedia* said they allowed each church "to practice open or close communion at its discretion,"[59] but provides no source for this information. If refusing correspondence with Salem sounds contradictory to this practice, perhaps the United Baptist Association did not approve of Salem's *exclusive* commitment to open communion and preferred to leave the decision to the churches. We cannot be sure about this.[60]

Regardless, it is clear that the early United Baptist churches *were not Free Will Baptists*. They held free will views of the atonement, conditional election, and human responsibility for the gospel. They did not hold to the possibility of apostasy, open communion as a definite commitment, or feet-washing as an ordinance of the church.[61]

---

[58] *The Christian Index*, Aug. 25, 1843, 538.

[59] *The Free Baptist Cyclopaedia*, 227.

[60] Interestingly, the 1851 minutes, 2, of the United Baptist Association show that their *committee* on correspondence recommended correspondence with Salem, so there must not have been any significant disagreement.

[61] It is clear enough that one does not have to hold to the possibility of apostasy in order to be "free will" in doctrine or "General Baptist." Asplund's *Register*, in 1794, for example, distinguished between "General Baptists, Who hold *Perseverance in Grace*" and "General Baptists, Who hold *final falling from Grace*." John Asplund, *The Universal Register of the Baptist Denomination*, Third edition (Boston, MA: John W. Folsom, 1794; reproduced by Arno Press, New York, 1980), 49.

Who Was Cyrus White?

Before taking up the thread of events again, beginning with the founding of the Chattahoochee United Baptist Association in 1835 or 1836, this seems the best place to provide more extensive information about Cyrus White as the minister evidently most responsible for the founding of United Baptists in Georgia.

White was born in Virginia February 3, 1783, and was brought to Georgia in his youth by his parents, Moses and Ann White.[62] Information about his boyhood is limited. In 1804, he registered for the land lottery in Franklin County, Georgia. There is some confusion in the records about the date of his marriage and name of his wife. Some say she was Derinda Harold, some Verlinda Harvey, the latter being better attested, I think. It is possible he was married twice, I suppose; but, given the similarity in the names, I think it more likely there was a miscopying in some source. Probably he married in 1811, at age 28, in Jasper County.

White was a Captain of his own company in Wimberley's Regiment, 3d Regiment of the Georgia State Troops, in the War of 1812. In 1814, he was on a committee "of respectable citizens" to express local sentiments, to be communicated to the Jasper County members of Congress. In 1815, he was on a Jasper County jury. In 1818 he was announced as a candidate for surveyor of a district in the recent land purchase from the Creek Indians.[63]

We know almost nothing of his education. One writer said it

> was of the crude sort, gathered at haphazard from such meager sources as were, at that early day, available to the pioneer farmer boys. Nature having endowed him with a mental capacity considerably above the average, he made the most of what was acquired in boyhood, adding to it by studious habits and teaching in his earlier years of manhood.[64]

---

[62] The Find-A-Grave site for White has the memorial ID number 181872524 and is available at https://www.findagrave.com/memorial/181872524?search=true. (RLV)

[63] The facts in these two paragraphs (and some that follow) are from "Genealogy Report: Ancestors of Osiris Merlin Johnson," printed 2001, November 30: https://www.genealogy.com/ftm/j/o/h/Osiris-M-Johnson/GENE1-0030.html (hereafter "Genealogy Report"). (RLV) For the surveyor announcement, see *The* (Milledgeville, GA) *Reflector*, Nov. 17, 1818, 3. (RLV)

[64] F. L. Cherry, "The History of Opelika and Her Agricultural Tributary Territory," chap. XXIII, *The Opelika Times*, Feb. 29, 1884, 4. This was subsequently reprinted in *The Alabama Historical Quarterly*, 15:2. (RLV)

Specific information about White's conversion and ordination is not available. His obituary (in 1844) indicated that he had been a member of the Baptist church for 31 years and a minister "upwards of 30."[65] This probably meant that he had been converted in about 1813, aged 30, and ordained a year or so later. I would guess that those momentous events took place during or shortly after his military experiences. Cherry, cited about White's education above, reported that he was mustered out at Charleston in 1814.

Cherry also said that he "acquired some note as a Baptist minister." The Genealogy Report already mentioned has assembled a listing of numerous items about him, mostly from newspapers, as follows.

—1821: minister of the Bethlehem Baptist Church in Jasper County.

—April 21, 1821: with Jonathan Nichols to preach at Fellowship, County Line, and Cainy Creek in May.

—December 18, 1822: with Jonathan Nichols, to preach at Little River and Sandy Creek in January.

—December 3, 1822: with Jonathan Nichols, to preach at Antioch, Eatonton, and Crooked Creek.

—January 16, 1824: with Francis T. Martin, constituted Bethesda Church.

—March 26, 1824: signed, as clerk (Jonathan Nichols, moderator), a report to churches of the Ocmulgee, relative to a meeting to discuss the need for revival.

—March 9, 1824: with Edward Shackelford, to preach at Crooked Creek, White Plains, and Powelton.

—July 12, 1825; April 26, 1826: notices of letters being held for him at Jasper Post Office.

—August 20, 1827: with Rev. James Reeves, constituting Macedonia Baptist Church near Newnan, GA.[66]

---

[65] *The Christian Index*, March 15, 1844, 40.
[66] Confirmed by one of J. P. Reese's "Cedar Creek Ripples" columns, c.1880. (RLV) J. P. (John Palmer) Reese (1827-1900; Find-A-Grave memorial #64535189) and his father James Rees (1801-1890; Find-A-Grave memorial #27134342)—the family name could be spelled either way—were ministers in the Chattahoochee (so was J. P.'s twin brother, H. C.), closely associated with Cyrus White, often living near him. James appears in the Chattahoochee minutes for 1848 and J. P. in 1851 as a licentiate. J. P.'s column, in the Newnan, Georgia, *Herald*, led to his nickname "Ripples." For James's obituary, see the (Columbus, GA) *Daily Enquirer-Sun*, Sep. 21 and 25, 1890, 3 and 7 respectively. (RLV)

—May 18, 1829: with Benjamin Wilson, traveling under the direction of Baptist State Convention; to preach at Bethel.

—? 1829: with H. B. Wilson, to preach in Fayetteville and at LaGrange.

—? 1833: preached the funeral of Stockley Morgan at Bethlehem Church, Jasper County.

A matter of relatively minor interest is that in 1831 a Sheriff's sale included the following items belonging to White: "Two bay horses, one about seven, and the other about twelve years old, 2 cows and calves, 15 head of hogs, 15 barrels of corn, and Gills commentaries." They were being sold by the sheriff to honor a "fi fa" levied against White in Baldwin Superior Court in favor of Charles Wheeler and Ambrose Witcher.[67] What makes this interesting is that the sale included the commentaries of John Gill, a well-known English Baptist theologian, thoroughly Calvinistic. One wonders if White voluntarily let them go because of Gill's theology—but that is too speculative to assume.

White's success as a preacher can be illustrated by a newspaper report in January 1828. During five Sundays in October, November, and December of 1827 he had baptized 149 persons: 48 at Hepzibah, 72 at New Hope, and 27 at Bethlehem.[68] Interestingly, these three churches were still part of the United Baptist Association in 1840, in the earliest minutes of that association we possess; New Hope and Hepzibah were in the Chattahoochee in 1842. The newspaper article goes on to observe: "The revival is still progressing, not only in these churches, but also in others in the upper part of Jasper, Morgan, Newtown &c. Multitudes are anxiously enquiring what shall I do to be saved."[69] This was apparently before controversy arose, but it is not difficult to suppose that White's view of universal atonement contributed to the energizing of his evangelistic zeal.

According to Cherry, White soon attracted attention as holding doctrinal tenets that were different, saying he "conceived and encouraged" a movement "contrary to the doctrine" of the Baptists with whom he was associated. White

---

[67] *The* (Milledgeville) *Georgia Journal*, Jan. 27, 1831, 3. (RLV). A "fi fa" is a *fieri facias* writ to execute judgment against a debtor. The sale would fulfill that writ.

[68] These add to 147 rather than 149.

[69] *The* (Middlebury, VT) *National Standard*, Jan. 22, 1828, 1, citing *The Georgia Journal*, Dec. 17, 1827. (RLV)

withdrew, he said, and "immediately had a respectable following," which "increased rapidly," until they were able to form "an Association, or united body, under the name and title of the Free Will Baptists, and were remarkable for their piety and zeal." One newspaper item reflects the difference between White and other Baptists: "June 12, 1830. Holly Springs Primitive Baptist Church, Covington, GA. moved and carried that Cyrus White be prohibited from preaching in this house while he holds the doctrine he now does and preaches it."[70]

Cherry was incorrect in using "Free Will Baptist" in this way, anachronistically reading back into the organization the name that United Baptists later came to wear (and wore in Cherry's day). Even so, it seems likely that he understood, correctly, that they were "free will" in sentiment from the beginning—by which I mean that they preached universal atonement, conditional election, and human responsibility for responding to the gospel.

The churches that identified with White were often called "Whiteites" or "Whiteite Baptists," as a number of sources attest—not that they officially adopted the name. This nickname continued to be used for many years.

Cherry went on to report that White was the first moderator of the first session of the new association—the United Baptist Association, as we have seen. He also reported that White "published a pamphlet about this time, taking the ninth chapter of Romans as a foundation, explanatory of his doctrine. This little book had a large circulation, creating considerable interest and agitating the mother church to its center. It was soon followed by another, 'On the Atonement,' which drew a reply from the late venerable Jesse Mercer."[71]

During the winter of 1835-36, White moved from Georgia to Russell County, Alabama (now Lee County), near Mechanicsville.[72] He built his first cabin about a mile and a half southwest of Nettle's Ferry, on the Chattahooche River. Because of the possibility of trouble from some Indians in the area, he and his

---

[70] "Genealogy Report."
[71] Cherry, 4.
[72] Michael Thomas (c.1795-1846), said to have been born in Ware County, North Carolina, apparently relocated from Georgia to southeastern Alabama in 1835-36—at approximately the same time as White—and immediately planted the first of the United Baptist churches there, to be known as Macedonia. Cherry described him as "a disciple and follower of the late Cyrus White." See F. L. Cherry, "The History of Opelika and Her Agricultural Tributary Territory," chap. XX, *The Opelika Times*, Jan. 18, 1884, 4. (RLV)

family and other settlers crossed the Chattahoochee back into Georgia. He was made captain of a voluntary defense force of those making camp there, perhaps because of his military experience. No hostile Indians appeared, however, and the refugees returned to their homes on the Alabama side.[73]

White became a teacher again and taught for several years at Mechanicsville and at Wacoochee Valley. We may assume that he continued preaching. At any rate, he spent the rest of his life in southeastern Alabama, near the banks of the Chattahoochee River, which separated Alabama from Georgia.

On February 7, 1844, White died. His obituary, written by long-time friend and fellow minister Prior Reeves, was published in *The Christian Index* and reads, in part:

> He had served his country in a military line and as a soldier, he was patriotic, valorous and obedient to orders as an officer. He was humane, charitable, and dedicated as a Christian. Studious and devoted to religious duties, benevolent to the indigent and needy of every class and we think truly a philanthropist. As to his ministerial character and career, I need say but little as the last fourteen years of his life has fully developed that. Though I will say so much, that he had great zeal for God's glory and for his own peculiar tenets. …
>
> In his illness he was visited by all classes and denominations of people, and he exhorted all to prepare for death and judgment. And Christians, he would urge to live a practical holy life; often expressing a full belief and decided preference in favor of the doctrine and sentiments he had taught for the last fourteen years. And would often express that he had "fought a good fight, & Etc." He was a decided friend to all benevolent enterprise, temperance and Sabbath School institutions. In his sphere he taught by precept and example. He often stated to all that the Lord to some extent had blessed his labors, yet he had nothing whereof to boast and should alone be saved by Grace. …
>
> I, and another intimate brother, two days before his death, conversed with him much on the subject of death and eternity. … He then requested, as he had often done, that I should preach his Funeral and not exaggerate his character. But to tell all, that he would have been glad that he had lived more holy, but under the circumstances of life, over many of which he could exercise no control, he had done about the best he could.

---

[73] Cherry, 4. A later report in "Cedar Creek Ripples" (an unsigned column conducted by J. P. Reese) in the *Newnan* (GA) *Herald*, Mar. 25, 1879, 3, says that White and the other settlers spent two or three months on the eastern side of the Chattahoochee, living in rail pens, and that "The women and children had a hard time, for it was rainy and wet, and provisions were hard to get." (RLV)

His funeral will be preached, if the Lord permit, on the fourth Sabbath in March, at Smyrna Church, Russell County, Alabama, where his membership was when he died. His remains now be interred by the side of his wife, (who died two years since of black jaundice) near the western bank of the Chattahoochee River.[74]

It is to be regretted that all of the minutes of the United Baptists in Georgia that still exist came after White relocated to Alabama. The result is that almost no record of his activities in those associations appears in the minutes we have. Even so, he was still remembered with honor. As late as 1851 the United Baptist Association minutes show that they were working to "inclose" the graves of Cyrus and his wife, and that they were doing this in cooperation with the Chattahoochee Association. This is confirmed in the 1850 and 1851 minutes of the Chattahoochee; in the latter the phrase is "entombing the remains."

Exactly what they intended to do is not entirely clear, but when the biographical sketch I have cited was published forty years later in 1876, Cherry bemoaned the situation. He said that the Whites "rest side by side in a family graveyard a half mile east of the old place, but in a dilapidated condition. ... It is a shame that the resting place of such a man should remain without a stone to mark the spot. A few years more and all trace of his grave will be lost to the living, unless more care is taken in the future than has been in the past." Apparently the efforts of the United and Chattahoochee associations to mark their graves, twenty-five years earlier, had not come to fruition.[75]

I should note that White was viewed positively by some in the Restorationist movement led by Alexander Campbell. The most extreme view, along these lines, is represented by Larry Whitehead, who appears to assume that White, during his later years in Alabama, identified with the Restorationists. But for all his optimistic observations, he fails to provide any evidence of this.[76] A more objective Disciples of Christ source, J. E. Moseley, said that White was more open-minded toward Campbell's movement than many other Baptists in Geor-

---

[74] *The Christian Index*, March 15, 1844, 40. (RLV)

[75] Apparently the grave sites are no longer known. They may be under water, given that much of the Chattahoochee in that area has been dammed up to form lakes.

[76] Larry Whitehead, "Cyrus White & The Whiteites," *The Alabama Restoration Journal: An Historical Perspective of Churches of Christ in Alabama*, vol. 5, no. 3 (Feb. 1, 2012), 25-26. (RLV)

gia. He reported that perhaps six or more "Freewill Baptist" churches—also called "Whiteites" or "Soft Shell Baptists," —went over to the Disciples, beginning as early as 1835. He praised White as having "assisted Disciples to receive a considerate hearing in several places," for which he suffered "misrepresentation, calumny, and defamation." He said White "broke bread" with many of the Disciples and possessed and read many of Campbell's writings. Even so, Mosely reported that White perceived that Campbell's writings, though Campbell disavowed creeds, had become the creed of many, and that though Campbell also disavowed sects, his sect would soon become as strong as any other.[77]

White's nephew, W. V. W. McLindon, sent a letter to Campbell's *Millennial Harbinger* in 1847. McLindon had identified with the new movement, withdrawn from the United Baptists, and recently relocated from southeastern Alabama to Michigan. Among other things, he reported that Prior Reeves, a longtime associate of White's, had been convinced of Campbell's views and had led a part of the church at Smyrna, in Alabama, into "reform."[78]

I assume that White's greater tolerance for and understanding of the Restorationists resulted from sharing similar free will doctrine with them. It seems clear, however, that White himself did not unite with Campbell's efforts.

The Chattahoochee United Baptist Association

The Chattahoochee would apparently become both the most influential of the United Baptist associations, in Georgia, and the one that first officially incorporated "Free Will" into its name. Its influence among Free Will Baptists was and is extensive. From it came most of the other associations in Georgia, as well as the earliest associations in southeastern Alabama and in the West Florida panhandle.

The exact date of the founding of the Chattahoochee Association of United Baptists is not certain. Williams, citing Jesse Campbell, notes:

> By 1836, the United Association was deemed too large, and the delegates agreed to divide into two associations. Campbell says, 'Those churches in Jas-

---

[77] J. Edward Moseley, *Disciples of Christ in Georgia* (St. Louis, MO:Bethany, 1954), 105. (RLV) One notes that Moseley, like Cherry, also used the name "Free Will Baptist" anachronistically.

[78] *The Millennial Harbinger*, ed. Alexander Campbell, Series III, Vol. IV (April 1847), 236-37. (RLV)

per, Henry, &c., retained the old name, and those in Harris and other western counties are known as the "United Chattahoochee Association".' "[79]

The 1851 minutes claim to be the sixteenth session, and that, too, would put the organization back to 1835 or 1836 (depending on how the organizational session was counted).[80] Another source indicates that Cyrus White was the first moderator of this association (as he had been of the United Baptist Association) when it was organized at New Teman Church in Henry County.[81]

The earliest minutes of the Chattahoochee we have are for 1842. In those minutes, White appears in the list of ministers and at Smyrna Church in Russell County, Alabama. He served on the Committee on Arrangements, preached on Sunday, and was employed as an itinerant preacher for the association. Prior Reeves,[82] who would write Cyrus White's obituary two years later, was clerk. The two men, along with Andrew Cumbie, were made a committee "to draft Rules of Decorum for the government of this body."[83]

Shortly before this 1842 meeting, White and Reeves announced their intention to publish a paper in the interests of the United Baptists. The notice appeared in a Columbus, Georgia, newspaper in November 1841. The new paper would be published there, monthly, and named *The United Baptist*. Its first issue was projected for January 1, 1842. The notice was headed "Prospectus of the United Baptist" and began, "Cyrus White and Prior Reeves propose to publish a monthly periodical, in which the Doctrine and Discipline of the United Baptists shall be fairly stated and vindicated." Content planned would include, among other things, "a plain account of the causes which led to the divisions now existing in the Baptist Denomination."[84]

---

[79] J. Campbell, 268 (written in 1847, about ten years after the event and so probably accurate), as cited by Williams, 16.
[80] Minutes, the Chattahoochee United Baptist Association, 1851, front cover.
[81] *Free Baptist Cyclopaedia*, 227-28.
[82] Prior (Priar, Prier) Reeves (1799-1865; Find-A-Grave memorial #28053426) was a close associate of Cyrus White, especially during his years in Alabama. He appears in the 1842 Chattahoochee minutes as a minister representing the Smyrna Church in Russell County, Alabama. His Find a Grave record includes a lengthy description of his ministry among the Churches of Christ after he aligned himself with the Restorationist movement.
[83] Minutes, Chattahoochee United Baptist Association, 1842, 4.
[84] *The Columbus-Enquirer* (Columbus, GA), Nov. 24, 1841, 1. (RLV)

The notice went on to give prices and solicit subscriptions. I do not know whether the plans came to fruition and am not aware that any copies of such a paper exist.

If we had the early minutes of the United and Chattahoochee associations, we could probably tell exactly which United churches formed the Chattahoochee. In 1840, there were twelve churches in the United: in Henry, Jasper, Upson, Pike, Newton, Campbell, and Fayette counties. The 1842 minutes of the Chattahoochee, two years later, do not list any of these but name twenty-three churches in Muscogee, Randolph, Marion, Stewart, Russell (AL), Harris, Early, Decatur, and Chambers (AL) counties.

In other words, after the Chattahoochee was formed, the churches of the United Baptist Association were in central western Georgia, in a relatively small area from just south of Atlanta to northeast of Columbus. The Chattahoochee churches were in a larger area to the south of the United churches. They were in the southwestern part of the state, many of them near the Chattahoochee River, reaching from just north of Columbus to the Blakely area. Six of the churches were across the river in southeastern Alabama.

One interesting item in the 1842 minutes catches attention: "We never did adopt the Sharon Confession of Faith; neither did we ever design so to do."[85] What was the motivation behind this? Williams suggests that it "bears witness to a more influential Arminian presence in Chattahoochee" (than in the United Baptist Association, I assume he means).[86] I wonder, instead, if it simply reflected a tendency (already indicated above) not to put too much stock in formal articles of faith. This view is supported by the fact that in 1848 the minutes show that the Chattahoochee "Agreed to re-publish, *as a summary of our doctrinal views*, what is usually termed the Sharon Confession of Faith"—and they did.[87] They did so again in 1850, calling it "*our* Abstract of Principles." This time they added one article, expanded two other articles with added notes, and affixed to

---

[85] Minutes, Chattahoochee United Baptist Association, 1842, 5.
[86] Williams, 17.
[87] Minutes, Chattahoochee United Baptist Association, 1848, 2, 4 (italics added).

each article a set of Scriptural references in support.[88] It is obvious, then, that they took this confession seriously and regarded it as expressing their views.[89]

The 1854 minutes of the Chattahoochee include a Circular Letter that adds yet more confirmation regarding their doctrinal stance.[90] The letter focuses on the atonement and eloquently emphasizes the free agency of human beings, along with the universal benevolence of God's eternal counsel and of the atonement. I was struck by the following sentence: "When the Holy Spirit opens the heart to attend to the claims and influence of the Atonement, there is no more violence offered to the freedom of the will, than there was in Christ showing his wounds to doubting Thomas, to make him 'not faithless, but believing.'" This expresses nicely the delicate balance between the necessity of God's drawing (prevenient grace) and man's freedom to respond or resist.

Equally interesting, the 1848 minutes include this: "Received the Report of the Committee appointed to set forth the causes of the division between the United Baptist [sic] and the Flint River Association, in 1830"—and published the report, which concludes as follows.

> In conclusion we readily admit a disagreement existing, and which has ever existed, between us and other Baptists, relative to the 4th article of what is termed the ORIGINAL CONFESSION OF FAITH, to wit: (We believe in the Eternal Election of a definite number of the human race, to grace and glory, and that there was a covenant of grace or redemption made between the Father and the Son before the world began, in which their salvation is secure, and that they in particular are redeemed.) Believing as we do that this doctrine is not in accordance with the Word of God, and inconsistent with christian and missionary operations. Finally, we say to the world that in accordance with the Doctrine and Principles set forth in these minutes, we heartily desire a union and co-operation with all Baptists.[91]

---

[88] Minutes, Chattahoochee United Baptist Association, 1850, 6-7 (as authorized on p. 2). (Italics added.)

[89] Williams, 13, 15, etc., might not agree with my assessment entirely, apparently thinking that the Sharon Confession and the later Chattahoochee formulation (perhaps utilizing the 1843 documents published in *The Christian Index*) were not in agreement. As I have said, I view the Sharon Confession as more direct in its expression of free will sentiments regarding universal atonement, conditional election, and human ability to respond to the gospel. But even if the 1843 document was somewhat muted, it might have been intended, at least, to allow room for the same "Arminian" views. Williams may well be right, that in those early days there were some differences in emphases that led some to prefer one expression over the other.

[90] Minutes, Chattahoochee United Baptist Association, 1854, 3-5. The entire letter is worth re-publishing.

[91] Minutes of the Chattahoochee United Baptist Association, 1848, 2.

The United Baptists and Interaction With Other Bodies

The last sentence of the previous extended quotation points to an important feature of the United Baptists of the Chattahoochee and other associations. They were interested in active fellowship with other like-minded associations, regardless of name.

One manifestation of this is seen in their associational correspondence with other associations, either in writing or in exchanging corresponding delegates to visit with each other. In 1840 and/or 1842, the United Baptist Association named delegates to the Mt. Zion, Duck River, Concord, Nolichucky, and East Tennessee associations in Tennessee, and to the Big Ivy Association in North Carolina. In 1849, only the Concord and Mt. Zion associations were named in this way, and in 1848, the Chattahoochee Association corresponded with these same two associations in Tennessee.

I do not have information about most of these associations, but at least the Mt. Zion and Duck River were Separate Baptists. If any of them were United Baptists, in name, I am not aware of that.

Another way the United Baptists showed their interest in a broader fellowship was in their effort, early on, to maintain some relationship with the Georgia Baptist Convention. In 1839, William Byars was messenger from the United Baptist Association to the Convention, bringing "contributions for missions and other benevolent objects."[92] The 1849 session of that Convention published a listing of Georgia Baptist statistics, which included the increase in members among the United Baptist Associations, amounting to 111 members.[93] Apparently, the United Baptists were still reporting to that body. The 1850 minutes of the Chattahoochee include this note: "Agreed to send a copy of the Minutes of this body to the Georgia Baptist Convention, by brother D. J. Apperson."[94]

Yet another manifestation of this reaching out beyond themselves is seen in an early attempt by the Chattahoochee to make friendly contact with the Free

---

[92] J. Campbell, 111.
[93] *The Milledgeville* (GA) *Federal Union*, Aug. 21, 1849, 1, 4-7. (RLV)
[94] Minutes, Chattahoochee United Baptist Association, 1850, 2. David J. Apperson (1810-1894; Find-A-Grave memorial #184445060) was one of the leading lights of the United Baptists, from his licensure to preach (in the Chattahoochee) in 1841 to his death in 1894. His obituary is in the Chattahoochee minutes for 1894, 7, with others in his Find-A-Grave memorial.

Will Baptists of North Carolina. In 1857, they sent a letter to the original General FWB Conference in North Carolina, urging "a convention for the purpose of a union of the Free Will Baptists South." Since that included the Chattahoochee, this makes clear that they regarded themselves as "Free Will Baptists," even if they did not wear that name.

We know about this from a history of the Free Will Baptists in North Carolina, which also makes clear that the Chattahoochee initiative was rebuffed.[95] This action in North Carolina tends to confirm, by the way, what seems already clear: namely, that the Georgia United Baptists did not owe their origins to the North Carolina Free Will Baptists. The record in Harrison and Barfield appears to imply that in 1857-58 those in North Carolina regarded the United Baptists in Georgia as being not entirely like them, even though the same record mentions earlier contacts in 1839 and 1856.[96] It may well be that the following sentence by those authors, written in regard to what they called "vigorous proselytizing by the Campbellites" in the middle 1840s, indicates the suspicious attitude that was involved: "Experience teaches a dear lesson, and we have learned in this school to watch those who visit our Conferences pleading for union."[97]

The most important manifestation of the United Baptists' interest in uniting their efforts with those of other Baptists of like doctrine in the South is seen in their participation in organized unity movements. There were at least two such movements near the end of the nineteenth century. One was led by B. W. Nash, a Union Baptist of North Carolina, the other led by A. D. Williams (with John L. Welch, Sr.), who resided in Nashville, Tennessee. Robert Vaughn and I have told this story, in detail, in another chapter in this volume. I will therefore only summarize briefly here.

---

[95] See the excerpted record of the General Conference for 1857 and 1858 in T. F. Harrison and J. M. Barfield, *History of the Free Will Baptists of North Carolina* (W. E. Moye, 1897), 245-46, 248. There is reference to this in the chapter in this volume dealing with unity movements that involved Free Will Baptists.

[96] Chester H. Pelt, *A History of the Salem Association of Free Will Baptists of West Florida*, (unpublished, 1987), 5. For the 1839 contact see Harrison and Barfield, 230-31, showing that the United Baptists were "requesting a correspondence" and a committee was appointed to correspond. For the 1856 contact see Harrison and Barfield, 244, which says only that two men were "appointed to correspond with the Georgia brethren." Apparently the 1857 rejection brought that to a close.

[97] Harrison and Barfield, 234-35.

The first of these movements was foreshadowed in 1859, in a convention called by the United Baptists in Georgia, held in a Chattahoochee Association church, Providence in Muscogee County. Those in attendance represented four states: Virginia, North Carolina, Georgia, and Alabama, and included Union Baptists, United Baptists, and Free Will Baptists. Probably because of the looming Civil War, no ongoing organization was formed.

Following the Civil War, efforts in this direction were renewed, leading in 1876 to the formation of the "Southern Baptist Association,"[98] which included Union Baptists, Free Will Baptists, and United Free Will Baptists. By this time, the United Baptists of Georgia had incorporated "Free Will" in their name, as will be observed below. Indeed the organization was perfected at the Deep Creek church in Georgia. Annual sessions continued for several years, at least through 1883, convening in Georgia, Alabama, Mississippi, North Carolina, South Carolina, and Tennessee. Apparently, an effort was made to revive this organization, or one similar, in Columbus, Georgia, in 1889.

The second unity movement in the South, typically referred to as "Southern Unity," was less successful, but, again, the Georgia United Free Will Baptists took part. Together with several other associations of churches in Alabama, Tennessee, and Texas, the Ogeechee and Chattahoochee United Free Will Baptist associations in Georgia called for a convention of all "Southern white Baptists who believe in free will, free salvation and free communion, on the basis of uniting on things in which we are agreed and of leaving points of difference to the several local bodies." The lengthy announcement appeared in a Nashville, Tennessee, paper in November, 1889.[99] That convention took place as scheduled and the "General Association of Baptists, believing in Free Will, Free Salvation, and Free Communion" was formed.

This organization was relatively short-lived. It apparently did not last any longer than 1897 or so. By then it had come to be known, more simply, as a "General Association" that included only Free Will Baptist associations in Tennessee. As early as 1890 the Chattahoochee, at least, had apparently lost interest,

---

[98] Not to be confused with the Southern Baptist Convention!
[99] *The* (Nashville) *Daily American*, November 27, 1889, 8. (RLV)

as the following item from its minutes shows: "The subject of the Southern Unity move was brought before the body, and Bro. A. D. Williams and others made some remarks, but the question was dropped without definite action."[100]

I am inclined to think that the organization of the Georgia State Convention of Liberal Baptists about this time reflected the same interest in broader organizations. I will say a little more about this organization below.

One of the UFWB ministers who played a role in these activities was J. H. Jenkins, who began publishing a small newspaper, known as *The Harvest Gleaner*, in Phoenix, Alabama, in 1894. We have just eight issues, being the first eight numbers of volume III, for September 16 through November 4, 1896.[101] Each is four pages, with only the back page giving information about goings-on among the "Free Will Baptists." Interestingly, Jenkins was not friendly toward any attempt by B. W. Nash to revive his unity movement, but was more open to the movement led by Williams and Welch. He was also friendly toward the effort of Thomas Peden to establish a General Conference in the South that rivaled the General Conference in the North.[102] The doctrinal statement published in the paper was the same as the one published by the Middle Georgia UFWB Association and the Georgia State Convention of Liberal Baptists, both in 1897[103]; these associations will be mentioned below. Jenkins also reported regularly on the work of A. M. Stewart, a Chattahoochee United Baptist minister who had migrated to Texas and planted the first continuing white FWB churches in that state.[104] One of the things promoted in these issues of the paper was a preaching tour by Jenkins and the famous FWB evangelist E. L. St. Claire.

---

[100] Minutes, Chattahoochee UFWB Association, 1890, 3.

[101] These we scanned from microfilm on interlibrary loan from Auburn University. According to the Chattahoochee minutes for 1896, Jenkins was pastor at Corinth Church in Marion County and at Providence and Columbus churches in Muscogee County, all in Georgia.

[102] I have told the story of this effort in a chapter in *Little Known Chapters in Free Will Baptist History*. There is a related appendix in the present volume.

[103] *The Harvest Gleaner*, III:1 (Sept. 16, 1896), 4.

[104] The story of Stewart and the Texas work is told in another chapter in this volume by Robert L. Vaughn.

The Multiplication of United Baptists Before the Addition of "Free Will" in the Name

In Georgia, the United Baptist movement grew, spreading into southeastern Alabama and the West Florida panhandle. Other United Baptist associations of churches were formed—most of them, I assume, by amiable agreement. Before the addition of "Free Will" to the name, this included, at least, the following associations:

The Salem UB Association. This association is referred to in the 1847 minutes of the Chattahoochee as one in "correspondence."[105] Mention has been made, previously, of references to it in the 1846 and 1851 minutes of the United Baptist Association. According to Jesse Campbell, it was organized in 1843 and had 19 churches, apparently in about 1846; and in 1845 Wiley J. Blewitt (mentioned in a footnote below) was its clerk.[106] We have no minutes or other information about this body, but the fact that Blewitt's address was in Bainbridge, in Decatur County, indicates that the association's churches were in deep southwest Georgia.

The New Salem UB Association. This association is referred to in a report of the 1859 convention, in Georgia, of "liberal Baptists" of the South (mentioned above).[107] Nothing else about it is known.

The Unity UB Association. We have one set of minutes for this body, in 1876, identified as the thirtieth annual session. This would put its organization back to about 1846 or 1847.[108] It was definitely an association of United Baptists; the minutes begin, "The United Baptist association met ..." and the Circular Letter attached begins, "To the churches composing the United Baptist Association."

Four churches are listed in the minutes and in the statistical table: Bethlehem in Jasper County, Corinth in Butts County, Nazareth in Pike County, and Union Grove in Franklin County. The first of these sounds like the church of

---

[105] Minutes, Chattahoochee UB Association, 1847, 2.
[106] J. Campbell, 288. (RLV)
[107] For additional information about this, see the chapter in this volume entitled "Free Will Baptist Participation in Unity Movements in the South, 1870 to 1910."
[108] More than a dozen churches, mostly in Randolph and Stewart counties and in Alabama, disappear from the rolls of the Chattahoochee between 1842 and 1848. It is tempting to think these might have gone to the Unity Association, but there is no way to confirm this. If so, none of them were still in the Unity in 1876.

which Cyrus White was pastor in 1829-30 and which was part of the organization of the United Baptist Association and was still in that association as late as 1840.

One of the emphases in 1876 was on the rejection of man-made creeds and sole reliance on the Bible as the rule of faith and practice. There is a resolution to this effect in the minutes, as well as a Circular Letter that is focused on decrying creeds. A key two-sentence part that more or less summarizes the letter is this: "We take the Bible for our law, the Holy Spirit for our guide. This is our reason for being United Baptists." The Circular Letter concludes with an expression of interest in unity with others, but of course that meant with others who would agree to speak in the same way about creeds and the Bible. Interestingly, there is an item recording that the churches had "generally" adopted the practice of feet-washing.[109]

I would *guess* that this *could* have been a small association of United Baptists that were holding out for their original principles, perhaps even resisting trends they saw among the other United Baptists. But saying this is speculation.

The Middle Georgia UB Association. We have minutes for one year, 1897, identified as the thirty-fourth annual session, which would take it back to about 1863—which might—or might not—have been before any United Baptists added "Free Will" to the name.

Interestingly, of its eight member churches, three are apparently the same churches as three of the four in the Unity Baptist Association (above) in 1876: Bethlehem in Jasper County, Corinth in Butts County, and Nazareth in Pike County. The other five are: Union Hill in Paulding County, Mt. Pleasant in Carroll County, Hebron in Jasper County, Rehoboth in Pike County, and Gladey Creek in Jones County. (A couple of these counties are more in northwestern than in middle Georgia.)

The minutes use only "United Baptist" in identifying the association, but they include a "Doctrinal Statement of General Principles Taught by United Free Will and other Liberal Baptists."[110] The list of beliefs that follows uses this

---

[109] *Minutes of the Thirtieth Annual Session of the Unity Baptist Association*, 1876, 3-7.
[110] Minutes, Middle Georgia Association of United Baptists, 1897, 6. (Cover page missing.)

form throughout: "As to [subject]," followed by plural Scripture citations and no man-made definitions. Perhaps they had decided that this would not violate their prior stance against man-made creeds.

Furthermore, the minutes mention receiving a letter from "our beloved brother J. H. Jenkins, of the Chattahoochee Association." (I have referred to Jenkins and his paper above.) They also mention a "State Convention" to which they voted to send a statistical report and delegates, and they resolved to consolidate the minutes of "all F. B.'s in Georgia together with the S. C. [State Convention]."[111]

What conclusions should we draw from this? It seems clear that those in the Middle Georgia Association had a sense of identity with both the Unity Baptist Association (above) and other United Baptists (like the Chattahoochee) who had added "Free Will" to their name. They themselves, however, still went by the name United Baptist. Since this association had begun while the Unity Baptist Association still existed in 1876, but in 1897 included three of the four churches that had been part of that body, it would seem likely that Unity Baptist Association had ceased to exist by 1897 and its surviving churches were now in the Middle Georgia United Baptist Association.

The "State Convention" referred to in these 1897 minutes was the Georgia State Convention of Liberal Baptists.[112] We have minutes for that body for the very same year, 1897, as well as the front cover of the minutes for 1895. Member bodies included the Chattahoochee, Middle Georgia, Martin, Liberty, Ogeechee, and Georgia Union associations. Of special interest is the fact that the minutes attached an article from the *Free Baptist Cyclopaedia* headed "Liberal Baptists" and reported that "Arrangement providing to have statistics of our members published in the Free Baptist Year Book has recently been set on foot."[113] This organization did not last very long; I find references to it, in the minutes of the Chattahoochee, as early as 1891 and as late as 1907.[114] The 1897

---

[111] Minutes, Middle Georgia Association of United Baptists, 1897, 3-4.
[112] "Liberal Baptists" was not meant as the name of a particular denomination, but as a broad term that could include all Baptists who held free will sentiments and practiced open communion. Williams, 24, notes—correctly, I think—that this did not necessarily imply belief in the possibility of apostasy.
[113] Minutes, Georgia State Convention of Liberal Baptists, 1897, 7.
[114] Davidson, 201, cites the 1919 minutes of the Chattahoochee to refer to this statewide body as existing

minutes say it was the seventh annual meeting, which would put its organization at 1890 or 1891.

United Baptists Become Free Will Baptists

It is clear that United Baptists were *unofficially* regarded as "Free Will" Baptists well before they added that designation to their name. As early as 1838, a letter from Wiley Pearce appeared in *The Primitive Baptist* and said, "We have a few Whiteites, or more commonly called Free Wills, or Soft shells, who appear to be walking in their silver slippers, as it is a pleasant time with them."[115] In 1843, *The Christian Index* in Georgia mentioned receiving minutes from the "Chattahoochee United (Free Will)" Baptist Association.[116] Another example is found in a letter to Alexander Campbell, dated January 24, 1847, written by Cyrus White's nephew W. V. W. McLindon, saying, "I was a member of the Free-Will Baptist Church of Georgia, sometimes known in that State by the name of Whiteite Baptists, from Cyrus White, the founder of that church, in the State of Georgia, about the year 1828, I think."[117]

No doubt they were thought of in this way because of their view of universal atonement and human responsibility in accepting or rejecting the gospel. Both in New England and in North Carolina, the Free Will Baptists had been called by that name well before they made it official. One did not have to believe in the possibility of apostasy to be thought of as a "free willer," and the

---

"from approximately 1885 through 1905" and that it had disbanded "because of lack of cooperation." But there must be a misprint here; this is not in the 1919 minutes and I could not find it elsewhere.

[115] *The Primitive Baptist*, vol. 3, no. 6 (Mar. 24, 1838), 85-86. Pearce apparently meant that the United Baptists were prospering. Davidson, 197-98, because of this early use of the name "Free Will Baptist" in referring to some in southwestern Georgia who were excluded from Richland Creek (regular) Baptist Church in 1835, considered the possibility that there were Free Will Baptists there that early, not related to the United Baptists. But Pearce's 1838 letter was in reference to the same persons, and he identified them as Whiteites. Furthermore, those who were expelled included Wiley Blewitt (and others in his family), who was active in the United Baptists. In 1840, he was a corresponding delegate from the Chattahoochee to the United Baptist Association and preached. The 1842 minutes of the Chattahoochee list him as a minister representing the Mount Pleasant Church in Decatur County, Georgia. And Jesse Campbell, 288, indicates that in 1845 he was clerk of the Salem United Baptist Association. Most likely, then, these were United Baptists being called by the popular—but unofficial—name of Free Will Baptists. For more information about this group, see John G. Crowley, *Primitive Baptists of the Wiregrass South: 1815 to the Present* (Gainesville, FL et al.: University Press of Florida, 1998), 69-70. (RLV)

[116] *The Christian Index*, June 9, 1843, 361.

[117] *The Millennial Harbinger*, ed. Alexander Campbell, Series III, Vol. IV (April 1847), 236-237. (RLV)

United Baptists of Georgia, southeastern Alabama, and West Florida did not at first make apostasy a part of their official doctrine. (More about their doctrinal development below.)

Exactly when United Baptists added "Free Will" to their name is not clear. The reason is that we have no minutes for the Chattahoochee (where the addition was apparently first made) between 1854, when they were "United Baptists," and 1879, when they were "United Free Will Baptists." As late as 1859, when the unity meeting referred to earlier took place, they were still United Baptists. As early as 1874, in the minutes of the Mount Moriah FWB Association in Alabama, a reference to the Chattahoochee United Free Will Baptist Association appeared. Consequently, it seems clear that they officially became Free Will Baptists during the fifteen-year period between 1859 and 1874.

Since we do not have a record of the change, we also do not know *why*, or under what influence, the change was made. It hardly seems fruitful to speculate. I am inclined to think that this came as a result of interaction with Free Will Baptists in the unity movements I have mentioned earlier. Or perhaps they had been called "Free Wills" so long they decided to accept the designation. Or both.

For the record, however, I mention the view of Chester Pelt that they became United Free Will Baptists as a result of a *merging* of some United Baptists with a body of Free Will Baptists in Southeast Alabama and West Florida at an unknown date before 1852. His view is based on his interpretation of a letter dated May 15, 1852, sent to Jeremiah Heath in North Carolina from Henry Boit (Boyt), living in Florida and serving a church in Henry (later Houston) County, Alabama. Boyt said, somewhat vaguely: "I wrote you my dear Brother respecting the United Baptist, But I am happy to tell you, that they are all standing in the ranks of the free will Baptist [sic], and we have all consolidated together."[118]

---

[118] Pelt, 6-10. Boyt mentions some other ministers, "Brother Hollis" (perhaps his brother Hollis Boyt?), Levy Griffin, and Benjamin Tipton, and two churches named Post Oak and Kind Providence, and says "We now have 13 churches and 12 ordained Elders" plus a number of licentiates. I have not found any of these names in the minutes of the Chattahoochee. This certainly raises the possibility, suggested by Pelt, that there was an association of Free Will Baptist churches there at the time. But it remains nothing more than a possibility, unlikely in my view; the meaning of Boyt's words is ambiguous. Even if there were such an association, unrelated to the United Baptists, the story in this chapter would not be different; but more

The implications are not clear. We know that the United Baptists in Georgia were not using the name United Free Will Baptists that early.

Regardless of the time of the change, there were several United Free Will Baptist associations that sprang up[119]—all from the roots of the Chattahoochee, apparently—between the time this became their official name and the end of the nineteenth century. And these included associations in southeastern Alabama and West Florida. The following are the ones we know about, named in chronological order by the year of their organization.

The Ogeechee/South Georgia UFWB Association (1876/77). Our earliest minutes are for 1903, when the association changed its name from the Ogeechee to the South Georgia Association. The minutes are identified as the twenty-seventh session of the Ogeechee United Free Will Baptist Association, thus tracing the organization back to 1876 or 1877.[120] I assume, therefore, that it was "United Free Will Baptist" at the time of its organization. (This is *not* the same as the current Ogeechee FWB Association, formed in about 1909.)

The Southeastern UFWB Association, of Alabama (1879/80). The 1879 minutes of the Chattahoochee recorded that there was a petition of the churches of the association located in Alabama, "asking leave to withdraw and form an association … on the same principles as this, to be called the South-east Alabama United Free-will Baptist Association, which was considered and granted."[121]

The Martin UFWB Association (1886/87). Our earliest minutes are for 1887, its "first annual session." There were twenty churches in the association at the time: Cedar Springs, Enterprise, Springfield, Open Pond, White Pond, and Zion in Early County; Bellview, Friendship, Macedonia, New Salem in Miller County;

---

research on the group mentioned by Pelt could prove interesting. Pelt, 13, thought this was the Southeastern Association, but we know for sure when it was organized, as indicated in the text to follow.

[119] Writing in 1847, J. Campbell, 111, said "If any churches of this order are now in existence, this fact is unknown to the author. Little did he know!

[120] My uncertainty in deriving the organizational date (for this and other associations) stems from the fact that associations often, *but not always*, counted the next session *after* organization as the "first" annual session (much as we count birthdays). (For that matter, they also sometimes got the numbers wrong!) Williams, 19, dates the Ogeechee to 1878.

[121] Minutes, Chattahoochee UFWB Association, 1879, 2. The *Free Baptist Cyclopaedia*, 228, says it was organized in 1882, but this does not fit the evidence. The Southeastern minutes for 1926, our earliest, claim to be the forty-eighth annual session, which tends to confirm the 1879 date. Since the names of the churches are not included in the 1879 minutes, we cannot be sure which churches these were.

Traveler's Rest and Live Oak in Baker County; Pleasant Hill and Bethlehem in Randolph County; New Prospect, Pleasant Grove, and Pleasant Springs in Calhoun County; and Pine Grove and Corinth in Decatur County.[122] All twenty had been in the Chattahoochee and were dismissed—amiably, it would appear—to organize a separate association.[123] The Martin was named for C. C. Martin, who had been a leader in the Chattahoochee and helped organize the new association.[124]

The (Alabama/Florida) State Line UFWB Association (1886). This association was apparently divided from the Southeastern UFWB Association, as reported in the *Free Baptist Cyclopaedia*.[125] The 1893 minutes, which are the earliest we have, claim to be for the eighth annual session.

The West Florida Liberty UFWB Association (1889). The minutes for the 1910 session of this body (the earliest we have) begin thus: "The Liberty United Freewill Baptist Association, of West Florida, and South East Alabama."[126] The Chattahoochee minutes for 1889 record that these churches petitioned for and were granted the right to organize as a separate association.[127] (Apparently, it was first called the Second District Association of West Florida.[128])

The Liberty UFWB Association (1892/93). For this *Alabama-Florida* association, our earliest minutes are for 1906, identified as the fifteenth annual session. Apparently the movement was spreading westward along the Alabama-Florida line, since this association was centered in the far southwestern part of Alabama and across the line in Florida, including churches in Escambia counties in both

---

[122] Minutes, Martin UFWB Association, 1887, statistical table. Such a table was often called a *scale*.
[123] Minutes, Martin UFWB Association, 1887, 2; Chattahoochee UFWB Association, 1885, statistical table.
[124] C. C. Martin (1827-1910; Find-A-Grave memorial #31538851) appears first in the Chattahoochee minutes for 1879, but might have been ordained well before that. He had three or four brothers who were also preachers; one, Isaac, was listed in the Chattahoochee minutes for 1842. Winnie Yandell (wvy), on the Find-A-Grave site for S. C. Martin, another of the preacher brothers, says that the family "had deep roots in the Horse Branch Free Will Baptist Church" near Turbeville, SC, but she does not provide evidence for this.
[125] *Free Baptist Cyclopaedia*, 228. Pelt, 14, records an account that this was because the Southeastern proposed to "abolish feet-washing as a church ordinance."
[126] Minutes, West Florida Liberty UFWB Association, 1910, 1.
[127] Minutes, Chattahoochee UFWB Association, 1889, 4. Pelt, 15, speculated that the Liberty of West Florida was formed out of the Southeastern, and for the same reason (feet-washing) as the State Line, but the Chattahoochee minutes show this to be incorrect.
[128] Minutes, Chattahoochee UFWB Association, 1890, 1-2.

states. This would become the Liberty UFWB Association No. 1 in about 1910 or 1911 when the Liberty UFWB Association No. 2 was organized from it, apparently amiably.

The Liberty UFWB Association (1893). For this *Georgia* association, we have minutes for 1893-1896, with the first of these identified as the meeting for organizing. The thirteen churches were: New Prospect and New Bethel in Worth County; New Shiloh in Erwin County; Greenwood and Friendship in Mitchell County; Hartsfield, Pine Hill, Magnolia, and Cool Springs in Colquitt County; County Line and Pleasant Home in Thomas County; Love's Chapel in Dooly County, and Free Will Union in Pulaski County.

The Georgia Union UFWB Association (1894/95). Our earlies minutes are for 1897, designated as the 3rd annual session. This would put the organization back to 1894 or 1895. Its five churches (in 1900) were Double Branch, Love Chapel, Pleasant Hill, and Oak Grove, all in Dooly County, and Free Will Union in Pulaski County. Love Chapel and Free Will Union apparently came from the Liberty Association.

The Salem UFWB Association (1897). This Florida association was organized, by mutual agreement, out of the West Florida Liberty Association, taking its name from the Salem church, which was the oldest of those in the new organization. The Salem church was organized by J. T. Knight, who had come to that part of Florida from the Chattahoochee Association.[129]

The Midway UFWB Association (1898/99). Our earliest minutes are for 1902, designated as the fourth session and thus dating the organization to 1898 or 1899. The twelve churches listed in the statistical table were: Open Pond, Zion, White Pond, Pleasant Grove, Oak Grove, Bethlehem, Traveler's Rest, New Light, Macedonia, New Enterprise, Damascus, and Live Oak. Many of these were in the Martin Association (and had been in the Chattahoochee), so the Midway was apparently divided from the Martin.

Even past 1900, associations were organized as United Free Will Baptists, including the Little River UFWB Association, in 1906 or 1907, and the Union

---

[129] Pelt, 16-17. This source includes, on pp. 18-21, the minutes of the organizational session of the Salem Association.

UFWB Association (merging the Liberty and Ochlocknee associations) in about 1926.

In addition to these, there are passing references to a Butts County Conference and an Ochlocknee Association, but we have no information about either of them. Davidson also mentions an earlier Liberty UFWB Association in northwestern Georgia that might have dated to the 1860s.[130]

The *Free Baptist Cyclopaedia* mentions also *The Spring Creek* (UB or UFWB?) *Association* (1872?) and *The Mt. Hosea* (UFWB?) *Association* (1887?). These two were made up of African-American churches. The first group was set off from the Chattahoochee not long after the end of the Civil War and organized by C. C. Martin, D. J. Apperson, and L. Gipson. The second was later divided from the first.[131] Whether these last two associations went on to become "United American Free Will Baptists," as the African-American Free Will Baptists in that area are now known, I do not know. This would be a good area for further research.

I have made no attempt to determine just when the various associations of this heritage dropped "United" from their name. No doubt Williams is correct in saying, "In the early twentieth century, the 'United' title was gradually dropped."[132]

The Development of Free Will Baptist Doctrine Among the United Baptists

I have already indicated enough about the theology of the early United Baptists in Georgia to make clear that they held free will sentiments in regard to universal atonement, conditional election, and the freedom of human beings to believe or reject the gospel. To be thoroughly Free Will Baptist in doctrine, however, requires more. I turn my attention, now, to that matter, dealing in turn with three important issues: the possibility of apostasy, washing the saints' feet, and open communion. In discussing each of these, I will explore first the views

---

[130] Davidson, 201, as cited by Williams, 18.
[131] *Free Baptist Cyclopaedia*, 228. Williams, 22-23 mentions an interesting obituary of an African-American member of the Bethlehem church found in the Unity Baptist Association minutes for 1876.
[132] Williams, 29, n. 95.

of the Chattahoochee and then expand from there to the rest of the United Free Will Baptists in Georgia, Alabama, and Florida.

1. *The possibility of apostasy.* Clearly, the first United Baptists in Georgia did not include this possibility in their official doctrinal statements, even if some of them believed it. That some did seems likely, since "the thorny question of falling from grace came before the body [the Georgia Baptist Association] in 1828" and was tabled. The next year the delegates "agreed to let it 'lie on the table.'" And this was "a spill-over from Cyrus White's teaching."[133] As already noted, the Sharon Confession said, "We believe that Saints will persevere in Grace to the end of their lives." (This was article 8 in the original but became article 9 in 1850.) This is unambiguous and affirms what we now call "eternal security."

There was no change from this, in the Chattahoochee, until the association wrote its own "Doctrinal Views." Because of the gap in minutes between 1854 and 1879, we cannot be sure exactly when this change occurred, but the new composition was in effect in 1879, saying (again, article 9):

> That the preserving attachment of true believers to Christ is the grand mark which distinguishes them from superficial professors; that a special providence watches over their welfare, and that they are kept, by the power of God, through faith unto salvation.[134]

This wording might have come from the 1843 articles of faith that were published in *The Christian Index* (which might, or might not, have been adopted by the United Baptists at that time, as discussed previously). There, item 40 in the "Declarative and Explanatory Views" had these very same words, prefixed by an additional clause that said, "That such only are christians as endure unto the end, that their persevering ...."[135]

This may require some interpreting. Williams thinks this signals "a movement away from absolute perseverance" without entirely repudiating that view.[136] In a way, it does make God's keeping "conditional," being "through faith." But it seems clear that this, as much as the previous form, affirms the

---

[133] Gardner, et al., 134. (RLV)
[134] Minutes, Chattahoochee UFWB Association, 1879, 15.
[135] *The Christian Index*, vol. 11, no. 34 (Aug. 25, 1843), 539.
[136] Williams, 20.

certain perseverance of all *true believers* in distinction from *superficial professors*: that is, those who only superficially make a profession of faith. There has always been a distinction between those who only profess and those who genuinely possess saving faith, and it appears likely that this was the distinction intended in this article.

Whatever was meant by the formal article, the ministers of the Chattahoochee had apparently accepted the possibility of apostasy, at least by 1902. The circular letter attached to the minutes that year was devoted, specifically, to the subject. Written by J. M. King, it said, forthrightly, "Scripture proves that a man can fall" and referred to this view as "our doctrine."[137]

Over the years, two changes took place in the form quoted above and included in the printed articles of faith. First, in 1908 or 1909, "preserving attachment" became plural: "preserving attachments"—even though the verb it governs remained singular: "is."[138] I suspect this was accidental and had no intended significance.

The other change was from "professors" to "possessors," which took place in 1913.[139] I find it difficult to decide whether this was intentional or accidental. If it was intentional, then perhaps they meant the first clause to say that "persevering attachments" to Christ serve to distinguish between true believers and those who superficially (but not deeply) possess Him. In that case, the final clause could then be interpreted to mean perseverance by faith, thus opening the door to the possibility of apostasy. However, I doubt that the change was intentional or that it was meant to open the door for apostasy. More likely, although there is no way to confirm what it meant (if anything) to those assembled in 1913, it continued to mean what it had always meant, even though the words themselves lack coherence.

Interestingly, this affirmation remained in the Chattahoochee minutes at least through 2012; more recent minutes print no articles of faith at all—perhaps assuming, appropriately, that the denomination's articles of faith in the national *Treatise* are readily available. I don't doubt for a moment that the people

---

[137] Minutes, Chattahoochee UFWB Association, 1902, 7-8.
[138] Minutes, Chattahoochee UFWB Association, 1909, 20. We do not have the 1908 minutes.
[139] Minutes, Chattahoochee UFWB Association, 1913, 13.

of the Chattahoochee had long since accepted the possibility of apostasy and would affirm the articles of faith of the National Association of Free Will Baptists. Even so, their official statement on the subject remained ambiguous and did not support that belief.

Among other United Free Will Baptists there was a quicker, clearer change. Articles about perseverance took at least three new forms, here and there, intentionally reflecting the possibility of apostasy. One of these appeared as early as 1893 in the Liberty and State Line associations: "Perseverance. None will be finally saved, but those who through grace, persevere in holiness to the end."[140] Strangely, the same Liberty minutes have another section, "Doctrinal Views," which include the old Chattahoochee article nine given above, regarding the "preserving attachment of true believers"—apparently not realizing the possible contradiction involved.[141] Interestingly, the Martin Association minutes for 1902 also contain the same two expressions.[142] The Georgia Union Association minutes for 1900 have only the "None will be finally saved, but ..." form.[143]

Williams regards this expression as "an almost middle ground between perseverance and apostasy."[144] But it has been used fairly widely among Free Will Baptists. Even the current short article on perseverance in the *Treatise* of the National Association of Free Will Baptists uses essentially the same form of expression on perseverance. It seems clearly meant to include, *by implication*, the possibility of apostasy for those who do not persevere in holiness.

A second way of expressing belief about perseverance appeared as early as 1903 in the minutes of the Ogeechee-turning-South Georgia Association: "We believe that good works are the fruits of a saving faith, and that in the use of the means of grace and not out of the use of those means eternal life is promised to men."[145] This, too, is a positive expression of conditional perseverance,

---

[140] Minutes, Liberty UFWB Association, 1893, 16. Cf. minutes, State Line UFWB Association, 1893, 14. A completely positive form of this same article appears in the current (short) articles of faith in the national *Treatise*: "*Perseverance*. All believers in Christ, who through grace persevere in holiness to the end of life, have promise of eternal salvation."

[141] Minutes, Liberty UFWB Association, 1893, 13. Indeed, these minutes contain a multiplicity of documents.

[142] Minutes, Martin UFWB Association, 1902, 18, 20.

[143] Minutes, Georgia Union UFWB Association, 1900, 9 (unnumbered).

[144] Williams, 20.

[145] Minutes, South Georgia UFWB Association, 1903, 11.

meant to imply the possibility that some of the converted may cease to appropriate the means of grace in their lives. This form has been used, from time to time, among Free Will Baptists in various places. But the Satilla Church (which apparently would have joined the Ogeechee/South Georgia Association), on its organization in 1880, adopted articles of faith that included the form to be mentioned in the following paragraph.[146]

Yet a third form of article on perseverance appeared in the minutes of the Southeastern UFWB Association of Alabama in 1926 (we have no earlier minutes of this association): "We do not believe under the Gospel dispensation, that any soul is elected to eternal life unconditionally. But that those who by faith persevere to the end will be saved. That it is possible for men who have been converted, to "Make shipwreck of the faith," turn again to sin and be finally lost." This is obviously the clearest expression of the doctrine. As just noted, this form was used as early as 1880 when the Satilla Church was organized.

I am aware that yet other wordings were used as time passed. It is clear, however, that the United Baptists of the Chattahoochee, and other associations descended from her, came to the historic Free Will Baptist position on apostasy, and that they did so at least by shortly before the turn of the century.

2. *Washing the saints' feet*. One should remember that the practice of washing feet, as a church ceremony (if not *ordinance*), was often discussed and somewhat widespread among churches in eighteenth and early nineteenth century America, by Baptists and others. This was not always made a matter of official denominational doctrine. Consequently, we should not be surprised that there is little about this in the early United Baptist statements, or that what is found appears in statements other than in their articles of faith.

As already noted, the Sharon Confession did not contain any expression regarding feet-washing. Neither did the lengthy document published in *The Christian Index* in 1843.[147] We have nothing affirming feet-washing, then, in the publications of the United Baptist Association or the Chattahoochee United

---

[146] "Organization of Satilla Church," 6, handwritten document in the FWB Historical Collection.
[147] *The Christian Index*, August 25, 1843, 537-540.

Baptist Association, through 1854, the last minutes we possess before a gap of twenty-five years.

The next Chattahoochee minutes we have are for 1879, where feet-washing does appear, although not in the section headed "Doctrinal Views." In the section headed "Church Decorum," article 32 reads: "Feet washing shall be attended to as the church sees proper"; and article 12, under "Government and Ordinances," does not include it: "That the Lord's Supper is an ordinance to be observed in the church till the Lord comes."[148]

In 1883, the Circular Letter attached to the minutes, written by T. H. Griffin, provided a lengthy and eloquent defense of feet-washing as something Christ commanded and as included in his commission to teach disciples to observe all he commanded.[149] In 1890, the minutes record that feet-washing was observed, along with the Lord's Supper, during the session.[150]

In 1891, article 12 ("Government and Ordinances") was changed to read: "That the Lord's Supper and washing of the Saints' feet is an ordinance to be observed in the church till the Lord comes,"[151] while article 32 in "Church Decorum" remained the same. One notes the singular verb: apparently they regarded the Lord's Supper and Feet-washing as two parts of a single ordinance. This change resulted from a deliberate action of the body: "The subject, feet-washing, was discussed, and, after remarks by several of the brethren, it was agreed by a unanimous vote of the body to amend the 12th article of our Government and Ordinances so as to mention "feet-washing" as well as "communion.""[152]

Things remained the same until 1908 or 1909 when the wording of this article became plural: "That the Lord's Supper and washing of the saints' feet *are ordinances* to be observed in the church till the Lord comes."[153] Apparently, they had begun to think of the practices as two ordinances. Meanwhile, article 32 in "Government and Ordinances" continued as it had been. The two remained as long as these documents were printed in the annual minutes, through 2012.

---

[148] Minutes, Chattahoochee UFWB Association, 1879, 12, 14.
[149] Minutes, Chattahoochee UFWB Association, 1893, 7-12.
[150] Williams, 20.
[151] Minutes, Chattahoochee UFWB Association, 1891, 11.
[152] Minutes, Chattahoochee UFWB Association, 1891, 3.
[153] Minutes, Chattahoochee UFWB Association, 1909, 18. (Italics added. We do not have the 1908 minutes.)

The rest of the United Baptist community apparently followed the example of the Chattahoochee in this. But the State Line Association (of Alabama and Florida) adopted a more direct statement as early as 1893, as article 15 of "Church Decorum": "We believe it the duty of the churches to commune and wash the feet at least one time a year, and if possible in the month of June and the expense paid by the church."[154]

Several of the associations printed, in their minutes, the same "Church Decorum" as the Chattahoochee, which included article 32, as quoted above. At the same time, under "Articles of Faith," they printed number 13, entitled "Gospel Ordinances," which named only baptism and the Lord's Supper.[155] Perhaps this reflected a view that feet-washing was a good practice but less than a full-fledged ordinance. These associations included the Liberty (1893), the Georgia Union (1900), and the Martin (1902).

The Ogeechee/South Georgia Association, however, printed an article in 1903 that included feet-washing in a list of a *number* of "ordinances," being item 15 under "Articles of Faith":

> We believe, as touching Gospel ordinances, in believers' baptism, laying on of the hands, receiving of the sacrament in bread and wine, washing the saints' feet, anointing the sick with oil in the name of the Lord, fasting, prayer, singing praise to God, and the public ministry of the Word, with every institution of the Lord we shall find in the New Testament.[156]

This reminds us of similar articles published by the Six Principle Baptists, and it tends to reduce the meaning of the word *ordinance* to anything commanded in the New Testament. This article appears, from one time and place to another, in other Free Will Baptist articles of faith.

It is clear enough that the United Baptist tradition came to regard feet-washing as an ordinance of the church. We have at least one newspaper record, in 1889, that one of the churches observed the rite: "The church at Macedonia will

---

[154] Minutes, (AL/FL) State Line UFWB Association, 1893, 13.
[155] Minutes, Liberty UFWB Association, 1893, 18, 25; Georgia Union UFWB Association, 1900, 9, 18; Martin UFWB Association, 1902, 14, 21.
[156] Minutes, Ogeechee/South Georgia UFWB Association, 1903, 11-12.

perform the duty of washing each other's feet on the second Sunday in June."[157] This church had been constituted by Cyrus White and James Reeves in 1827, as already noted.

3. *Open communion.* It has not been traditional to express, in formal articles of faith and practice, the conviction that the Lord's Supper should be open to all believers. Indeed, the short articles in the current Free Will Baptist *Treatise* do not do so, even though the longer statement under "The Faith of Free Will Baptists" does. It is not surprising, then, that there is not much said about open communion in the formal documents of the United Baptists in Georgia. As already noted, the Sharon Confession said nothing about this.

In the 1843 document published in *The Christian Index* (see above), however, under the heading "Government and Ordinances," the final item was as follows: "29. That the Lord's Supper is an ordinance to be observed in the church till the Lord come; and that none are entitled to partake of this ordinance but orderly members of a gospel church, who have been received into the church in the divinely appointed way, even by baptism."[158] It is difficult to know what this was intended to communicate about open or closed communion. It sounds more like the latter.

I have already mentioned the action of the United Baptist Association in 1851, refusing a relationship with the Salem United Baptist Association because the latter affirmed open communion—perhaps because the United felt it important to leave this decision to the churches. Indeed, as early as 1848, David Benedict said, of the Whiteites in Georgia, that "*Open Communion*, to some extent, was practiced among them at first."[159]

At any rate, it seems clear that by 1859 the United Baptists in Georgia were practicing open communion. I say this because the broad convention held that year to promote unity among "Liberal Baptists" of the South included the Union Baptists of North Carolina and Virginia led by J. W. Hunnicutt and B. W. Nash; and open communion was touted by them as one of the marks of

---

[157] *The* (Newnan, GA) *Herald and Advertiser*, May 17, 1889, 5. (RLV)
[158] *The Christian Index*, Aug. 25, 1843, 538.
[159] David Benedict, *A General History of the Baptist Denomination in America and Other Parts of the World* (New York: Lewis Colby and Co., 1848), 744, cited by Williams, 16,

"liberal" Baptists. If not by this date, then at least by 1876, when the Southern Baptist Association was formed and included the Chattahoochee, belief in open communion would have been essential to participation.[160] I have referred to this unity movement above, and one chapter in this volume is devoted to that story.

So far as I can tell, the Chattahoochee never made a published expression of commitment to open communion, although I assume this was part of their practice.

Some of the other United Free Will Baptist associations had more to say about this. In 1893, the (Alabama-Florida) State Line Association included two articles in its "Articles of Faith" that affirmed open communion. Article 10, regarding "Gospel Ordinances," affirmed that all three ordinances are "to be perpetuated under the gospel of universal salvation, and to be observed by all true believers." Article 11, regarding the Lord's Supper in particular, affirmed that it "was instituted for Christians and that all Christians should unite in performing the sacred service, regardless of name, denomination, or distinction."[161]

This was also the article (but ending "regardless of names or denominational distinctions") adopted by the Satilla Church on its organization in 1880, which apparently joined the Ogeechee Association (to become the South Georgia Association in 1903).[162]

Also in 1893, the Martin Association said essentially the same thing—about baptism and the Lord's Supper—as the State Line's article 10. So did the Georgia Union Association in 1900.[163] The Southeastern UFWB Association, in Alabama, used almost the same wording in 1926, in its article about the Lord's Supper, as the State Line's article 11.

---

[160] Perhaps the issue of open versus closed communion was strongly contested at about that time. In the Ebenezer Church near Glenville, that controversy arose early in 1878 and "was fiercely debated during the summer," which led to the formation of two different congregations later that year. The open communion group ultimately prevailed and possessed the church facility. (This may be about the time the church joined the United Free Will Baptists.) See *Ebenezer Free Will Baptist Church 1843-2008*, 1-3 (unnumbered).

[161] Minutes, (AL/FL) State Line UFWB Association, 1893, 14.

[162] "Organization of Satilla Church," 7, handwritten document in the FWB Historical Collection. There is no article regarding feet-washing in the document.

[163] Minutes, Martin UFWB Association, 1893, 8 (unnumbered); Georgia Union UFWB Association, 1900, 9-10 (unnumbered).

In 1897, the Georgia State Convention of Liberal Baptists printed, on the front cover of its minutes, "Free Grace, Free Will, Free Communion." It was made up only of United Free Will Baptists.

It is clear, then, that the United Baptists of Georgia, Southeast Alabama, and the Florida Panhandle practiced open communion. Indeed, it is clear that they adopted all the traditional doctrines of Free Will Baptists, and that they did so, at least for the most part, by the end of the nineteenth century.

Concluding Observations

There are two things that I think need to be said. The first harks back to the introduction to this chapter and is, simply, this: the origins of Free Will Baptists in Georgia—as well as in Southeast Alabama and West Florida—lie first in the United Baptists of Georgia in the first half of the nineteenth century. These United Baptists subsequently took the name United Free Will Baptists, before the end of that century, and later dropped the "United." Given that nearly all the contemporary FWB associations in that region were originally United Free Will Baptist and descended directly from the Chattahoochee United Baptist Association, I don't see how this conclusion can be legitimately questioned, even if later research adds to the story.

Furthermore, it seems likely that, in spirit, those who founded these United Baptists represented the Separate Baptist tradition of the two bodies which, in 1787 in Virginia, merged and created the United Baptists.

Significantly, the influence of the United Baptists in Georgia goes well beyond their early outreach into Alabama and Florida. Many from the Chattahoochee migrated westward and carried their influence with them. Included among them was A. M. Stewart, who planted the first continuing, white FWB church and association of churches in Texas. That story makes up yet another chapter in this volume.

My second observation is equally important. This origin does not rule out an important contribution from the Free Will Baptists of the General Baptist heritage represented in the Palmer movement originating in North Carolina. From their earliest existence, the Georgia United Baptists interacted with many influences outside themselves, including B. W. Nash's Union Baptists, Separate

Baptists, and more traditional Free Will Baptists, both of the North and of the South. They would have had access to *The Morning Star*, published in New England, and to *The Free Will Baptist*, published in Ayden, North Carolina. There are evidences of interaction with those in the Palmer movement. One example has been mentioned in this chapter: namely, an 1852 letter from Henry Boyt in West Florida to Jeremiah Heath in North Carolina. Another chapter in this volume mentions another example: namely, that two preachers from the Cape Fear Conference in North Carolina ministered in Southeast Alabama for a few years beginning in 1868, when in fact two churches there joined the Cape Fear.[164] No doubt many other interactions occurred.

To return to the metaphor I have introduced in the Preface, when tributary streams enter a mainstream, they feed it and are likewise fed. The flow downstream from that joining is not exactly what it was in either stream before. The United Baptists influenced the course of Free Will Baptist history in various ways, especially in the geographic region covered in this chapter. And the mainstream Free Will Baptists, in various ways, changed who they were. It may well be that some or all of the doctrinal development I have traced in the latter part of this chapter is the best example of that effect.

Even so, Free Will Baptists with a United Baptist heritage, like Free Will Baptists in other places, make up an important part of the Free Will Baptist people as we know them today. Their heritage is part of our heritage.

---

[164] See chapter 7 in this volume.

4

The Founding of the Free Will Baptist Work in Texas

The Story of A. M. Stewart From Georgia

by Robert L. Vaughn

Editor's note: One of the latest studies in FWB history is From the Red to the Rio Grande: a History of the Free Will Baptist Work in Texas, 1876 to 2014, *by Thurmon Murphy.*[1] *It is the most comprehensive treatment of FWB history in Texas available, and I highly recommend it.*

Not long after Murphy's volume was published, I was put in touch with Robert Vaughn, who lives at Mt. Enterprise, Texas, who has discovered additional information that was not available to Murphy when he wrote. (Which is the way writing history always works!) Vaughn is not FWB but is interested in the history of all branches of Baptists and is a gifted researcher. He published the material in this chapter in the form of a booklet entitled Angus McCallister Stewart: Man of God, Friend of All Mankind, and the Founding Father of the Free Will Baptist Church in Texas. *He has kindly allowed me to republish that material, edited to fit the style of this volume, and I am pleased to offer it here for a wider audience.*

FWB historians have long associated A. M. Stewart's name with the beginning of the FWB work in Texas, but they simply did not know who he was. Typically, they identified him as a product of the FWB movement in the North, and so they credited the founding of

---

[1] Thurmon Murphy, *From the Red to the Rio Grande: a History of the Free Will Baptist Work in Texas, 1876 to 2014* (Columbus, OH: FWB Publications, 2017).

the work in Texas to the Randallites. Significantly, however, Vaughn now shows us that this was not the case, that Stewart came from Georgia and was part of the FWBs in the South. Furthermore, Vaughn has uncovered a great deal of information about Stewart, helping us round out our understanding of the man and his ministry and the FWB work in Texas.

This is not to say that there was no Randallite influence in Texas during the formative years. As Murphy has reported, Randall FWBs began work, at first, among African-Americans there. No doubt some of the white FWB churches, too, were organized by some from the North who shared our denominational name, migrating to Texas. But what this chapter makes clear, and what we didn't know before, is that FWBs from the South were also actively involved and planted the earliest white FWB churches in the state.

—Robert E. Picirilli

Introduction

A. M. (Angus McAllister) Stewart came from Georgia to Texas by 1876 and organized the first continuing Anglo Free Will Baptist work in Texas, beginning with a church at Clayton in Panola County in 1876. He also organized the first association in the state, the Texas Free Will Baptist Association, in 1878, from several churches he had gathered. Despite his importance to the history of Free Will Baptists in Texas, little biographical information seems to be available on him. This chapter will begin to rectify that situation.

This study resulted from the confluence of several interests. First is my study of the Old Prospect Baptist Church and Sand Flat Community, south of Mt. Enterprise, Rusk County, Texas. In this search I found that one community patriarch, James Pierce Lunsford, started a Free Will Baptist Church called Old Prospect in 1887. Second is my interest in the ministry of the community pastor of my youth, Barney Atlas Grant. The extent of his ministry among the Free Will Baptists, before coming to the Missionary Baptists, was unknown to me and I began to research it. Third, in trying to sort out the history of Free Will Baptists in East Texas, the ministry of A. M. Stewart caught my attention and was fanned into a flame I was unable to ignore until I took a closer look.

Early Years

Stewart entered this world at Cedar Springs, Early County, Georgia, and left it from Carthage, Panola County, Texas. In the miles and years between, he became an educator, pastor, and evangelist. He was the "Founding Father" of the first Free Will Baptist church in Texas: that is, of the first Anglo-American Free Will Baptist work historically connected to the current Free Will Baptists in the state.

Stewart was the son of John M. and Hulda Stewart. The censuses of Early County, Georgia, are confusing at this point, giving different parental names for what is clearly the same group of siblings. The 1850, 1860, and 1880 censuses list the father's name as John M., but as Norman in 1870.[2] Also in 1870 and 1880 John M/Norman's spouse is listed as Susan, which might have been another name for Hulda; or the change may indicate a second marriage after the death of his first wife.[3] It is not uncommon for names to vary from first name to second name from one census to another. Otherwise, the change might be a simple error made by one of the enumerators of the censuses.

Angus McCallister Stewart was born August 25, 1853, grew up on a farm, and attended the public schools in Early County. Altogether the 1850, 1860, and 1870 censuses list him with four other siblings: Amanda, Martha, Wesley, and Kilby (or Kelby). Angus also appears in the 1880 Early County census, living alone and teaching school.

We have very little information about his siblings. In 1880, Amanda was a widow. She and her three children were living with John and Susan Stewart. She had married Martin L. Sheffield in January 1870. He died in 1877. She and her children subsequently moved to Texas and were living in Panola County, Texas, when that census was taken in 1900. It is uncertain what happened to the others.[4]

---

[2] It seems likely that the initial M was an error for N.
[3] I suspect that the John N. Stewart (1821-1885) buried at Cedar Springs Cemetery in Early County is A. M.'s father. If this is correct, and if the note on the Find-A-Grave memorial page for John Norman Stewart (#30833583, maintained by Glen Spurlock) is correct, A. M. Steward was the grandson of David and Hannah Stewart. I also suspect that the Franklin W. Stewart (1855-1864) buried there is A. M.'s brother, Wesley, who appears only in the 1860 census.
[4] E. K. Stewart, a school teacher in the 1880 census in Nacogdoches County, Texas, has enough in common with Kilby Stewart to be him, but there is not enough information available to make the identification certain.

At about age seventeen Angus entered the Buford Academy in Gwinnett County, Georgia,[5] some 250 miles north of his home in Cedar Springs. During that year, he professed faith in Christ and was ordained to the ministry the next year. We do not know who baptized or ordained Stewart. This might have been at a church in Gwinnett County, or perhaps at a Free Will Baptist church in Early County, especially if he were home for the summer.[6] "While a student at the Buford Academy he was employed as an assistant instructor, which was the beginning of his life's work, while yet a boy, of teacher and minister of the Gospel."[7] From this small beginning he would soon make his mark on Texas.

Founder

A. M. Stewart's venture to Texas brought him to the Marshall area in Harrison County, "where he taught his first school." While teaching at Marshall he preached "whenever opportunity afforded, and to him belongs the honor of organizing the first Freewill Baptist church to be founded in Texas."[8] This church was constituted in Panola County near Clayton, Texas, in 1876; a 1911 map of the county is nearby.[9] Though in Texas in 1876, Stewart returned to Georgia by 1880, leaving his fledgling organi-

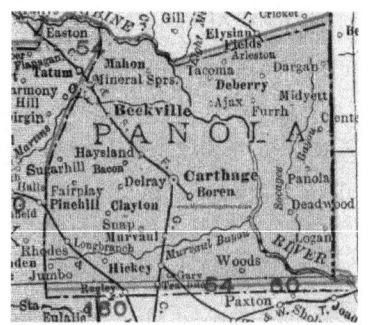

---

[5] "Rev. A. M. Stewart Passes Away," *The Panola Watchman*, September 24, 1913, 8. He probably enrolled in the fall of 1870. A. M. Stewart is listed with his parents in Early County in the 1870 census, which is dated July 5, 1870. Buford Academy may be the one mentioned in the *Annual Report of the Commissioner of Education for the Year 1883-'84* by the United States Office of Education (Washington, DC: Government Printing Office,1885), 487. According to this record the Academy was not organized until 1872. Perhaps the 1872 date is in error or the Stewart obituary is off a few years regarding Angus Stewart's age when he entered the Academy.

[6] There is a Cedar Springs Church at Cedar Springs in Early County, listed in the 1879, 1881-1883 Chattahoochee FWB Association minutes that I inspected.

[7] "Rev. A. M. Stewart Passes Away."

[8] Ibid. See also *History of Free Will Baptist State Associations* (Nashville, TN: Randall House, 1976), 100.

[9] Some sources identify the church name as Liberty FWB Church of Clayton, but perhaps it should be Friendship FWB Church of Clayton instead (or perhaps the name was Liberty and then changed to Friendship). When the Texas State Association met at Friendship at Clayton in 1940, E. S. Jameson stated "that they were meeting in the first Free Will Baptist church to be organized in the state of Texas, 62 years ago"; Murphy, 79. Friendship FWB Church "was located halfway between Clayton and Delray communities just off present-day Farm Road 1970"; Jane Metcalf, *Beckville, Texas: History of the Town and Its Schools* (n.p., n.d.), 208.

zations in the hands of others. He is found that year in the census at Cedar Springs, Early County, Georgia—single, living alone, and a school teacher. He was apparently still living in Georgia in 1881 and 1882, when he attended the Chattahoochee United Free Will Baptist Association.[10]

Stewart had returned to Texas by the time the Chattahoochee Association met November 10-12, 1883. He married Emma Eugenia Ross on November 7, 1883, in Panola County, Texas. Their marriage occurred at the Ross homestead, which was near Clayton. One may guess that Emma was a member of that first Free Will Baptist church.[11] Her mother, Sarah Jane Davis Ross, wife of Arthur Brown Ross, Sr., was certainly a charter member, as confirmed in a 1930 obituary: "Friendship Church: Our beloved sister and mother in Israel, Mrs. S. J. Ross, who was a charter member of the first Free Will Baptist Church in Texas."[12]

Burgess and Ward in the *Free Baptist Cyclopædia*, as well as other writers, credit six more early East Texas Free Will Baptist churches to the labors of Stewart, in addition to the Clayton Church: Lone Star and Rape's Chapel[13] in Cherokee County; Beckville and Union Chapel[14] in Panola County; and Good Hope[15] and

---

[10] Minutes, Chattahoochee UFWB Association, 1881, 13; 1882, 2, 14.

[11] Emma Ross might not have been a *charter* member there, being about 13 years old when the Clayton church was organized. If not, she was probably a member by the time she married Stewart. The report of the Committee on Obituaries at the 1926 Texas FWB Association (Minutes, 8; this association later became the East Texas FWB Association) reveals two other charter members: Jack Brinson Duke and his wife Lucinda Carolina Fallwell Duke. "Brother and Sister Duke were charter members of the first Free Baptist Church in Texas. They had been faithful for nearly 49 years. Their posterity has shown their training by their faithfulness to the church."

[12] Minutes, Texas FWB Association, 1930, 10.

[13] I have not located Rape's Chapel in Cherokee County or elsewhere, but my working assumption is that it was probably located in Cherokee County, Texas. Perhaps the name was passed down incorrectly.

[14] Believed by some to be the same as "Union Arbor," sometimes listed as "Union Harbor" in minutes. This is called into question by the fact that Union Chapel and Union Arbor/Harbor churches are both listed in the 1894 and 1899 minutes of the Texas State Association. See also Metcalf, 209; Murphy, 319.

[15] A question must be raised concerning the Good Hope FWB Church. She counts her existence from 1875; see Good Hope Church website and Murphy, 306. Yet Free Will Baptist historians apparently consistently agree that the first Anglo Free Will Baptist church organized in Texas was organized at Clayton, in Panola County in 1876. Pastor E. S. Jameson, who was from the Good Hope community, in the 1940 minutes of the Texas State Association of Free Will Baptists spoke of the Clayton church as the first Free Will Baptist church in the state. The Texas FWB Association (the East Texas Association, organized in 1878) has several such references in the minutes. So Good Hope counts her beginning in 1875 without apparently asserting any claim ahead of the Clayton Church in 1876. This creates something of a quandary. Perhaps a group at Good Hope was gathering by that time but not constituted as a church? Perhaps Good Hope was organized as a Missionary Baptist Church and then later changed to Free Will Baptist? Edna Mae Watson's piece about "Thomas Franklin B. Jimmerson"—in *Rusk County, Texas, History 1982* (Henderson, TX: Rusk

Union Springs in Rusk County.[16] With these first churches as constituent members—at least the ones already organized by the time—Stewart organized the Texas Free Will Baptist Association in 1878.[17] Doubtless Stewart licensed and/or ordained the first Free Will Baptist ministers raised up in East Texas, such as James Pierce "Jim" Lunsford[18] and Doctor Reubin Gideon ("D. R." or "Dock") Jimmerson.[19]

Later Stewart moved his center of operation to Central Texas, where he is credited with organizing several churches. The first Free Will Baptist Church of Brazos County (and the vicinity) was Bright Light, organized by P. H. Adams in 1886. At times Stewart is credited as a co-organizer of Bright Light, but perhaps he simply followed up the constitution of the church with a revival meeting. "The church was organized in the summer of 1886 by the Rev. P. H. Adams... Soon after the church was organized, a revival was held under a brush arbor with the Rev. A. M. Stewart as evangelist."[20] Stewart suggested the name of the church.[21] After the organization of Bright Light in 1886, eleven other churches were organized by W. T. Wood and A. M. Stewart, including Concord, Tyron Hall, and Wellborn in Brazos County; Givens' Creek, Iola, and Spring Hill in

---

County Historical Commission, 1982)—says that the Jimmerson family first joined the Missionary Baptist Church at Zion Hill when they came to Texas. Some members of the Jimmerson family were members of Ebenezer and Mission Springs Missionary Baptist churches (both organized later than Good Hope). That Good Hope changed from Missionary to Free Will is a theory, of course, as is the idea that it might already have been meeting but not yet a church. D. R. Jimmerson, E. S. Jameson and others would have been in a position to know whether Good Hope was an older Free Will Baptist church than the one at Clayton, yet they never claimed that.

[16] G. A. Burgess and J. T. Ward, eds., *Free Baptist Cyclopædia: Historical and Biographical With Illustrations* (Chicago, IL: Free Baptist Cyclopaedia Co., 1889), 642 (hereafter *Cyclopaedia*); see also G. W. Million and G. A. Barrett, *A Brief History of the Liberal Baptist People in England and America: from 1606 to 1911* (Pocahontas, AR.: Liberal Baptist Book and Tract Company, 1911), 298; et al.

[17] *Cyclopædia*, 642: "The Good Hope and Union Springs churches, in Rusk County, and the Union Chapel and Beckville churches, in Panola County, all gathered by Rev. A. M. Stewart, entered into the organization," implying that the Lone Star and Rape's Chapel churches either were not yet organized or did not enter the organization at the beginning. The article inexplicably fails to mention the Clayton Church, which surely was a constituent member.

[18] One descendant of Lunsford records that he was ordained in 1877 by the "1st Free Will Church" in Cherokee County. In correspondence, Elaine Maduzia revealed that she has lost most of her records in a computer crash, and that this one online is all that survived; so she could not document the source of this information.

[19] The obituary of A. M. Stewart in the Carthage newspaper records Jimmerson's stating at the funeral that "to him Bro. Stewart gave license to preach."

[20] "250 Visit Harvey for Homecoming at Bright Light," *The Bryan Eagle*, May 18, 1954, 5.

[21] Murphy, 282.

Grimes County; and Hollis, High Prairie, Plain View, and Willow Hole in Madison County.[22] Stewart was a charter member and the first pastor of the Bryan Free Will Baptist Church, which he organized in 1894.[23]

Evidently, Stewart was instrumental in organizing some other churches not mentioned in the sources just cited. Evergreen Church in Grimes County must be added to the list,[24] as well as a church at Grass Bur.[25] This brings to about twenty the total number of churches believed to have been organized by him alone or together with other ministers.

Educator

A. M. Stewart was primarily a Free Will Baptist minister, but he also engaged in society for civic improvement, especially in the field of education. He taught school in Georgia and Texas, and perhaps in other places. He also organized schools. Former Texas Speaker of the House R. T. Milner said:

> of the Free Baptist college movement, they have a fine man at the head of it in the person of Rev. A. M. Stewart. I have known him for a number of years. He was engaged in school work in East Texas for ten years and built up two splendid schools in that section, Lone Star Institute and Hewett Institute. He combines splendid executive ability with the other qualifications necessary for successful school work."[26]

Together with Colonel Thomas A. Cocke, Stewart established the Lone Star Institute, a private school, in Lone Star, Cherokee County, Texas, in 1889.[27] The Institute "emphasized cultural accomplishments in music and elocution" and "attracted broad attention." "Many families moved to Lone Star to enroll their

---

[22] "Free Will Baptists," *The Bryan Eagle*, August 1, 1897, 4. This does not make clear whether all were started by the two men together or some by one and some by the other. The article lists Iola and Spring Hill as two churches; Thurmon Murphy (in an email) says they were the same.

[23] Some sources give 1897, which appears to be incorrect. "First Free Baptist Church, Bryan, Texas," *The Bryan Eagle*, April 22, 1913, 24; "Bryan Free Will Baptist Church launched in '94," *The Bryan Eagle*, October 25, 1939, 22; see also Murphy, 292.

[24] Evergreen at Keith in Grimes County was organized by Stewart in 1895. W. T. Wood was the first pastor. See Murphy, 283.

[25] "Rev. A. M. Stewart recently organized a Free Baptist Church at Grass Bur (Bowman's school house)," *The Bryan Eagle*, May 4, 1899, 6.

[26] "Another School Secured," *Bryan Morning Eagle*, June 9, 1902, 2.

[27] Hattie Joplin Roach, *The Hills of Cherokee: Historical Sketches of Life in Cherokee County* (n.p., 1952), 58.

children in it. Some of the teachers and music instructors in its four years of existence were Perry I. Wallace, a Mr. Weaver, and Erma Jones."[28] According to the Texas State Historical Marker, Lone Star "began to decline after a disastrous fire in 1893," and this coincides with the demise of the Institute. Stewart established a Free Will Baptist Church at Lone Star, probably earlier.[29]

He also started the Hewitt Institute (pictured nearby) at Beckville in Panola County. It was in operation by 1891, was the third school in Beckville, and continued operation until 1911. According to Lelia LaGrone, Stewart was hired as the president of Hewitt in 1891 for a period of five years, in which time the school prospered. The school year was extended to 10 months during his tenure.[30] "Legend says that professor Stewart coined a school motto, "Hew to the line!" and this became the background for the name "Hewitt Institute."[31]

Stewart was a leading figure in establishing a Free Will Baptist school at Bryan, Texas. In 1899, the Texas Association's Committee on Schools and Education discussed "the necessity for the establishment of a Free Baptist school" with the "concensus [sic] of opinion that the school should be located at Bryan."[32] By May of 1900, Stewart had "started on an extensive trip through the State, his object being to raise money for the erection of a Free Baptist college at

---

[28] Bernard Mayfield, "Lone Star," in *Cherokee County History* (Jacksonville, TX: Cherokee County Historical Commission, 2001), 59, 210. He *could* be the same as the Angus Stewart who "operated a cotton gin and grist mill" in nearby New Summerfield in Cherokee County about that time (same source), but more likely this was Angus Lorenzo Stewart, who is buried at Myrtle Springs near New Summerfield. The two men by that name do not seem to have been related.

[29] Mrs. H. A. Wheeler, "Early History of Free Will Baptists," *The Free Will Baptist* (Ayden, NC), February 3, 1943, 5.

[30] Lelia Bell LaGrone, *Know Your Heritage* (Carthage, TX: McDowell Printing, 1977), 52. *Hewitt* is spelled *Hewett* in some records. See George Smith, *Biennial Report of the Secretary of State of the State of Texas, 1892* (Austin, TX: Ben C. Jones & Co., 1893), 18 (listed under "Miscellaneous Charters Filed"). The Hewitt Institute building, the Methodist Church, and some homes were wrecked by a storm in November of 1892; see *The Galveston Daily News*, November 2, 1892, 3; and *History of Panola County* (Carthage, TX: Circulating Book Club, 1936). The school nevertheless continued in operation until 1911. See also *Report of the Commissioner of Education for the Year 1897-98, Volume 2* (Washington, DC: United States Office of Education, 1899), 2326; *The Bartlett Tribune*, February 9, 1906, 6; Metcalf, 225; LaGrone, 52.

[31] LaGrone, 52. While this might be an "apocryphal" story, it may explain the origin of the name "Hew it" Institute. There do not appear to be any prominent Hewitt/Hewett places or persons' names in the vicinity of Beckville.

[32] "Free Baptist Association," *The Eagle*, October 26, 1899, 13. I found no evidence that Stewart was a teacher or administrator at the Allen Academy in Bryan, but he owned and sold the property on which it was situated; see "Allen Academy," *The Bryan Eagle*, June 8, 1899, 6.

or near this place [Bryan]."[33] By March 1901, he had concluded the money-raising trip, and the school opened in the fall of 1902.[34] Lay leader J. L. Edge was the secretary and A. M. Stewart the principal of the Academic and Collegiate Institute—presumably the same institution called the Free Will Baptist Academy in its formative stage.[35] The Bryan Academic and Collegiate Institute was co-educational, opening with "primary, academic and collegiate departments." As well as being president over the school, Stewart was also head of the collegiate department. The new school's curriculum embraced "science, languages, literature, and later on, theology."[36] During this period, Stewart was a partner in Bryan Grocery, which interest he sold late in 1904 or early in 1905.[37] In 1906, the Bryan Academic and Collegiate Institute was moved to Lancaster in Dallas County, Texas, consolidating with a military school there, and "President Stewart [remained] at the head of the consolidated school."[38] For reasons unknown, he apparently only stayed there one year.

THIRD SCHOOL. HEWITT INSTITUTE

A. M. Stewart was directly involved in education as teacher and founder. He also promoted education through the Free Will Baptist associations. In 1894, the Texas Association's Committee on Education and Publication, of which

---

[33] *The Houston Daily Post*, May 12, 1900, 5.
[34] *The Galveston Daily News*, March 8, 1901, 3.
[35] "Academic and Collegiate Institute," *Bryan Morning Eagle*, September 2, 1903, 2.
[36] "Another School Secured," *Bryan Morning Eagle*, June 9, 1902, 2. See also Alton Loveless, *The Burial Locations of Free Will Baptist Ministers, Volume II*, 557-558; and Murphy, 292. The board of directors was made up of 10 men and 1 woman: 8 of them from Texas and one each from Arkansas, Indian Territory (now Oklahoma), and South Dakota.
[37] "Rev. A. M. Stewart has sold his interest in the Bryan Grocery company to his partners, T. A. Searcy and Allen Smith, who will continue the business under the same firm name"; "Business Matters. Changes at Bryan," *The Houston Post*, January 6, 1905, 2. He had purchased the interest with Searcy in 1900; "Business Change," *The Bryan Eagle*, April 5, 1900, 5.
[38] "Bryan, Texas, May 4.—The Bryan Academic and Collegiate institute of this city will be removed to Lancaster, Dallas county. The president, Rev. A. M. Stewart, under direction of the board of directors, has contracted for the military school property at Lancaster, consisting of a main building and two dormitories, and the two schools will be consolidated. President Stewart will remain at the head of the consolidated school"; "School to Be Moved," *The Houston Post*, May 5, 1906, 7; see also *Bryan Morning Eagle*, May 4, 1906, 2.

Stewart was Chairman, recommended "For our ministers, Butler and Dunn's Theology,"[39] and further:

> We think the churches should exert themselves for the education of the ministers that come from their ranks. We think our circulating library should be looked after, the several volumes collected and a good librarian elected, and our ministers be required to use, if they have not, and connect several like reading. Our ministers should have a yearly course of reading prescribed by our board of examiners."[40]

Currently, little detail is known of Stewart's own educational qualifications, though they appear respected throughout the state by those who knew him. A *Bryan Daily Eagle* article on the opening of the new Free Will Baptist institute in Bryan refers to Stewart as A.B. and A.M. (with these letters following his name).[41] With the background that is currently available, it must be assumed that Stewart received his Bachelor of Arts and Master of Arts degrees from the Buford Academy. His obituary included this: "After his marriage, feeling the need of a better equipment for his ministerial work, he took a course in the Theological Department of Chicago University, from which institution he was granted a diploma."[42] His diploma from the University of Chicago was for completing a course in religious or pastoral studies.[43]

Angus Stewart also participated in the Brazos County Teachers' Institute.[44]

Many ministers of the day were bi-vocational in order to support their families, and Stewart's professional pursuit as an educator no doubt contributed to that end. He is listed as a minister of the gospel only in the U. S. Federal Census of 1900. It is not unusual for bi-vocational preachers to list as their occupations the ones from which they derive their primary incomes, and this was probably

---

[39] John Jay Butler and Ransom Dunn, *Lectures on Systematic Theology* (Boston, MA: Morning Star Publishing House, 1892).

[40] Minutes, Texas FWB Association, 1894, 5-6. The minutes continue: "Joseph Apperson was appointed librarian."

[41] "Another School Secured," *Bryan Morning Eagle*, June 9, 1902, 2.

[42] "Rev. A. M. Stewart Passes Away."

[43] "It is possible he could have attended the first University of the Baptist Theological Union but not gotten a degree (even if he got a 'diploma' but not an actual degree)—we don't have records for those possible students"; email from Tyler L. Hough (Assistant Director, Constituent Relations, U of Chicago Alumni Association), October 23, 2017.

[44] "Brazos County Teachers," *The Bryan Eagle*, March 22, 1903, 5.

true of Stewart as well. The 1870 census (before his ordination) lists him as a "farm laborer"; in 1880, a "school teacher"; and in 1910, involved in "real estate." At one time, as already mentioned, he was part owner in a grocery store at Bryan. In addition to selling real estate, at times he also sold insurance.[45]

Patriarch

As already noted, after Stewart returned to Texas from Georgia, he married Emma Ross. Her mother, Sarah Jane Davis Ross, was a charter member of the first FWB church at Clayton, as probably was her father, Arthur Brown Ross, Sr. Her father was the sheriff of Panola County in the 1870s.[46]

The union of A. M. and Emma was blessed with five children: Norman Arthur (1885-1953), Ross Angus (1887-1962), McAllister Franklin (1888-1910), Bernard Hadley (1894-1921), and Eva Juanita Stewart Storrie (1905-1996).

Emma was a supporter of her husband's ministry and often had to keep the home fires burning when he was away in revivals, touring the country to raise money, and such like. Though records of her works are not readily available, she engaged in labors of her own in the church. In 1894, "Mrs. E. E. Stewart" was one of three women who served on the eight-member Mission Board of the Texas Free Will Baptist Association.[47] When a Free Baptist Young Peoples Society of Christian Endeavor was organized in 1898, "Mrs. A. M. Stewart" was elected president.[48] She was a teacher at a B.Y.P.U. Training Class in Bryan in February 1923.[49] In May 1922, the widow Emma Stewart (pictured nearby in 1942) married Angus Bolton McSwain at the home of Rev. and Mrs. J. J. Tatum in Brazos County.[50] McSwain and his first wife, who had died

---

[45] "For Old Line life insurance see A. M. Stewart, Carthage, Texas," *The Panola Watchman*, April 17, 1912, 8.
[46] *East Texas Family Records*, vol. 5, no. 3 (Tyler, TX: East Texas Genealogical Society, Fall 1981), 20.
[47] Minutes, Texas FWB Association, 1894, 6.
[48] "New Christian Endeavor," *The Bryan Daily Eagle*, May 11, 1898, 4.
[49] "The B.Y.P.U. Training Class Opened Monday," *The Bryan Weekly Eagle*, February 1, 1923, 1.
[50] "McSwain-Stewart Wedding," *The Bryan Weekly Eagle*, May 11, 1922, 1; "At the home of Rev. and Mrs. J. J. Tatum this afternoon at 4 o'clock A. B. McSwain of Rock Prairie and Mrs. A. M. Stewart of Carthage, Texas were united in marriage, Rev. Tatum officiating...Mr. and Mrs. McSwain will reside at the beautiful farm home of Mr. McSwain in the Rock Prairie community."

in 1916, had united with Bright Light Free Will Baptist Church by profession of faith in July 1886, and they were very active in Free Will Baptist work in Brazos County.[51] They had even named one son Angus Stewart McSwain.

Consistent with Stewart's views on and promotion of education, the occupations of the Stewart children—Norman (druggist), Ross (insurance agent), Franklin (law student), Bernard (druggist), Eva (school teacher)—indicate they received education beyond the high school level.[52] Norman served as a commissioner of the city of Bryan, and was mayor from April 13, 1933 to April 12, 1935.[53]

Norman had three sons and Eva had one son, but I do not know whether any of A. M. Stewart's descendants are currently active in Free Will Baptist churches.

Preacher

Though his main field was Texas—organizing and pastoring a number of churches in East and Central Texas—Stewart scattered the gospel seeds widely. "The life's work of Mr. Stewart extended over many States, including Oklahoma, Missouri, Illinois, Minnesota and Colorado, yet Texas was his principal field of labor."[54] Georgia, the place of his nativity, must be included on the list; no doubt he preached there after being licensed and ordained, before relocating to Texas. When he returned there he was pastor at two churches in the Chattahoochee Association: Pleasant Springs, Calhoun County, in 1881; and Pleasant Grove, Randolph County, in 1881 and 1882. He also preached to the Association in 1882, on Sunday at 11 o'clock.[55]

---

[51] "Mrs. Mattie C. McSwain: A Noble Christian Wife and Mother Finds Her Reward," *The Bryan Weekly Eagle*, July 27, 1916, 5.
[52] U. S. Federal Censuses 1910, 1920, 1930; Ross's and Bernard's World War I draft registrations; "Former Local Girl Weds Aviator," *The Bryan Eagle*, July 8, 1929, 1.
[53] *Mayors, Councilmembers and Appointed Officials, City of Bryan, April 9, 1889 to Present* (Bryan, TX: Office of City Secretary, 2014), 18-19, 21 (not numbered).
[54] "Rev. A. M. Stewart Passes Away."
[55] Minutes, Chattahoochee FWB Association, 1881, 13; 1882, 2, 14. The statistical tables included here show that the Pleasant Grove Church was one of the leading churches in baptisms during the two years of Stewart's tenure, which was consistent with his evangelistic success in Texas and perhaps elsewhere.

In Texas, Stewart was pastor at about a dozen churches: Bright Light and Bryan in Brazos County; Lone Star and Rape's Chapel[56] in Cherokee County; Evergreen in Grimes County; Beckville, Clayton, Tatum, and Union Chapel in Panola County; and Good Hope and Union Springs in Rusk County.

Some of the other places of Stewart's ministry are also known. (1) He preached from January to April 1880 at Bristol Baptist Church in Bristol, Virginia. This church was a member of a group of "free will" churches known as the Southern Baptist Association.[57] (2) He was pastor in Hampton, West Virginia, beginning in about 1887.[58] One of the Stewarts' sons, McAllister Franklin, was born in West Virginia in 1888. (3) In 1907, he was pastor at Champlin Free Baptist Church in Champlin, Minnesota, affiliated with the Hennepin Quarterly Meeting of Free Baptists.[59] Thus, even though he did not come to Texas from the Randall Free Will Baptists, he became known and preached among them and apparently attended at least one of their General Conferences.[60]

Stewart was also a writer. In 1895 a book of his appeared, entitled *Key to the Book of Job, or the Plan of Redemption through the Lineage of Esau*. It used the Biblical story of Job (which Stewart insisted was historical) as an analogy for the church, comparing Job's initial prosperity to the prosperity of much of the lukewarm church.[61]

---

[56] The location of Rape's Chapel in currently unknown.

[57] *Not* to be confused with the Southern Baptist Convention! The Southern Baptist Association was founded by B. W. Nash, S. G. Scoven and others in 1876; see *History of Tennessee from the Earliest Time to the Present: together with an Historical and a Biographical Sketch of from Twenty-five to Thirty Counties of East Tennessee* (Chicago, IL: Goodspeed Publishing Co., 1887), 918-919; *Bristol News*, January 13, 1880, 3, and April 20, 1880, 3; *Bristol, Tennessee/Virginia: A History, 1852-1900* (Johnson City, TN: Overmountain Press, 1992), 312. Bristol is a "state line" city, but the church building was in Virginia. The Bristol Baptist Church was established by Zachariah Lyles Burson, who "being tops among the richest men in town, went down on the Virginia side of Main Street and there, in the 800 block, shelled out $8,500 and built his own church, the finest building in town at the time"; Bud Phillips, "The dancing Major of Bristol was 'legendary'" (Pioneers in Paradise column), *Bristol Herald Courier*, November 9, 2009 (accessed online). For another reference to this, see the chapter in this volume dealing with unity movements in the South.

[58] "Brother [J. E.] Cox writes that the church at Hampton, W. Va., is now self-supporting, and has called Rev. A. M. Stewart of Texas to the pastorate, while Brother Cox goes to Charleston, intent upon the upbuilding of our cause in that city"; "Report of the Home Mission Society," *The Freewill Baptist Register and Year-Book, 1888* (Boston: F. B. Printing Establishment, 1887), 20.

[59] *The Bryan Eagle*, March 15, 1907, 5; and *Star Tribune* (Minneapolis, MN), June 10, 1907, 5.

[60] A "Rev. A. M. Stewart" is mentioned in the *Minutes of the Twenty-Ninth General Conference of Free Baptists*, October 2-8, 1895 (Boston,MA: Morning Star Publishing House, 1896), 59.

[61] A. M. Stewart, *Key to the Book of Job, or the Plan of Redemption through the Lineage of Esau* (St. Louis, MO: Na-

I have discovered almost no information about his ministry in Colorado, Illinois, Missouri, or Oklahoma. It is not hard to imagine that a ministry in Oklahoma could have occurred while he resided in Dalhart, Texas, which is only about 30 miles from the Texas-Oklahoma state line.[62] Campo, Colorado is only about 75 miles from Dalhart, which is less than half the distance of his travel between Beckville, Texas, and Bryan, Texas. Some of Stewart's ministry in other states might have been as an evangelist rather than as a pastor.

Indeed, A. M. Stewart labored extensively as an evangelist. Much of his early ministry in Texas of necessity was that of a missionary and evangelist, but such labor seems to have been part and parcel of his ministry. His successes as an evangelist have been captured in brief newspaper reports, such as these [with italics mine]:

> The revival at the Free Will Baptist church conducted by Rev. W. T. Wood, and Rev. A. M. Stewart the Free Will Baptist evangelist of St. Louis, closed Sunday with *24 accessions* to the church.[63]

> A very successful meeting, conducted by Revs. Sandel of the Methodist church and Stewart of the Free Baptist church, closed here [Wellborn, Brazos Co., Tex.] last night, resulting in *thirty-two accessions* to the two churches.[64]

> Bryan, Texas, May 17.—The tent revival conducted by Rev. A. M. Stewart closed Sunday night. There were *twenty-six accessions* to the church, twenty-one by experience and baptism and five by letter. The new converts were baptized Sunday afternoon in Carter's creek, about three miles from town. It was a glorious revival.[65]

---

tional Baptist Publishing Co. Press, 1895). An advertisement for this appeared in the back of the minutes of the Chattahoochee UFWB Association for 1895, to be ordered from the publisher of *The Harvest Gleaner* in Phoenix, Alabama, which was published by J. H. Jenkins, a FWB minister in the Chattahoochee UFWB Association. (Reprints of the book—with pages 1-5 apparently missing—are available through Amazon.com.)

[62] According to Wikipedia, "Dalhart is located closer to six other state capitals than to Texas' capital of Austin."

[63] "Bethel Briefs," *Bryan Daily Eagle*, August 19, 1896, 1. If the reference to St. Louis is correct, this announcement identifies a time when Stewart was in Missouri. *The Harvest Gleaner* supports this conclusion; issues from September 23 to October 7, 1896, list Stewart's address in St. Louis. But the issue for October 14, 1896, notes that he "has changed P. O. from St. Louis, Mo. to Bryan, Tex."

[64] "Methodist and Baptist Revivals," *The Galveston Daily News*, August 3, 1896, 2.

[65] "Successful Revival," *The Temple Times*, May 20, 1898, 7.

Rev. A. M. Stewart closed a meeting at Brightlight Free Baptist church Sunday in which he was assisted by Rev. W. T. Wood and Rev. Hughes.[66] There were *twenty-one accessions* to the church, seventeen being by baptism. The ordinance was administered Sunday morning at 10 o'clock at D. P. Cole's tank by Rev. A. M. Stewart the pastor.[67]

A number of similar reports could be added to these.[68] As an evangelist, Stewart engaged in revivals that over a century later appear both numerous and successful. Some of the revivals lasted three weeks, perhaps longer.

In revival campaigns Stewart sometimes had charge of the music: "The choir under the direction of Mr. Stewart aids in the services with splendid music."[69] He also engaged noted singers of the day, such as W. C. Frasier and J. E. Thomas.[70]

Stewart cooperated with other denominations in ways consistent with his own beliefs, as shown in the 1896 revival at Wellborn and other union meetings in which he participated. But for his part, the accessions for the Baptists were quickly followed up with immersion baptism of the converts, often in local creeks and stock tanks—as was common at the time.

In that same spirit, A. M. Stewart promoted unity among Baptists of the "liberal" or "free will" persuasion. I have already made reference to his preaching for a Southern Baptist Association church in Virginia. He was also active in an effort to unify Southern Free Will Baptists. His name is found among the ministers calling for a convention to unite Baptists in the South "who believe in free will, free salvation and free communion." This convention was scheduled to meet at the First Free Will Baptist Church (later named Cofer's Chapel FWB Church) at Nashville, Tennessee, on December 5, 1889.[71]

---

[66] J. M. Hughes of Waller County had been a member and minister of another denomination. He was admitted to membership in the Free Will Baptist church at Bryan and "regularly ordained" to preach just prior to helping in the revival; *The Bryan Eagle*, August 7, 1898, 3.

[67] "Meeting at Brightlight," *Bryan Morning Eagle*, August 16, 1898, 3.

[68] See "The Revival," *The Bryan Daily Eagle*, April 26, 1898, 4; "The Revival," *The Bryan Daily Eagle*, May 4, 1898, 4; "Continued Meeting," *The Bryan Morning Eagle*, April 26, 1899, 3; *The Bryan Daily Eagle*, May 16, 1913, 2.

[69] "The Revival," *The Bryan Daily Eagle*, May 4, 1898, 4.

[70] A Professor Hensley of Waco is also mentioned. "Prof. Hensley, the singer who assisted Rev. A. M. Stewart in the meeting held here, returned home to Waco yesterday"; *The Bryan Eagle*, June 1, 1899, 11.

[71] "Free Will Baptists, A Convention to Be Held Here Next Week," *The Daily American* (Nashville, TN), November 27, 1889, 8. See also the chapter in this volume dealing with unity movements in the South.

In August 1910, an unspeakable tragedy invaded the Stewart home. While living in Dalhart, Texas, the Stewarts' son McAllister Franklin committed suicide. According to the census and a newspaper article, "Mack" was a law student. He developed paranoia and was under a doctor's care. The intent was to place him in the sanitarium on Friday, but he fatally shot himself on Thursday. His mother Emma was at the home when the tragedy occurred.[72] This event no doubt colored their lives with grief and might have precipitated their move back "home" to Panola County, Texas. By late 1912 they were residing in Carthage.[73]

I have found no record that Stewart served as pastor after moving back to Carthage, but he remained active in the ministry; and a few references to his "regular appointment" (in the *Panola Watchman*) could mean that he served the Friendship Church again. He performed weddings and assisted at funerals. He preached "at the Christian Church at the 11 o'clock hour" on March 3, 1912, and on a regular basis there.[74] He preached the commencement sermon at the Beckville school,[75] gave the invocation and pronounced the benediction at the High School graduation exercises in Carthage,[76] led the devotional exercises at the Panola County Teacher's Institute in August,[77] occupied the pulpit of the M. E. Church in Timpson in October,[78] and delivered a sermon at a community Thanksgiving service.[79] He also hosted Z. F. Griffin, a missionary from India, well known among the Free Will Baptists of the North.[80] He even had cataract surgery in Dallas![81]

---

[72] "Ends His Life with a Bullet," *El Paso Herald*, August 11, 1910, 9. The article calls A. M. Stewart a Presbyterian minister. This may simply be an error or may indicate that he was filling the pulpit at a Presbyterian church at the time. The article also says that "the family came from Bonham, Texas," intimating that the Stewarts were living there before moving to Dalhart.

[73] See *The Panola Watchman*, October 9, 1912, 8; or October 2, 1912, 1.

[74] *The Panola Watchman*, February 28, 1912, 1. An August issue mentions his having a "regular appointment" there; *The Panola Watchman*, August 14, 1912, 8. In October, this is identified as every third Sunday of the month. "Notice. Until further notice there will be services every Lord's Day at the Christian church. V. R. Stapp will preach the first, second and fourth Lord's Days and A. M. Stewart on the third. V. R. Stapp." *The Panola Watchman*, October 2, 1912, 1.

[75] *The Panola Watchman*, May 15, 1912, 8.

[76] *The Panola Watchman*, May 29, 1912, 4.

[77] *The Panola Watchman*, August 21, 1912, 6.

[78] *The Panola Watchman*, October 2, 1912, 8.

[79] *The Panola Watchman*, November 27, 1912, 1.

[80] *The Panola Watchman*, November 13, 1912, 16. This missionary was Zebina Flavious Griffin.

[81] *The Panola Watchman*, April 16, 1913, 5; April 23, 1913, 8; May 7, 1913, 8.

Beyond these civic and cross-denominational activities, Stewart continued to minister among Free Will Baptists. He moderated the 1912 Texas Free Will Baptist Association.[82] He "filled his regular appointment in Clayton" in April.[83] He "attended the Southern Free Baptist convention in Earlsboro, Okla." and was quoted as saying he "had a most enjoyable trip."[84] He conducted revivals in Ore City and Bryan. The meeting in Bryan was a three-week tent revival "with great results accomplished."[85]

Sickness and Death

In 1913, another tragedy visited the Stewart home. A. M. Stewart had an unlikely and seemingly insignificant accident. He stepped on a tack, which punctured his foot. The puncture healed outwardly, but became infected inwardly. Blood poisoning set in and eventually doctors determined to amputate part of his leg to save the patient. All of this was to no avail. At 9 o'clock a.m. on Wednesday, September 13 "his body gave up the struggle and his great, noble soul leaped from its earthly tenement to meet its Creator." His funeral was described as "possibly the largest gathering of people ever assembled in the Christian Church."[86]

By the time the Texas Free Will Baptist Association met in October 1913, Angus McAllister Stewart had gone to his long sought home. "Rev. D. R. Jimerson being the oldest minister present assumed the Chair as Moderator on account of the death of the former Moderator."[87] Their committee on obituaries submitted the following resolution:

---

[82] I do not have access to the 1912 minutes, but this is implied in the 1913 minutes. Stewart had moderated the 1899 session (*Bryan Eagle*, October 26, 1899, 13) and probably many other sessions whose records are lost or missing.

[83] *The Panola Watchman*, April 17, 1912, 8. Though not clarified, one assumes this means the Free Will Baptist church in Clayton.

[84] *The Panola Watchman*, November 20, 1912, 10. This was the Southwestern Freewill Baptist Convention. Stewart was one of 112 licensed or ordained ministers from Texas who attended the session; Murphy, 13-20, 261-262; see also William F. Davidson, *The Free Will Baptists in History* (Nashville, TN: Randall House Publications, 2001), 261-62.

[85] *The Panola Watchman*, July 24, 1912, 8; *The Bryan Daily Eagle and Pilot*, May 16, 1913, 2.

[86] "Rev. A. M. Stewart Passes Away."

[87] Minutes, Texas FWB Association, 1913, 1.

To the memory of the organizer and promoter of the Freewill Baptist church in Texas:

Inasmuch as our Heavenly Father in his wisdom has seen fit to remove from our midst our Leader and Co-worker, Rev. A. M. Stewart,

And whereas, he was organizer of our church in Texas, and always a promoter of anything for its interest and welfare, not only among people of his own church, but always lending a hand to all Christianity,

And whereas, another one of God's Noblemen has gone, his presence will be missed in our ranks, but the members of the Ministers' Association in the town where he lived, one after another, stood at the funeral and expressed the keen sense of their loss, it is needless to say that his family is heartbroken. Yet he is better off, far, than we, and soon those, who follow his Christ, may enter the same joys.

Therefore, be it resolved; first, that our association extend to the family our sympathy and our prayers.

Second, that we commend our church to his God and advise that our people follow Him in the same earnest spirit, which our brother manifested.

Third, that a copy of these resolutions be spread on our minutes and a copy furnished the family.

Done by order of the association in session, this 3rd day of October, 1913.

E. S. JAMESON, Chairman Committee.[88]

A. M. Stewart's remains were laid to rest at the Odd Fellows Cemetery in Carthage, Panola County, Texas (picture of gravestone nearby). Friends in Bryan described him as "a man of sound intellect, a forceful speaker, an energetic worker, and happiest when ministering to the wants of the sick and needy."[89] In a little over 60 years Angus McAllister Stewart became preacher, pastor, organizer, business man, educator, evangelist, and the "Founding Father" of the Free Will Baptist Church in Texas.

---

[88] Minutes, Texas FWB Association, 1913, 6-7.
[89] "Death of Rev. A. M. Stewart," *The Eagle*, September 17, 1913, 5.

Concluding Observations

As the founder of the first Anglo-American Free Will Baptist church with historical continuity to present-day Free Will Baptists, we may pronounce Stewart the "Founding Father" of Free Will Baptists in Texas. There was a prior "spontaneous" work that emerged from the "Regular" Baptists that had a brief existence circa 1850 in the area of Sabine County, Texas.[90] Furthermore, the African-American St. Paul Freewill Baptist Church in Lancaster, Texas, preceded Stewart's church in Panola County by six years. Other Anglo Free Will Baptists entered Texas independently of Stewart and also started churches that have continued to the present, albeit arriving and organizing later than he did. Nevertheless, through his life and ministry, Angus McAllister Stewart made an original, unique, and lasting contribution to the founding of Free Will Baptists in Texas.

One of the implications of this study is that Georgia Free Will Baptists provided a primary source of influence on the Free Will Baptists of Texas, specifically in East and Central Texas where Stewart labored profusely. This is an important influence, previously unnoticed and unaddressed, and especially involving the Chattahoochee UFWB Association in Georgia. Stewart himself was born, reared, educated, licensed, and ordained within the pale of that association.

There are additional connections between Georgia and Texas. Joseph Apperson, moderator of the 1894 session of the Texas Free Will Baptist Association and pastor of New Prospect church in Cherokee County, was already an ordained minister in the Chattahoochee Association in Georgia before he came

---

[90] The Free Will Missionary Baptist Association was formed by churches that withdrew from the Sabine Baptist Association. The Sabine Association was not "Primitive" but was opposed to Missionary Societies and Fraternal Orders and (apparently) held to a Calvinistic soteriology in general. In contrast, the Free Will Missionary Baptist Association adopted the name "Free Will" and held the distinctive Free Will Baptist doctrines: general provision, the free response to the universal call of the gospel, open communion, and apostasy, as well as adopting "pulpit affiliation" (i.e., exchanging pulpits with different orders of Baptists and/or other denominations, which neither the Anti-Missionary Society, Missionary, nor Primitive Baptists allowed). Z. N. Morrell, *Flowers and Fruits from the Wilderness* (Boston, MA: Gould and Lincoln, 1872), 192-93. One of this new and short-lived Free Will Association's leaders, Peter Eldredge, originally ministered in the same area of Georgia as the Chattahoochee Association (though apparently in the Bethel Association) and seems to have embraced the "Free Will Baptist" viewpoint before leaving Barbour County, Alabama, for Texas.

to Texas, at least by 1886. His father, David J. Apperson, served as moderator of the Chattahoochee Association about 30 years. Hezekiah Dunn, who settled in Rusk County, Texas, by 1883, came from Miller County, Georgia. Dunn's father's obituary appears in the 1885 Chattahoochee minutes. The Edge and Cloud families in Brazos County came from Schley County, Georgia, where D. J. Apperson lived—although it cannot presently be shown that they were connected with the Free Will Baptists there. Joshua Timothy Lee and Joseph Andrew Jackson Sheffield of the Southeast Texas Free Will Baptist Association came to Texas from southwest Georgia.[91]

Furthermore, there appears to be some kinship between the documents of the Chattahoochee and those of the Texas Free Will Baptist Association. The "Church Decorum" and "Government and Ordinances" documents recorded in the minutes of the Texas Free Will Baptist Association show dependence on, or at least correspondence to, these same documents in the Chattahoochee minutes. For example, the "Church Decorum" articles are the same, except that there are 30 instead of 34 articles. The "Government and Ordinances" articles are the same, except that there are 9 rather than 13 articles.[92]

Interestingly, however, the "Articles of Faith" of the Texas Association were *not* fashioned after the "Doctrinal Views" of the Chattahoochee—at least not if we assume (as seems likely) that those found in the Texas Association minutes for 1894 (the earliest we have) and thereafter were still the same as in 1878 when the association began. These articles—included in an appendix below—are succinct and biblically oriented, consisting mostly of Scriptural citations. There are only five brief articles, one each on God, Free Will, Baptism, the Lord's Supper, and the Bible. There are no articles about apostasy or feet-washing, although the latter is briefly addressed in the 29th statement of the "Church Decorum."

---

[91] The information in this paragraph reflects what is found in Chattahoochee FWB Association minutes, U. S. censuses, and Find-A-Grave memorials 110181425, 28090843, and 5617013.

[92] Articles 5, 11, 31, and 33 in the Chattahoochee "Church Decorum" and articles 3, 6, 11, and 12 in the Chattahoochee "Government and Ordinances" are missing from the Texas document (and Article 13 of the latter is truncated). These observations compare the "Church Decorum" and "Government and Ordinances" in the Chattahoochee minutes for 1879, 10-14, with those of the Texas Association for 1894, 12-18. Because we do not have the 1878 minutes of the Texas Association, assumptions must be made that the 1894 articles corresponded to those in 1878.

These Articles of Faith are unique among Free Will Baptists anywhere.[93] It may be that Stewart, either alone or working with someone else, composed them. We cannot be sure of that, of course, but as the founding minister of the new organization he would have been actively involved.[94] Otherwise we have very little to indicate the doctrine that Stewart would have promoted, although we can assume that he subscribed to the doctrinal views of the Chattahoochee Association. At the turn of the century, his church in Bryan emphasized the "free communion" aspect of its doctrine, as seen in its newspaper listing: "Free Communion Baptist—A. M. Stewart, pastor; Services every Sunday night in each month; Sunday school 10 a.m."[95]

A. M. Stewart's work is done. He kept his faith. *The Panola Watchman* reminded its readers regarding this "man of God, friend of all mankind" who was "loved by all with whom he had acquaintance":

Weep not that his toil is over;

Weep not that his race is run.

God grant we may rest as sweetly,

When, like his, our work is done.

APPENDIX: The Articles of Faith of the Texas FWB Association, 1894 (now the East Texas Association),

OF GOD.—Article 1. There is one God and Mediator between God and men, the man Jesus Christ, who gave Himself a ransom for all, to be testified in good time.

OF FREE WILL.—Article 2. We believe that the human will is free, and that all who have heard and who have learned of the Father have the ability to accept or reject the conditions of salvation.

OF BAPTISM.—Article 3.

---

[93] Robert Picirilli compared articles of faith of 55 different associations from eleven states (in the South and Southwest), all in existence in 1894, and reported that "there are no articles of faith like those in any of these associations. Not even close!"—email correspondence dated Friday, November 17, 2017.

[94] I considered the possibility that these articles were modeled after those of the Southern Baptist Association, an organization with which Stewart had some sympathies, but that now seems unlikely since they do not match the articles of that association printed in *The Baptist Review* (Goldsboro, NC), January 30, 1905.

[95] *Bryan Morning Eagle*, September 24, 1900, 4.

Mode—And Jesus, when He was baptized, went up straightway out of the water.—Matt. 3:16.

And it came to pass in those days that Jesus came from Nazareth and was baptized of John in Jordan.—Mark 1:9.

Buried with Him in baptism, wherein ye are also risen with Him through faith of the operation of God who hath raised Him from the dead.—Col. 2:12

We are buried with Him in baptism, into death, that like as Christ was raised from the dead by the glory of the Father, even so we also walk in newness of life. For if we have been planted together in the likeness of His death, we shall be also in the likeness of His resurrection.—Rom. 6:4-5.

For ye are dead and your life is hid with Christ in God.—Col. 3:3.

Subjects—Go ye therefore and teach all nations—Matt. 28:19.

Then they that gladly received His word were baptized—Acts 2:41.

And they spake unto him the word of the Lord, and to all that were in the house. And he took them the same hour of the night, and washed their stripes; and was baptized, he and all his straightway. And when he had brought them into his house, he set meat before them and rejoiced, believing in God with all his house.—Acts 16:32-34.

If thou believest with all thine heart thou mayest.—Acts 8:37a.

Object—The like figure whereunto baptism doth also now save us (not putting away the filth of the flesh, but the answer of a good conscience toward God) by the resurrection of Jesus Christ.—1 Peter 3:21.

THE LORD'S SUPPER.—Article 4. But let a man examine himself, and so let him eat of that bread and drink of that cup.—1 COR. 11:28.

Object.—This done in remembrance of Me.—Luke 22:19.

THE BIBLE.—Article 5. All Scripture is given by inspiration of God and is profitable for doctrine, for reproof, for correction, for instruction in righteousness.—2 Tim. 3:16.

5

Free Will Baptist Participation in Unity Movements in the South, 1870 to 1910

Robert L. Vaughn and Robert E. Picirilli

Preface

Recently come to light is the fact that a number of Free Will Baptists in the South actively participated in cross-denominational (and intra-denominational) unity movements in the late 1800s and early 1900s. Most of this is new information about us, which has not previously been given any significant attention.[1] It is an interesting story, in two parts, and it deserves to be more widely known.

The first part of the story begins with a small group of Baptists—Union Baptists—in the eastern part of Virginia and North Carolina, and with one of their leaders, B. W. (Bushrod Washington) Nash, whose name or influence appears often in the minutes of Free Will Baptist bodies of his time. Nash devoted

---

[1] G. W. Million and G. A. Barrett, *A Brief History of the Liberal Baptist People in England and America From 1606 to 1911* (Pocahontas, AR: Liberal Baptist Book And Tract Company, 1911), 179-80, devoted just twelve lines to B. W. Nash and the Union Baptists, the subject of the first part of this chapter. Michael R. Pelt, *A History of Original Free Will Baptists* (Mount Olive, NC: Mount Olive College Press, 1996), devoted about four pages to them in the North Carolina context but did not treat the Southern Baptist Association. Dodd and Davidson give no attention to the matter. None of the historians treat the movement involved in the second part of this chapter.

a great part of his energies toward uniting "liberal" Baptists[2] of the South into one body, and Free Will Baptists were significantly involved.

I. Union Baptists, B. W. Nash, and the Southern Baptist Association

Union Baptists

The Union Baptist Church was formed in Virginia by James Wesley Hunnicutt.[3] He was born in 1814 in Pendleton District, South Carolina. Around 1832, he became a minister in the Methodist Church and attended Randolph-Macon College at Boydton, Virginia.[4] At some point Hunnicutt decided against infant baptism and withdrew from the Methodists. By 1841 he had formed the Union Baptists, and in 1842, he published *A Summary of the Doctrines, Held and Maintained by the Union Baptists: to which Is Annexed a Recantation of Infant Baptism.*

Hunnicutt, perhaps with others, formed congregations in Virginia and North Carolina.[5] In 1845 he began publishing, in Richmond, Virginia, a monthly newspaper entitled *Union Baptist Banner and Pioneer*, "devoted to the interest of the Union Baptist Church."[6] Subsequently, the name of this publication was

---

[2] "Liberal" Baptists, at that time, meant those who held to the freedom of the will, universal atonement, and other Arminian teachings about soteriology, as well as to open communion.

[3] This group should not be confused with another group of "Union Baptists" that owed their origin to the American Civil War. The national political conflict, secession, and war divided Baptist churches and associations, especially in the Border States. Pro-Union Primitive Baptists often joined Union Leagues. The Primitive Baptists did not allow members to hold membership in secret societies. Considering the Union League a secret society, they often excluded these members from their churches, or the churches that held such members from their associations. The Mountain Union Association, formed in 1867 by some of these that were excluded, was the first "Union Baptist" association on this order, having no connection to the Union Baptists formed by Hunnicutt.

[4] Randolph–Macon College was founded at Boydton by Virginia Methodists in 1830. In 1868, it relocated to Ashland, Virginia, where it remains in operation today.

[5] Charles Crossfield Ware, *North Carolina Disciples of Christ: A History of Their Rise and Progress, and of Their Contribution to Their General Brotherhood* (St. Louis, MO: Christian Board of Publication, 1927), 102, reported that Hunnicutt evangelized in Eastern North Carolina before the Civil War and established churches in Lenoir, Beaufort, Carteret, Craven, Duplin, Greene, Jones, Pender, Sampson, and Wayne counties; "In these ten counties, in 1858, there were fifty Union Baptist Churches with over four thousand three hundred members." Attributing all these churches to Hunnicutt, apparently, glosses over details that are more correctly presented in the text of this chapter. Pelt, 147, credits Nash with organizing several Union Baptist churches in eastern North Carolina.

[6] "The 'Union Baptist Banner and Pioneer' shall be devoted to the interest of the 'Union Baptist Church,' to a fair and full exposition of their doctrines, usages, &c., &c., and to an untiring Christian defence [sic]

changed to the *Christian Banner*.[7] He supported the union of the nation and after the War took a Radical Republican position,[8] which apparently damaged his credibility among the Union Baptist churches and the people of Virginia and Carolina generally.[9] We have found no record of his involvement, after the Civil War, with the denomination he founded; perhaps he became disconnected with the Union Baptists entirely. Thereafter B. W. Nash became their leading figure and promoter.

As for the original faith and practices of the Union Baptists, Hunnicutt's 1842 *Summary* is the obvious source. It was in effect a treatise of fourteen brief articles, each buttressed by extensive Scripture quotations. Any Free Will Baptist could easily agree with the document, except that Hunnicutt's ordinances did not include washing the saints' feet. Especially interesting is the reason given, in the Preface, to explain why they could not unite with Free Will Baptists: "because of their ultra-abolition principles; they denounce all slave-holders and their apologists, and do not recognize them as christians." Hunnicutt had contacted the *Morning Star*, weekly paper published by the Free Will Baptists of the North, and its editor had responded with an article saying,

> We shall send brother Hunnicutt the Treatise on our Faith, our Register, &c., and hope to hear further from him. He should understand that the oppo-

---

of the same. Its constant aim will be to promote unity among all evangelical denominations of Christians." *Richmond Enquirer*, Friday, August 22, 1845, 2. The ad was signed by "Jas. W. Hunnicutt."

[7] The online Virginia Encyclopedia article cited below says, "Hunnicutt moved to Fredericksburg in 1847 and the next year established a weekly newspaper, the *Christian Banner*." This may express the relationship between the two periodicals more accurately.

[8] Before the war broke out, Hunnicutt opposed the secession of the Southern states, but from a pro-South (and pro-slavery) stance. After the war, as a Radical Republican, he supported full citizenship rights for the former slaves and became very involved in Virginia politics. See the online Encyclopedia Virginia, "James W. Hunnicutt (1814–1880)," contributed by Matthew S. Gottlieb and the Dictionary of Virginia Biography; accessed April 5, 2018, at https://www.encyclopediavirginia.org/Hunnicutt_James-_W_1814-1880#start_entry. The article includes a photograph of Hunnicutt and cites his *The Conspiracy Unveiled: The South Sacrificed; or, the Horrors of Secession* (Philadelphia, PA: J. B. Lippincott & Co., 1863).

[9] The *Religious Herald* (of mainstream Baptists in Virginia) for June 19, 1862, quoted the *Richmond Examiner* to say that the *Christian Banner* had "gone over to the enemy," welcoming the "re-appearance of the 'Stars and Stripes' in Fredericksburg." The same note observes that "the negroes and Yankees" were now calling Hunnicutt a "Free Will Baptist," which (along with at least one other reference in this chapter) goes to show that many regarded the Union Baptists and Free Will Baptists as equivalent in doctrine if not in name and organization.

sition of the Free Will Baptists to the whole system of slavery is invincible,—that they do not fellowship slave-holders or their apologists as christians.[10]

Apparently Hunnicutt did not realize that the Free Will Baptists of the North and of the South were two entirely independent denominations.

We also have some later publications by Nash that indicate the Union Baptists' teachings. In an 1885 newspaper article, he would say, "The doctrines on which the organization is based, is [sic], free agency, free grace, free communion and immersion as the only mode of baptism."[11] This straightforward statement summarized accurately the faith of the Union Baptists. Hunnicutt's *Summary* also clearly affirmed the doctrine of apostasy, and those who disagreed on the point took note. The Cape Fear Association (of Regular or Missionary Baptists, which required re-immersion of members received from the Union Baptists) said: "The Union Baptists are followers of Hunnicutt, are advocates of loose communion and of the privilege of falling from grace."[12] (One may not appreciate their sarcasm!)

That the Union Baptists did not practice feet-washing is also clear in the record of a Union Convention in December of 1867, held at Hookerton in Greene County, North Carolina (more about this meeting below). It included delegates from the Disciples, Free Will Baptists, and Union Baptists. The fourth resolution for consideration said, "While we do not regard the washing the saints' feet as an ordinance of the Christian Church, still we look upon it as a good work, designed to teach the Lord's people the great lesson of humility; and that all Christians should be at liberty to assemble when, where, and as often as they please for this purpose." This resolution was "voted for by the Disciples and the Union Baptists, and voted against by the Free Will Baptists."[13]

---

[10] James W. Hunnicutt, *A Summary of the Doctrines, Held and Maintained by the Union Baptists: To Which Is Annexed a Recantation of Infant Baptism* (Richmond, VA: P. D. Bernard, 1942), 6-7. We are grateful to Gary Barefoot, curator of the Free Will Baptist Historical Collection at the University of Mount Olive in North Carolina, for a scan of this document. *The Religious Herald* for July 31, 1851, evaluated this statement as being "closer to Arminianism than Calvinism—holding to free will, and rejecting predestination," calling the Union Baptists a "new sect." The article also indicated that Hunnicutt was baptized "by a minister connected with the Reformers" but had disagreed "on some points with that church."

[11] *Goldsboro* [NC] *Messenger*, October 8, 1885, 1.

[12] "Cape Fear Association," *The Biblical Recorder*, November 3, 1869, 2.

[13] Ware, *North Carolina Disciples*, 104-06, has the minutes of this meeting.

The grand mission of the Union Baptists, according to Gary Barefoot and others, was to urge "the necessity of union between all liberal Baptists."[14] Hunnicutt's first paper, as already mentioned, had promoted "unity among all evangelical Christians"; apparently there was a more specific goal for Baptists with Arminian tendencies. C. C. Ware said that "the effort of Rev. J. W. Hunnicutt … [was] to unite all the wings of the open communion Baptists in one grand, aggressive body, under the name and style of the Union Baptist Church."[15] Histories written by Disciples of Christ and Free Will Baptists often emphasize that the Union Baptists failed "to unite all stripes of Baptists into one denomination and so this movement ceased to have existence."[16] While this is true, one may also say that they ceased to exist because individuals and churches ultimately united with Disciples and Free Will Baptists and were no longer distinctly known as Union Baptists.

B. W. Nash

According to the announcement of his death, Nash was 86 years old when he died on January 27, 1911.[17] This would mean he was born in about 1825, but his tombstone gives 1831 as the date of his birth. We have no information about his early life, but he apparently entered the ministry, as a Union Baptist, under the tutelage of J. W. Hunnicutt in Virginia. A Methodist minister of his time described Nash as "an educated man—a true Christian and a first-rate preacher; he was gifted as an orator."[18]

According to his own account, Nash was transferred from Virginia to North Carolina in the summer of 1858 and did mission work there. He had found "the skeleton of 12 churches, with about 300 members," and after two

---

[14] Gary F. Barefoot, Alan K. Lamm, Michael R. Pelt, Ricky J. Warren, *A History of the Cape Fear Conference of Original Free Will Baptists 1855-2010* (Executive Committee of the Cape Fear Conference, 2011), 3.
[15] Ware, *North Carolina Disciples*, 321.
[16] Million and Barrett, 179-80; see also Ware, *North Carolina Disciples*, 102-03: "The last standing Church property of this group was old Lousan Swamp. It burned after the death of Nash. In its ashes is the last material vestige of Nash's movement among the Baptists."
[17] "Rev. W. B. [sic] Nash," *The Morning Star* (Wilmington, NC), January 27, 1911, 7.
[18] E. A. Barnes, "Scenes in My Early Ministry," *North Carolina Christian Advocate*, October 25, 1906, 4.

years could report (in 1860) "16 churches, with between twelve and fourteen hundred members."[19]

Of special interest is the fact that these were, at least for the most part, Free Will Baptist churches when Nash arrived. In the same article Nash relates that in 1852 the Annual Conference of Free Will Baptists in North Carolina had split over the issue of local church autonomy in dealing with Freemasons. Both groups had claimed to be the "original" Free Will Baptists, but in 1858 one of the two groups, "who favored secret orders," he said,[20] joined the Union Baptists and became the Grand Council of Union Baptists of North Carolina. R. K. Hearn said, referring to this same faction, "The other party bore the name [Free Will Baptist] a few years, then a portion of them united with Rev. Mr. Hunnicut, under the name of Union Baptist."[21] These were apparently the churches that had but three hundred members when Nash came to the state, and about which he said, "This was the best that we could do, out of a Free Will Baptist Conference, that claimed a membership of two thousand, the year before."[22] There is nothing here to suggest that there were other Union Baptist churches already in North Carolina, but that may simply be information that is missing.

---

[19] "Union Association of Baptists," *Goldsboro Messenger*, October 15, 1885, 1. That he was "transferred" may suggest that the Union Baptists practiced a more authoritarian form of government. So also his saying that the Union Baptists, "with head quarters [sic] at Fredericksburg, sent out a minister in search of brethren of like faith and order." In this, Nash might have been referring to someone other than himself or to himself indirectly.

[20] This was the group known as the Alfred Moore faction; they supported the authority of the conference to prohibit churches from expelling members because they were masons. The James Moore faction insisted that each local church had the right to determine this for itself. According to George Stevenson, the split came in 1853. Stevenson also said that the thirteen articles of faith of the Union Baptists reflected a revision (seven "almost word for word") of the articles of the North Carolina Original FWBs, which in turn was the Free Will Baptists' 1812 revision of the Brief Confession of 1660 of the English General Baptists; see his note attached to the 1857 minutes of the Alfred Moore faction of the North Carolina Original FWBs.

[21] Rufus K. Hearn, "Origin of the Free Will Baptist Church of North Carolina," reprinted in D. B. Montgomery, *General Baptist History* (Evansville, IN: Evansville Courier Co., 1882), 176; the entire article is on pp. 148-178 and can be accessed at https://archive.org/details/generalbaptisthi00mont. It originally appeared in the *Toisnot Transcript*, May 20-June 17, 1875. It can also be accessed at https://fwbhistory.com/?page_id=123.

[22] "Union Association of Baptists," *Goldsboro Messenger*, October 15, 1885, 1. Pelt, 148, notes that before the original North Carolina Conference divided, in 1851, there were 36 ministers and 45 churches; and afterward, 17 ministers and 17 churches.

Surprisingly, a record of the 1858 session of those Free Will Baptists has been preserved in a newspaper article.[23] They met at Lousan Swamp, Lenoir County, in November. Nash preached the introductory sermon. After adopting resolutions to join the Union Baptists and change their name to Grand Council, they received Nash as a member, transferring from the Grand Council of Union Baptists of Virginia. They employed Nash and S. J. Carrow[24] as "itinerant ministers to travel and preach" for the ensuing year. They seated visiting brethren from Virginia, adopted the articles of faith, church constitution, and church government of the Union Baptists of Virginia, recommended Hunnicutt's *Christian Banner* as the organ of the denomination in North Carolina, and appointed delegates to attend the next meeting of the Grand Council in Virginia. J. W. Hunnicutt and James H. Hundley of Virginia preached on Sunday.

The First Unity Meeting Involving Union Baptists and Free Will Baptists

Once Nash was established in North Carolina and helped convert a faction of the Annual Conference of Free Will Baptists into Union Baptists, he and Hunnicutt proceeded to attempt to realize their vision for the union of Baptist bodies, in the South, holding free grace, free will, and free communion. A convention toward this end took place, beginning April 30, 1859, at the Providence Church in Muscogee County, Georgia. This was a church of the Chattahoochee United Baptist Association, soon to become United Free Will Baptists.

A record of this meeting has also been preserved in a newspaper article at the time,[25] and some additional detail appears in a later recollection of Nash himself.[26] Nash said it was "called by the United Baptists" of Southwest Georgia.[27]

---

[23] *American Advocate* (Kinston, NC), November 16, 1858, 3. The article is apparently headed "Congratulations," but the middle part of the word is covered and unreadable. All information about this meeting is from this article.

[24] S. J. Carrow had been a minister in the Alfred Moore faction of the General Conference of original Free Will Baptists of North Carolina; see the minutes, 1857, 6.

[25] "Georgia Convention," *American Advocate* (Kinston, NC), June 2, 1859, 3. All information about this meeting is from this article and the one in the following note.

[26] "The Southern Baptist Association," *Baptist Review*, January 30, 1905, 2-3. All information about this meeting is from this article and the one in the preceding note. Special thanks to Gary Barefoot, curator of the Free Will Baptist Historical Collection at the University of Mount Olive, North Carolina, for a scan of this issue.

[27] This seems likely. The Chattahoochee had made an unsuccessful effort to enlist the original General FWB Conference in North Carolina in "a convention for the purpose of a union of the Free Will Baptists

Delegates were present from four states—Virginia, North Carolina, Georgia, and Alabama— and included "several orders of Union, United, General[28], and Free-will Baptist denominations," including the Grand Council of Union Baptists of North Carolina, New Salem United Baptist Association, Chattahoochee United Baptist Association, and Mount Moriah (Alabama) Free Will Baptist Association. Attending this meeting were prominent leaders such as Ellis Gore of Alabama and James E. Brodnax and D. J. Apperson of Georgia.[29] J. W. Hunnicutt of the Union Baptists of Virginia was present, preached, and played a leading role. Nash was a delegate from the North Carolina Union Baptists but was not as active as Hunnicutt. Gore was elected moderator[30] and Hunnicutt clerk.

Of interest is the fact that during this meeting Hunnicutt read the articles of faith and government and the constitution of the Union Baptists of Virginia and North Carolina. Then Gore read those of the Mount Moriah FWB Association. There followed extensive discussion of the names Free Will Baptist and Union Baptist and of the articles of faith and government of the two denominations. As clerk, Hunnicutt recorded that "the discussion was continued for some time, with considerable zeal on the part of the speakers." Included were observations by J. H. Hundley of Virginia to the effect that the Union and United Baptists involved would benefit from uniting. In the end, a resolution recommended, to the New Salem and Chattahoochee United Baptists (and other United Baptists in the South) the propriety of adopting the name and the articles of faith and government of the Union Baptists. One gets the feeling, from reading all this, that the Mount Moriah Free Will Baptists were less inclined to make changes in their name or articles of faith and government. And we know, from subsequent

---

South" in 1857, which had been rejected. See the record of the General Conference for 1857 and 1858 in T. F. Harrison and J. M. Barfield, *History of the Free Will Baptists of North Carolina* (W. E. Moye, 1897), 245-46, 248.

[28] Any General Baptists at the meeting are not identified and perhaps were present as visitors.

[29] For other references to Apperson and Brodnax, of the Chattahoochee Association, see the chapters in this volume devoted to United Baptist origins in Georgia and to A. M. Stewart and origins in Texas.

[30] Nash, in the *Baptist Review* article cited, said that Gore, in his own testimony at the meeting, said so much about the Freewill Baptists of the Randall movement that others took him to be an abolitionist and at first did not want to seat him; but Nash spoke up for him and he was seated. There is a good bit of information about Gore in this article.

events, that the Chattahoochee United Baptists (and perhaps the New Salem United Baptists?[31]) went on to become "United Free Will Baptists."

At any rate, the meeting, although it seems to have concluded with good feelings and general resolutions of unity, apparently did not lead to any continuing organization. It seems apparent that any additional efforts toward uniting were halted by the gathering clouds of war and the torrent that burst from them. The Civil War devastated the South and would certainly have prevented any more such conventions while it raged.

Although Nash was having success with some (former) Free Will Baptists in North Carolina, he was not so successful with those that remained in the mainstream there. This does not mean that he did not try. His basic method was to visit the conferences and urge cooperation in forming a union with others of the same general persuasion. He was especially active in the Cape Fear Conference, which had been formed in 1855. In 1858, he and Hunnicutt from the Union Baptists of Virginia, along with Owen Jones of the Union Baptists of North Carolina, were seated as visiting ministers. The Cape Fear named delegates to the next session of the Grand Council of Union Baptists of Virginia[32] and to the Grand Council of Union Baptists of North Carolina (which, as seen above, was formed primarily from Free Will Baptist churches of the Alfred Moore faction that broke away from the original Conference that same year). In 1859, Nash was present again and was granted permission to "preach in the bounds of the Cape Fear

> **THE BAPTIST REVIEW,**
> **An Independent Religious Newspaper.**
>
> It supports and defends the doctrine of free agency, and Personal Accountability. It advocates the doctrine of the unlimited atonement; and believes that salvation is attainable by all persons who hear and understand the gospel. It advocates the Union and Communion of all Christians at the Lord's table regardless of Denominational or Sectarian distinctions. And vindicates the cause of Christian Union upon the basis of the New Testament. It recognizes Christians of all evangelical Churches as members of the Church of Christ; and advocates co-operation among the protestant denominations in the work of evangelization. It advocates Immersion as the only proper mode of baptism and believers as the only subjects. Our motto is:
>
> FREE SALVATION, FREE COMMUNION AND IMMERSION.
>
> SUBSCRIPTION RATES
> One year $2 00
> Six months.............................. 1 25
> Three months............................ 75
> REV. B. W. NASH,
> La Grange, N. C.,
> Editor and Publisher.

---

[31] So far we have not been able to learn anything about the New Salem Association of United Baptists. In 1847, the Chattahoochee had correspondence with a Salem United Baptist Association, but we cannot say whether there was a connection. It seems likely that the association was in Georgia. There is a little information about the Salem Association in the chapter, in this volume, about United Baptists in Georgia.
[32] This bit of information, not in Pelt, is from Harrison and Barfield, 357.

Conference for the present."³³ There is, however, no evidence that the Cape Fear, as such, took part in the unity meeting in Georgia in 1859.

Nash, the Union Baptists, and the *Baptist Review* After the Civil War

The Civil War lasted from 1861 to 1865 and Reconstruction even longer. By the 1870s, however, the South had begun to recover. Nash—now without Hunnicutt—was re-energized in his attempt to promote Union Baptists and the vision of uniting various Baptist bodies holding "free will" sentiments. Around July 1873, to this end, he began publishing the *Baptist Review* at La Grange, North Carolina.³⁴ Apparently, Hunnicutt's *Christian Banner* had ceased during the Civil War and the new paper became the official organ of the Union Baptists and Nash's cause.³⁵

Nash's advertisement for his *Baptist Review* (pictured nearby) spelled out a number of his beliefs, including free agency, unlimited atonement, and "that salvation is attainable by all persons who hear and understand the gospel."³⁶ He also came to advocate for prohibition.³⁷ A later issue (1905) would also inveigh against the current efforts of "the holiness gang" (in North Carolina and

---

[33] The information in this paragraph is from Pelt, 152. Essentially the same information is in *A History of the Cape Fear Conference of Original Free Will Baptists 1855-2010*.

[34] *Carolina Messenger* [Goldsboro, NC], July 17, 1873, 3. *Geo. P. Rowell & Co's American Newspaper Directory* [New York, 1879], 259, lists the *Baptist Review* at La Grange, NC, as a four-page weekly, with Rev. B. W. Nash as its editor and publisher. In his own description in "The Baptist Review," *Baptist Review*, January 30, 1905, 3, Nash relates that in discouragement he had suspended publication in the fall of 1874 but revived it in 1875; it prospered and he relocated it to Goldsboro in 1882, where a fire in November of 1884 had led to another disruption in publication. It was "revived in about the date of 1886." In reference to this fire, the editor of the *Free Will Baptist* would say, "We are pleased to see that Bro. B. W. Nash of the *Baptist Review* has recovered from the great disastrous fire in Goldsboro in 1884. The *Baptist Review* is well printed and deserves a hearty support by the denominations of Christians which it advocates"; *The Free Will Baptist*, July 23, 1886, 3. This confirms the 1886 date for the republication of Nash's paper; it also tends to suggest that the editor of *The Free Will Baptist*, while respecting Nash's paper, thought it was not so useful *outside* the churches of Nash's group as *within*.

[35] Hunnicutt published until May 1861, then began again in the spring of 1862; but he soon left—"when General R. E. Lee's veterans marched in"—and apparently spent the rest of the war years in Philadelphia. He returned to Virginia after the war and began a politically-oriented publication, *New Nation*. He ran for governor of the state twice but was not elected, and he died in 1880. See "John W. Hunnicutt (1814-1880)"; and Charles Crossfield Ware, *Hookerton History* (Wilson, NC: self-published, 1960), 8 (accessed April 30, 2018, at https://archive.org/stream/hookertonhistory#page/8/mode/2up).

[36] "The Baptist Review," *The Morning Star* (Wilmington, NC), August 22, 1874, 4.

[37] *The* [New Bern, NC] *Daily Journal*, July 26, 1882, 1. See also "The Union Baptists," *Goldsboro Messenger*, October 8, 1885, 1. The editor of *The Daily Journal* appreciated Nash's advocacy of prohibition but did not like his linking that cause to the conflict between Republicans and Democrats.

Alabama) to take over open communion Baptist churches with their doctrine of a "second blessing" that "has filled the land and country with such strife and confusion and sin as had never visited the earth before them."[38]

In 1905, at least, the *Baptist Review* was published twice monthly—on the first and fifteenth, or the fifteenth and thirtieth of each—and a year's subscription price was one dollar[39]—as compared to the two dollars in the 1874 ad pictured above. Nash did his own publishing and this led to the establishment of a printing business. In addition to the *Baptist Review*, the "Baptist Review Job Office" printed other things, including associational minutes. That imprint can be found on a number of minutes of Free Will Baptist associations, including, for examples, those of the Cape Free FWB Conference of North Carolina, and the Mt. Moriah, Vernon, and Jasper associations of Alabama—mostly in the late 1800s and early 1900s.[40]

Nash also published hymn books;[41] his *Baptist Harmony* was adopted by various Free Will Baptist associations in the South. As early as 1877, the South Carolina FWB Conference recommended it.[42] In 1890, the Jasper FWB Association in Alabama adopted a resolution endorsing *The Baptist Review* as "our denominational organ," adding, "We also have the Baptist Harmony, which is of convenient size, and the best selection of hymns in use. It is neatly bound in morocco, and the retail price is 50 cents. For sale by Rev. B. W. Nash, Goldsboro, N. C."[43]

---

[38] "The Southern Baptist Association," *Baptist Review*, January 30, 1905, 2-3. He also referred to them as "hypnotism holiness." In yet another editorial, reprinted approvingly as "Slander and Abuse" in the *Goldsboro Messenger* for June 18, 1887, 2, Nash defended white Southerners against newspapers in the North who, he said, were accusing them of being "enemies of the negroes" and trying to "sink them into abject heathenism."

[39] "The Baptist Review," *Baptist Review*, January 30, 1905, 3.

[40] The 1897 minutes of the Vernon Association, 3, show that they voted "to allow Bro. Nash the option of printing the minutes if he would print them as cheap as anyone else." So Nash printed the 1898 minutes—and included a lengthy note of his own, on page 10, emphasizing how much better his printing was and saying he cleared only eight dollars after expenses!

[41] These were *Baptist Harmony: A New Collection of Hymns and Spiritual Songs* (LaGrange, NC: The Author, 1876); and a second edition, *Baptist Harmony: A Collection of Hymns and Spiritual Songs* (Goldsboro, NC: Baptist Review Job Office, 1884). Nash's sons continued the business as Nash Brothers Printing; it existed until recently as Nash Printing in Goldsboro.

[42] Minutes, South Carolina FWB Conference, 1877 (in *Minutes of the South Carolina Conference of Free Will Baptists 1858-1930*, transcribed from the handwritten record book by Clara L. and Robert E. Picirilli, 2000, 34).

[43] Minutes, Jasper FWB Association, 1890, 3.

In addition to his publishing, Nash continued visiting associations to enlist them in his cause. His efforts with the Cape Fear FWB Association continued. In 1874, he was present and spoke, "urging the necessity of union between all liberal Baptists." He was there again in 1875 and 1876.[44] In 1878, two other delegates were present from the Mt. Zion Baptist Association, the new name of the Union Baptists (as will be noted below).[45] And again in 1884 and 1888.[46]

Furthermore, Nash also attempted, from 1867-1870, to influence the older Free Will Baptist body in the state, the original General Conference.[47] In 1867, this conference seated visiting brethren from the Disciples and the Union Baptists. The delegate of the latter group, Irvin Jones,[48] invited them to send delegates to a convention at Hookerton "for the purpose of trying to unite the three denominations." Ten Free Will Baptist men were appointed for this, led by Rufus K. Hearn. That convention took place beginning December 27, 1867, at which three men (including Nash for the Union Baptists and Hearn for the Free Will Baptists) were appointed to write a preamble and resolutions to be considered. The first resolution affirmed to "take the Word of God for our only rule of faith and practice." The fifth affirmed to "regard all denominational names as unscriptural" and committed to be called only *Christians*.[49] (The fourth resolution has been mentioned above.) These were obviously heavily influenced by the Disciples.

The next year, 1868, two visiting delegates from the Union Baptists were seated in the Free Will Baptist General Conference. They asked the Conference to vote on whether it was willing to make some concessions on the name in order to unite with the Union Baptists. Although the majority voted No, the Conference appointed delegates to attend the next Grand Council of Union

---

[44] The information in this paragraph, to this point, is from Pelt, 152-53. Essentially the same information is in *A History of the Cape Fear Conference of Original Free Will Baptists 1855-2010*.

[45] Harrison and Barfield, 370.

[46] Minutes, Cape Fear FWB Association, 1884, 3-6; 1888, 7-8. Pelt mentions the 1884 presence but says "Finally." That was, however, *not* Nash's final effort with the Cape Fear.

[47] The information in this paragraph is from Pelt, 157-159. Essentially the same information is in *A History of the Cape Fear Conference of Original Free Will Baptists 1855-2010*.

[48] Irvin Jones had been a delegate from the Hookerton FWB Church to the Alfred Moore faction of the General Conference of the original Free Will Baptists of North Carolina in 1857; see minutes, General FWB Conference, 1857, 4.

[49] The minutes of this convention appear in Ware, *North Carolina Disciples*, 104-106.

Baptists of North Carolina. In 1869, then, Nash was present and seated as a visiting minister again. Rufus K. Hearn persuaded the Conference to vote to send three delegates to a convention (time and place not yet named) of free communion Baptists in the state, and to send three to the next Grand Council of Union Baptists of North Carolina. Finally, in 1870, with visiting delegates from both the Disciples and the Union Baptists present, James Moore made a motion that "we dismiss from our conference the subject of uniting with other denominations." That passed and apparently brought the matter to an end in that conference.

Name Changes and Alignments Among the Union Baptists

We have no detailed history of the Union Baptists during this period, but some key events are known as a result of Nash's correspondence and publication. Beginning with a resolution in 1867 and consummated in 1870, the Grand Council of Union Baptists became, simply, the "Baptist Association." In 1876, this became the Mount Zion Association of Baptists.[50] A record of the 1881 session of this organization has been preserved in a newspaper article.[51] Those who preached included Nash (who was "quite feeble from recent sickness"), W. C. Vause, and J. F. Hill. Hill was visiting from the Cape Fear FWB Conference and Vause was from the Eastern FWB Conference.[52] Support for the *Baptist Review* was "earnestly urged by the Committee on Denominational literature."

In 1883, this association, together with the Piny Grove Association of Baptists and Central Association of Baptists, formed the Union Association of Baptists, based on "free agency, free grace, free communion and immersion as the only mode of baptism."[53] A record of the 1885 session of this organization appeared in a newspaper article at the time.[54] It convened at Thunder Swamp

---

[50] "Union Association of Baptists," *Goldsboro Messenger*, October 15, 1885, 1. Ware, *North Carolina Disciples*, 106, links these changes to the fact that the Union Baptists broke up "the old order" of their organization in 1867, followed by the departure of many—at least seven of their ministers—for the Disciples.

[51] "Proceedings of the Mount Zion Association, held at South West on the 20th, 21st, and 22nd of October, 1881," *Kinston* (NC) *Journal*, October 27, 1881, 2. All information about this meeting comes from this article.

[52] He is identified in this way in the Minutes of the Cape Fear FWB Conference, 1894, 7.

[53] "Union Association of Baptists," *Goldsboro Messenger*, October 15, 1885, 1. We have no information about either of these two associations, both apparently in North Carolina.

church near Mount Olive, North Carolina. Nash was elected moderator and reported, as "agent" to investigate title to church property, that the deeds of several churches were defective: namely, Pleasant Grove and Hookerton in Greene County; and Lousan Swamp, Bethel, South West, and Hickory Grove in Lenoir County. The session adjourned to meet at Lousan Swamp in October 1886.

By 1885 yet another, broader, organization had been formed by this Union Association of Baptists and the Cape Fear Conference of Free Will Baptists (with churches in Johnston, Sampson, Cumberland, Harnett, and Wake counties). It was named the United Baptist Conference[55] and apparently did not require that either of the associations involved lose their distinctive identity. It was scheduled to meet at Hood Swamp FWB Church, east of Goldsboro, in October 1885. We have no records of this association, but the 1884 minutes[56] of the Cape Fear Conference, when Nash was present and preached, show that a majority of the churches had voted "to continue their connection with the United Baptist Conference." There was also a vote that each church should send one or more representatives to the United Conference in 1885, and another to approve holding that conference with the Hood Swamp Church in Wayne County, on Thursday before the fourth Sunday in October. There is also a note that "The Union subject" was "harmoniously discussed by Elders Nash, Johnson, Byrd, and others."

Nash's good relationship with the Cape Fear Association apparently continued at least until 1888, when the minutes show him present and preaching again and making "some remarks concerning Union movements." He reported that he had "visited and preached to several of the churches in our connection," and he "offers us the [*Baptist*] *Review*, a very neat little religious newspaper."[57]

The *Baptist Review* became known among many Free Will Baptists over a wide geographic area. The Territorial FWB Association in Oklahoma, for example, in 1896, adopted the publication "as our organ or church paper" and

---

[54] "The Union Baptists," *Goldsboro Messenger*, October 8, 1885, 1. Nash would write the paper a week later to correct the editor's use of "Union Baptists" in the heading, a name they no longer used.

[55] "Union Association of Baptists," *Goldsboro Messenger*, October 15, 1885, 1.

[56] The information in the rest of this paragraph is from the Minutes of the Cape Fear FWB Association, 1884, 3-6.

[57] Minutes, Cape Fear FWB Association, 1888, 7-8.

recommended it to the association's churches "as a faithful advocate of our doctrine."[58] The State Line FWB Association, of Alabama-Florida, in 1893, recommended the paper, "published by Bro. Nash."[59] So did the Cumberland FWB Association in Tennessee, as early as 1878, recommending "that every one of them [our brethren] take it."[60]

The paper was also known in Nebraska, where A. D. Williams edited, on behalf of the Randall movement Free Will Baptists in the West, a paper named *The Western Free Baptist*. In an 1877 issue Williams included this brief notice:

Funny

Our good Bro., Rev. B. W. Nash, editor of the *Baptist Review* ("Free Will Baptist") Goldsboro, North Carolina, objects strenuously to uniting with the Freewill Baptists—"North," as he phrases it,—because, as he avers, they are "amalgamationists." The thing is funny, there being so much more actual "amalgamation" at the South than in the North, and we know of no Freewill Baptist who is in favor of it.[61]

This shows several things, one being that editor Williams regarded Nash and the Union Baptists as equivalent to Free Will Baptists, and that Nash (if not Hunnicutt) had come to realize that the Free Will Baptists of the South were not the same denomination as those of the North. What he meant by *amalgamation* is not entirely clear: probably having the African-American Free Will Baptists in the same organization as the whites—and perhaps in the same churches. (More about Williams and Nash in Part II of this chapter.)

The Southern Baptist Association

Nash's broadest achievement came in 1876, with the formation of the Southern Baptist Association—not to be confused with the Southern Baptist Convention, and having nothing to do with the people we now know as Southern Baptists. This organization represented the culmination of his efforts to bring together "liberal" Baptists of the South, and his reach through the *Baptist*

---

[58] Minutes, Territorial FWB Association, 1896 (page not numbered).
[59] Minutes, State Line FWB Association, 1893, 4.
[60] Minutes, Cumberland FWB Association, 1878, 5.
[61] *The Western Free Baptist*, July 1887 (III:4), 3. *Amalgamation* was sometimes a code word for interracial marriage, but probably not here.

Review no doubt helped bring about its establishment. What is apparently his own description of how this came about appeared in a newspaper article in 1887[62] and includes helpful information.

In 1874, the publication of the *Baptist Review*, started the previous year, had led to a "spirit of union" among Baptists, in the South, who held to "free grace, free agency and free communion." The editor (Nash) had visited the Cape Fear FWB Association that year, as well as the Chattahoochee United FWB Association in Georgia and the Mount Zion Baptist Association in North Carolina. All three had welcomed him and his plan and named delegates to attend any meeting that should be convened for the purposes of union. In 1875, then, Dr. S. G. Scoven of Emmanuel County, Georgia (who had been a close communion Baptist[63]), after reading Nash's *Baptist Review*, organized the Deep Creek church in Emmanuel County and brought it into the Chattahoochee United FWB Association.[64] After considerable correspondence between Scoven and Nash, a convention was scheduled—for May 25, 1876, at the Deep Creek church—and announced in the *Baptist Review*. On his arrival there, Nash found, to his great disappointment, that he and Scoven were the only delegates who had come.

The two men considered what to do. In consultation with the members of the Deep Creek Church they decided to proceed with organization, using church members as "proxies" for delegates from the other bodies they had expected. They recognized that whatever they did would have to be approved by those other bodies if the organization were to continue. They adopted a constitution and articles of faith and government, chose the name *Southern Baptist Association*, and set the next session for the Friendship Church in Wayne County,

---

[62] "The Southern Baptist Association," *Weekly Transcript and Messenger* (Goldsboro, NC), May 6, 1887, 8. The information in the next two paragraphs comes from this article. The article, though unsigned, was copied from the *Baptist Review*; and it seems clear that Nash was the only editor of that publication.

[63] Scoven, a medical doctor, had begun his ministry as a Methodist missionary. The *Minutes of the Georgia Annual Conference of the Methodist Episcopal Church, South* (Macon, GA: Telegraph Steam Power Press, 1861), 13, include: "Bethel Mission, Rev. S. G. Scoven, Missionary, is reported in an improving condition." When he became a Baptist is not clear.

[64] At this point, because of gaps in the minutes, we cannot be sure exactly when the Chattahoochee changed from United Baptists to United Free Will Baptists, but at least by 1874. We have no minutes between 1853 and 1879.

NC, to begin September 20, 1877. That session took place as scheduled and a number of other bodies, having approved the 1876 results, were represented.

The articles of faith of the Southern Baptist Association were published in the *Baptist Review* in 1905, and we assume they were the same then as previously. Interestingly, they were *not* taken from the *Summary* published by Hunnicutt in 1842, but the basic doctrinal stance was the same. As in Hunnicutt's articles, there was no provision for feet-washing.[65]

Apparently, some associations felt that joining the Southern Baptist Association was inimitable with maintaining denominational identity. In 1878, the South Carolina FWB Conference dismissed two ministers (R. A. Gause and S. P. Gibbons) and "their" churches (New Hope, Thompson Branch, and Mount Moriah, N.C.) "for the purpose of uniting with Southern Baptist Association."[66] It is not clear whether this indicates hostility to Nash and his program, since the year before (1877) the Conference had endorsed Nash's *Baptist Review* in glowing terms as "the organ of our denomination in the South. It is an able paper, sound in doctrine, independent in spirit, and distinguished for its motto: free salvation, free communion and immersion."[67]

While we have no minutes of the Southern Baptist Association, there are enough references to put together a list of its (known) meetings, as follows:

1876: Deep Creek FWB Church, Emmanuel County, GA.

1877: Friendship Church, Wayne County, NC.[68]

1878: New Hope Church, Williamsburg County, SC. (Lark O'Neall, moderator).[69]

---

[65] *The Baptist Review*, January 30, 1905, 3.

[66] *Minutes of the South Carolina Conference*, 1878, 37. Harrison and Barfield, 395, say that Nash and "R. F. Gause of South Carolina tried to get the conference to join the Southern Baptist Association. The majority of the conference opposed the move; but, through the influence of Elders Nash and Gause, a few of the churches withdrew from the conference."

[67] *Minutes of the South Carolina Conference*, 1877, 34.

[68] There was a Friendship FWB Church (changed to Casey's Chapel in 1893) in the Cape Fear Conference in this county at this time; it seems likely that this was the church where the association met.

[69] The New Hope church was probably the one dismissed in 1878 from the South Carolina FWB Conference (see above) so that it could join the Southern Baptist Association. O'Neall, of Edgefield County in South Carolina, was referred to by Nash (in the article already cited) as "our venerable old brother." He was a former Methodist minister who had become Baptist and had adopted open communion six or eight years before his death in 1881. He had published "an able pamphlet" on this latter subject. See his obituary in *The Newberry* (SC) *Weekly Herald*, April 13, 1881, 3.

1879: Mount Moriah FWB Church, Pinkins [Pickens] County, AL (Ellis Gore, moderator).[70]

1880: Ebenezer Church, Tatnall County, GA.[71]

1881: Concord Church, Columbus County, NC.[72]

1882: Union Grove Church, Henry County, AL.[73]

1883: Union Church, Lee County, MS (Z. L. Burson, moderator).[74]

1884(?): Bristol Baptist Church, Sullivan County, TN.

1889: Columbus, GA.

Whether the 1884 session took place is uncertain. It was definitely scheduled: "Rev. Z. L. Burson has returned from the South, and informs us that the next session of the Southern Baptist Association will meet in Bristol, in November next."[75] And in 1905, Nash wrote that the 1883 session "adjourned to meet in Bristol, Tenn., Thursday before the second Sunday in November, 1884."[76] But he also said, in the same place, that the association "held four more sessions" after the one in 1879; and, in another writing in 1887,[77] he said that "The last session was held in November, 1883."[78] Perhaps, then, the 1884 session did not take place; the newspaper announcements were made almost a

---

[70] Nash, in reporting this, referred to Gore as "one of the best men that ever lived or died in the State of Alabama."

[71] This is probably the Ebenezer FWB Church near Glennville, GA, a member of the South Georgia FWB Association in 1917 (see those minutes); we have no earlier minutes of that association. A brief church history (*Ebenezer Free Will Baptist Church 1843-2008*, 1-3, appears to indicate that it joined the Free Will Baptists in about 1878, having decided for open versus closed communion.)

[72] This might not have been a Free Will Baptist church; if not, it might have been in the Piny Grove or the Mt. Zion associations, both of Baptist churches in North Carolina and involved with Nash.

[73] This was probably the Union Grove FWB Church belonging to the Southeastern FWB Conference.

[74] The minutes of the Vernon Association for 1893, 7, record that the session of the Southern Baptist Association was changed from the Evergreen Church to the Union Church, "8 miles Northwest of Tupelo," so it must have been part of that association; the same minutes record the creation of the Tupelo FWB Association out of churches from the Vernon and Union Grove associations. The Jonesborough, Tennessee, *Herald and Tribune*, November 1, 1883, 3, noted that Burson was going to the Southern Baptist Association at Tupelo, Mississippi, and reported that he was the moderator and had been for about four years. According to the *Bristol News*, May 13, 1879, Nash had preached "at Mr. Burson's church" in the city.

[75] (Bristol, TN) *Herald and Tribune*, December 6, 1883. 3. A similar announcement appeared in the (Memphis, TN) *Daily Appeal* for December 1, 1883, 2: "Bristol is to be honored next year with at least three important ecclesiastical conventions," one of them "in November the Southern Baptist Association."

[76] "The Southern Baptist Association," *Baptist Review*, January 30, 1905, 2-3.

[77] Theoretically, this was published in 1887, picked up from Nash's *Baptist Review*, and the original *might* have been written before an 1884 session; but that seems highly unlikely.

[78] "The Southern Baptist Association," *Weekly Transcript and Messenger* (Goldsboro, NC), May 6, 1887, 8.

year in advance of that, right after Burson had returned from the 1883 session in Mississippi. We do know there was a fire in Goldsboro that destroyed Nash's office, evidently in the same week the association was scheduled to convene in 1884,[79] and that event might have contributed to a cancellation of the meeting. And we know that Burson's church, in late 1885, ceased to exist as a separate congregation.[80] But whether any of this was related to an 1884 session of the association, or lack thereof, is not clear. Interestingly, A. M. Stewart, founder of the white Free Will Baptists in Texas, preached at the Bristol Baptist Church from January to March 1880.[81]

The 1889 meeting, however, seems certainly to have taken place, in view of an 1889 newspaper report in Goldsboro, NC, saying: "Rev. B. W. Nash left the city yesterday evening for Columbus, Ga., to attend the Southern Baptist Convention [sic for Association?] which meets in that city tomorrow, lasting three days. We wish him a pleasant journey."[82] Perhaps Nash and/or others were attempting to rejuvenate the organization after a lapse—if the word in this announcement should have been "Association" rather than "Convention."[83]

Perhaps Convention was the intended word and this meeting was *not* viewed as a re-convening of the Southern Baptist Association that had met last in 1883 or 1884. The minutes of the Chattahoochee FWB Association for 1889 include this: "Resolved, That this Association recommend a general convention of the Free-Will Baptist Association[s] in the South to meet in Columbus, Ga., or at some center point as early as possible, and that all the Associations be notified through the Baptist Review of the time and place agreed upon. We appoint as our delegates to this convention, J. M. Bray, W. A. Hooks, W. C. Duffell and J.

---

[79] "The Southern Baptist Association," *Baptist Review*, January 30, 1905, 2-3. Indeed, this is the very next sentence in Nash's 1905 account and so might have been intended by him to imply that the scheduled meeting did not occur.

[80] "The organization was maintained as a member of the Southern Baptist Association, until September 7, 1885, when an honorable adjustment of the difficulties with the parent church, was effected, and the two organizations were merged together, under the name of the Bristol Baptist Church." *History of Tennessee from the Earliest Time to the Present: together with an Historical and a Biographical Sketch of from Twenty-five to Thirty Counties of East Tennessee* (Chicago, IL: Goodspeed Publishing Company, 1887), 918-19.

[81] See the chapter in the present volume for the story of Stewart and the work in Texas.

[82] *The Goldsboro Headlight*, November 6, 1889, 5.

[83] The better known Southern Baptist Convention met in May of that year in Memphis, Tennessee.

R. Brown."[84] This sounds like the Chattahoochee was taking the initiative and was using the word convention to refer to an assembling rather than an organization. Note also that the convention was to be for "Free Will Baptist Association[s]" specifically, and not necessarily for "liberal" Baptists more generally.

Furthermore, in 1890, the Jasper Association in Alabama endorsed "the proceedings of the Southern Baptist Convention held at Columbus, Ga. in November, 1889,"[85] thus using the same terminology. Apparently, this session had been spoken of as a "convention"; Nash himself spoke of it in that way.[86] Beyond this, we have no actual record of any other sessions.

Interestingly, in the same year (1889) the *Morning Star*, weekly organ of the Free Will Baptists of the North, ran a series of articles about liberal Baptists of the South, with the author identified as "Pilgrim"—apparently Ransom Dunn, traveling in the South for that very purpose.[87]

In one report he referred to those "more or less associated with Rev. B. W. Nash in his Southern Baptist Association," having heard the estimates of their numbers as ranging from 300 to 1,000.[88] In another issue he included a longer report:

> Then there is an association, called the "Union Baptist Association," under the leadership of Rev. B. W. Nash, which, while repudiating the name of "Freewill," and not generally practicing feet washing, is still both Armenian [sic] and Free Communion. It numbers 485 members. Mr. Nash, however, claims that there are others, in other States, which occupy a like position, and more or less closely affiliate with him, enough to bring the number up to four or five thousand. Mr. Nash publishes a semi-monthly paper, called *The Baptist Review*, which does not lack in pointedness. The feeling between the Originals [the main FWB conferences in NC and SC] and the Nash people is not generally very cordial.[89]

---

[84] Minutes, Chattahoochee UFWB Association, 1889, 4. The association also adopted Nash's hymn book at this session.
[85] Minutes, the Jasper FWB Association, 1890, 2.
[86] B. W. Nash, "Circular Letter in Self Defense" (a single sheet otherwise unidentified but apparently printed in Goldsboro by Nash Printing in 1889). Thanks to Gary Barefoot, curator of the FWB Historical Collection at the University of Mount Olive, NC, for a scan of this document.
[87] A subsequent article (*Morning Star*, May 2, 1889, 140) appears to identify the writer as Dunn.
[88] *The Morning Star*, January 24, 1889, 28.
[89] *The Morning Star*, March 7, 1889, 74, 76.

The Southern Baptist Association apparently continued to exist as an organization for a few more years after 1889, even though Nash said, in 1905, that the Association "proved to be [a great success] as much as ten years thereafter," meaning after the 1879 meeting.[90] Even so, in the same 1905 article, he seemed to speak of the organization as though it still existed and printed the articles of faith of the Association. Furthermore, we know that on October 4, 1890, the Philadelphia FWB Church of Charlton County (near Folkston), Georgia, adopted the articles of faith, covenant, and constitution of the Southern Baptist Association.[91] Also (as Nash reported in 1905), in 1892 the Mount Moriah FWB Association in Alabama voted to rejoin the Southern Baptist Association, only to sever the relationship two years later in 1894.[92] One assumes, then, that there were meetings of the association, but not regularly; and that at least the structure of the organization must have continued to be in place.

The minutes of the Jasper FWB Association, in Alabama, show that they elected delegates to meetings of the Southern Baptist Association in 1892 and 1893, the first of these at Antioch church in Fayette County (in the Mount Moriah Association),[93] and the second at Mt. Olive church in Marion County (in the Jasper Association).[94] It seems strange that two consecutive sessions would have been scheduled in the same state. Perhaps some of the Alabama Free Will Baptists were trying to keep the organization going, or to revive it after lapses. This possibility seems confirmed in the 1892 minutes of the Mount Moriah Association, where, after reaffirming support for the Southern Baptist Association (during the annual session), the delegates (during the Union Meeting) first resolved "That this body consider the proposition made by Rev. B. W. Nash, for the consolidation of all Freewill and Free communion Baptists in the South" and then adopted this:

> After consideration it was unanimously agreed that we invite delegates from the various Associations of liberal Baptists to meet with the Mt. Moriah

---

[90] "The Southern Baptist Association," *Baptist Review*, January 30, 1905, 2-3.
[91] "Philadelphia Free Will Baptist Church – Charlton County, GA," accessed April 6, 2018 at https://umo.edu/elegy-to-a-country-church-yard/philadelphia-free-will-baptist-church-charlton-county-ga.
[92] "The Southern Baptist Association," *Baptist Review*, January 30, 1905, 2-3.
[93] Minutes, Jasper FWB Association, 1892, 4.
[94] Minutes, Jasper FWB Association, 1893, 4.

Association, for the purpose of considering the propriety of union among all our Associations in the South. Also that the Clerk inform brother Nash of the action of this body, and request him to be with us at the next session of our Association.[95]

As for the scope of the Southern Baptist Association, in 1879, according to Nash, there were 83 churches with 72 ministers and 3,296 members. In 1883, there were 121 churches with 102 ministers and 4,440 members. *Appletons' Annual Cyclopaedia* for 1879, in its article on "Free-Will Baptists," listed the Southern Baptist Association as "one of the associations of Baptists in North America whose doctrine and polity are in general agreement with Free-Will Baptists" and reported that it had 66 churches, 68 ministers, and 3,108 members and "holds correspondence with the Chattahoochee, South Carolina, Tennessee River, and Butts County Conferences, and is represented by the 'Baptist Review,' LaGrange, N.C."[96] *Appleton's* was apparently relying on the *Freewill Baptist Register* for 1879, which reported these same statistics; but they were for 1877, not 1879. It reported that the association was also in correspondence with bodies in South Carolina, Georgia, and Tennessee that apparently represented an additional 50 ministers and 2,000 members.[97] The next year's edition of the *Register* (apparently referring to the 1878 session but still giving the 1877 statistics) added that the association embraced the Mount Moriah Association in Alabama, the Ogeechee in Georgia, and the Mount Zion, Piny Grove, Cape Fear, and Pee Dee in North Carolina; the ones "with which it held correspondence" were the Chattahoochee in Georgia and the South Carolina, Tennessee River, and Butts County Conferences.[98] It appears that most of these were Free Will Baptists, the exceptions being the Mount Zion and Piny Grove in North Carolina and perhaps the Butts County Conference, which is unknown to us.[99]

---

[95] Minutes, Mount Moriah FWB Association, 1892, 1, 4-5, 7.

[96] *Appletons' Annual Cyclopaedia and Register of Important Events of the Year 1879*, Volume 4 (New York, NY: D. Appleton and Company, 1880), 70.

[97] *The Freewill Baptist Register* (Dover, NH: Freewill Baptist Printing Establishment, 1879), 74. The meaning of the wording regarding the "corresponding" associations is not entirely clear. Such "correspondence" was often by letter rather than by personal presence.

[98] *The Freewill Baptist Register* (Dover, NH: Freewill Baptist Printing Establishment, 1880), 79. The association is not mentioned in subsequent issues of the *Register*, at least through 1889.

Summary: Nash's Influence Among Free Will Baptists

It seems helpful, here, to focus specifically on the extent to which Nash, the Union Baptists, and the Southern Baptist Association involved Free Will Baptists, state by state. This survey is limited by the fact that we lack many of the minutes of the associations in these areas. Were there more minutes, there would no doubt be more information to report.

In North Carolina. Nash apparently led in influencing the Alfred Moore faction of the original North Carolina Free Will Baptist Conference to become United Baptists in 1858. Although he was not finally successful, after the Civil War, in involving the mainline Free Will Baptist Annual Conference, he made an active effort to court them (c. 1867-70) and they participated in some meetings. Apparently, one of their leaders, Rufus K. Hearn, was sympathetic with his efforts. But Nash was much more successful with the Cape Fear FWB Conference. At least through 1888 he was still welcomed there and at least succeeded in getting them to join with the Union Association of Baptists to form the United Baptist Conference. And at least one report of the Southern Baptist Association, in 1878, included the Cape Fear as within the embrace of the Association. All this has been given in detail above and need not be repeated here.

In South Carolina. The South Carolina FWB Conference, directly descended from the mainline annual conference in North Carolina, was aware of Nash and the *Baptist Review*, recommending (in 1877) that publication to the churches. At least three churches left the Conference to unite with the Southern Baptist Association. Apparently, the 1878 session of the Southern Baptist Association met at one of these churches, New Hope in Williamsburg County.

In Georgia. The associations in this state that played the largest role in the Southern Baptist Association were originally "United Baptists," the name they bore in 1859 when an early unity meeting was convened in the state. They became "United Free Will Baptists"—and one wonders if that was a result of that 1859 meeting—at least by 1874 when they were identified that way in the min-

---

[99] The only Butts County that comes up when googled is in Georgia. There is enough said in the online history of the Macedonia Baptist Church of that county to indicate that there might have been a Butts County Conference of United Free Will Baptists; but that is not certain.

utes of the Mount Moriah FWB Association. The first session of the Southern Baptist Association met in Georgia in one of their churches in 1876.

The Georgia associations involved were the Chattahoochee, the Ogeechee, and perhaps the New Salem and the Butts County. We have only the minutes of the Chattahoochee during the period involved, and only for the years 1879, 1881-83, 1885, and 1892. On at least one occasion a church in this association hosted the Southern Baptist Association. Nash said (as indicated earlier) that he visited this association in 1874 and the association had approved of his plan and elected four delegates to attend that first session.[100] The Association's minutes show that he also visited it in 1892, when he was well received and preached at the 11:00 o'clock service on Sunday morning, even though nothing appears in the minutes about his cause.[101] No doubt there were other visits. The Chattahoochee showed a continuing interest in reaching out, via correspondence at least, to other "Liberal Baptists."[102] And D. J. Apperson, one of the Association's leaders, questioned, apparently in 1889, Nash's motives in proposing another convention toward union after the Southern Baptist Association had not met for a few years.[103] Apperson, in the same piece, mentioned that the Martin Association had also shared an interest in the movement toward unity, but it is not clear whether this was for the Southern Baptist Association.

Furthermore, in 1880 the Southern Baptist Association met at Ebenezer Church near Glenville, Georgia. This church was in the Ogeechee United FWB Association, which changed its name to the South Georgia FWB Association in 1903.

In Alabama. As we have shown above, the Mount Moriah FWB Association was involved with Nash's cause from the beginning. Probably Nash enjoyed his greatest success with that association. Ellis Gore, its founding leader, was moderator of the 1859 meeting in Georgia and a strong supporter of Nash's goal of union for Baptists of the free will variety.

---

[100] "The Southern Baptist Association," (Goldsboro, NC) *Weekly Transcript and Messenger*, May 6, 1887, 8.
[101] Minutes, Chattahoochee UFWB Association, 1892, 3-4.
[102] Minutes, Chattahoochee UFWB Association, 1882, 3; 1883, 4.
[103] B. W. Nash, "Circular Letter in Self-Defense."

Again, we are hindered by the fact that we only have minutes of the Mount Moriah for 1874, 1885, 1889-92, 1897, and 1899 for the period in question, several of them printed by Nash's firm. They show an ongoing involvement with the movement for unity in the South. In 1874, Gore was appointed to correspond with the Chattahoochee United FWB Association.[104] In 1881, a resolution stressed the importance of supporting Nash's *Baptist Review* and referred to the minutes of the Southern Baptist Association and the possibility of a theological school "somewhere within the bounds of" that body.[105]

By 1889, the Mount Moriah was expressing interest in "Southern unity," a different plan that will be discussed in the second part of this chapter. But in 1892 Nash visited the Mount Moriah again and was well received. He preached "in support of our liberal Baptist Doctrines." The Committee on Publication reported as follows:

> Whereas, we the Mount Moriah Freewill Baptist Association, feel the great importance of closer union with our sister Associations and a more thorough understanding and education of the principles of the liberal Baptist [sic] in the South, and whereas we have been and still claim to be a constituent member of the Southern Baptist Association, and whereas The Baptist Review is the organ of the above named Association, and that the Review has been adopted by this Association:
> Resolved 1st. That we adopt the Southern Baptist Association and the Literature of the same.[106]

As already noted, this led to scheduling another convention for union within the Mount Moriah Association—apparently later that year. But the Mount Moriah turned back away from Nash and the Southern Baptist Association in 1894.

The Vernon and Jasper Associations were of the same lineage as the Mount Moriah. For the Vernon we have only the minutes for 1892, 1893, and 1897 during the relevant time period. For the Jasper we have only 1887-90 and 1892-93. We have already included references to those minutes; the Vernon was concerned as to whether Nash should print their minutes, and the Jasper elected

---

[104] Minutes, Mount Moriah FWB Association, 1874, 1.
[105] Minutes, Mount Moriah FWB Association, 1881, 5, 8.
[106] Minutes, Mount Moriah FWB Association, 1892, 1, 4-5, 7.

delegates to what it regarded as sessions of the Southern Baptist Association in 1892 and 1893.

In 1882, the Southern Baptist Association met in Henry County, Alabama, at a Union Grove Church that was apparently in the Southeastern United FWB Association. These Free Will Baptists were of the lineage of the Chattahoochee Association in Georgia (as were some in West Florida) and would likely have experienced Nash's influence. We have no early minutes of this association to confirm.

The End of a Movement

B. W. Nash died in 1911, and his wife Elizabeth C. Nash, "a member for many years of the Free Will Baptist church," died in 1914.[107] There is no evidence that any of the organizations Nash was involved with survived, as such, beyond him.

The Southern Baptist Association, for example, even if it continued to function into the 1890s in some measure, apparently did not last much beyond 1900 if that long. In the 1905 article we have cited several times, Nash, sounding bitter or at least defeated, appeared to be making one last appeal for support from other free communion Baptists, both for the Association and for the *Baptist Review*. This was issued when the Southern Baptist Association was no longer meeting and when a competing movement called Southern Unity (see Part II, below) had also failed. Nash's words are revealing:

> The Review now comes to the front with a motion to reconsider the whole matter and see if any thing can be done to save our cause; and the most substantial way to second the motion will be to write and let us know where you stand—which side you are on, life or death—to speak in the still small voice is life, to keep silence is death. All I ask of you brother preachers, in this emergency, is your influence. ... Nothing but prompt and immediate action will do in this case.

---

[107] "Goldsboro News Items," *Greensboro Daily News*, November 15, 1914, 11. The notice indicates that she was 75 and was survived by three sons and a daughter. Since Nash's death notice (referenced earlier) indicated three sons and *two* daughters, apparently one daughter had died between his and his wife's deaths.

Among other things he cited the fact that the Mount Moriah Free Will Baptists had turned away from him after Ellis Gore's death, led by Woods Springfield, who had once supported him, and W. H. McGee.[108] Another Alabama FWB association growing out of Ellis Gore's legacy, the Vernon, had apparently followed Mount Moriah's lead.[109]

Indeed, even at its heyday, the Association had the support of a relatively limited number of organizations. Nash named five associations in Alabama that were the fruit of Ellis Gore's labor, plus brethren in Southeastern Alabama, Central Georgia, and North Carolina; he estimated the total membership at between five and six thousand. All of these appear to have been Free Will Baptists, United Baptists who added Free Will to their name, and the small group of Union Baptists. The fact that he did not include Virginia may imply that the original Union Baptists there were no longer with those in North Carolina—if they continued to exist by that name.

Nash himself continued to be active past the turn of the century. There are newspaper notices about his preaching at Bethel, for example, as late as May 1900. Perhaps this is the same church as Bethel Union Baptist in Lenoir County, which had reorganized and joined the Disciples of Christ in November-December, 1870.[110] If so, some of the members had apparently remained true to the Union Baptist faith, or else the Disciples congregation was allowing Nash to preach for them. On the other hand, in 1884 the Bethel where Nash often preached is called a Baptist church.[111] Newspaper searches from 1900 to 1911 show B. W. Nash also preaching at Lousan Swamp (1900, 1904), the chapel in Kinston (1903), and Airy Grove (1903, 1904).[112]

---

[108] "The Southern Baptist Association," *Baptist Review,* January 30, 1905, 3. When the Mount Moriah rejoined in 1892, Woods Springfield was chairman of the committee making the recommendation. See Minutes, Mount Moriah FWB Association, 1892, 4.

[109] In "The Southern Baptist Association," *Baptist Review,* January 30, 1905, 2-3, Nash said that there were five associations resulting from "the life work of Elder Ellis Gore." These would have included Mount Moriah, Vernon, Jasper, and two others that need to be identified.

[110] Ware, *Hookerton History,* 8.

[111] Ware, *North Carolina Disciples,* 106-07; Pelt, 158; *The* [New Bern, NC] *Daily Journal,* February 27, 1884, 1; *The Daily Free Press,* May 29, 1900, 1.

[112] These are very brief news bites, and we have chosen not to document them. They can be located by searching at Newspapers.com.

We do not know just when publication of the *Baptist Review* ceased. Only one issue of that paper is known to exist, published June 30, 1905 (and cited often in this chapter). Apparently there was, in its pages, some discussion—perhaps debate—as to the preferred denominational name. In 1904, one lady wrote to the *Free Will Baptist* in reference to the *Baptist Review*, saying: "I see in both papers considerable dispute over denominational names. It seems to me that the prefix or term Free Will is a more desirable name than that of the antagonist's"—by which she seems to have meant Nash's views.[113] At any rate, as late as 1908 the minutes of the Jasper FWB Association in Alabama were still saying, "We don't know anything better than to recommend the Baptist Review as it is our only Denominational paper."[114] In 1909, however, they recommended *The Free Will Baptist*.[115]

As for the Union Baptists, simply "Baptists" after 1870 (but probably stuck with the old name in common usage), they had already begun dwindling well before Nash's demise. C. C. Ware reported that "many of them came to the Disciples. In 1887, they had but fifteen churches and 535 members. Five years later they had lost two more churches and their membership had declined to 442. Nash continued with a remnant."[116]

It seems likely that more of the Union Baptist churches became Disciples, who were also promoting the unity of all Christian churches under the simple name of *Christian*.[117] Indeed, J. L. Winfield said, as early as 1872, that a union between the Disciples and the "most prominent" Union Baptists had already been effected.[118] Some of the Union Baptist churches apparently returned to (or joined) the Free Will Baptists. Million and Barrett said, without providing evidence, "A great many of the churches and members ... came back and became

---

[113] *The Free Will Baptist*, December 11, 1904, 4. We thank Gary Barefoot of the University of Mount Olive, NC, for this.
[114] Minutes, Jasper FWB Association, 1908, 6.
[115] Minutes, Jasper FWB Association, 1909, 6.
[116] Ware, *North Carolina Disciples*, 102.
[117] Indeed, Nash's description of the objectives of his *Baptist Review*, quoted earlier, sound very much the same as the things that were said by Alexander Campbell and the Christian churches (Disciples) he led.
[118] Ware, *North Carolina Disciples*, 107. Winfield himself had moved from the Union Baptists to the Disciples.

reconciled with the old body."¹¹⁹ Some might have remained independent or found their way into the Southern Baptist Convention. At least one became a Methodist Church: Hickory Grove, "in the rich whortleberry section of Lenoir County ... about 5 miles southeast from LaGrange."¹²⁰ Interestingly, one newspaper had placed Nash at that church in 1882.¹²¹

The Legacy of the Union Baptists

From one perspective, and in agreement with other historians, we may observe that Nash and his movement ultimately failed to achieve their goal of union, a goal that a number of Free Will Baptists shared with them. It seems clear, by the way, that Free Will Baptists were by far the most numerous in the Southern Baptist Association.

Even so, the legacy of Nash and the Union Baptists lives on in the Disciples of Christ and Free Will Baptists in North Carolina—although the name of Nash is not highly respected among Free Will Baptist historians there, no doubt because he was the reason for the loss of a number of churches by the denomination. Perhaps the aim of Hunnicutt and Nash to promote unity was fulfilled in a way they did not hope or expect: by the demise of the Union Baptists and the union of their churches into other denominations.

For that matter, and of special interest to Free Will Baptists, there is yet another way the Union Baptists have "survived." In a note, Matt Pinson (the online editor of Rufus K. Hearn's "Origins in North Carolina") says: "It is interesting to note that, not long after this [that is, after the Alfred Moore faction of the original Free Will Baptist conference in North Carolina united with the Union Baptists in 1858], a group of these Union Baptists migrated to Oklahoma, and, in 1954, the Union Baptists of Oklahoma became a part of the Oklahoma State Association of Free Will Baptists."¹²² That note, in turn, was dependent on Damon Dodd, who only said that "some years ago" a group of Union Baptists from North Carolina "moved westward into Oklahoma and

---

[119] Million and Barrett, 180.
[120] Barnes, 4.
[121] *The* [New Bern, NC] *Daily Journal*, July 26, 1882, 1.
[122] Rufus K. Hearn, "Origins of the Free Will Baptist Church of North Carolina," accessed April 30, 2018, at http://fwbhistory.com/?page_id=123 [note 7].

Kansas," and that those in Oklahoma united with the Oklahoma State FWB Association.[123] Indeed, the minutes of the Oklahoma State FWB Association confirm this. The report of Delbert Akin, the Executive Secretary of that association, recommended that provision be made to receive this association of Union Baptists, and that was done.[124] The Union Association of Free Will Baptists continues to this day.

II. "Southern Unity," A. D. Williams, and the General Association

As Nash's Southern Baptist Association was losing ground, a different movement toward union of liberal Baptists in the South developed. Like a shooting star, it seemed to burn brightly for a time but then faded out. It developed, and ended, quickly; the effort was over in less than ten years, and most of what we know took place in 1889 and 1890. The movement would be known by the phrase "Southern Unity," and the short-lived organization that it produced was the General Association.

B. W. Nash was very much aware of this movement and did not welcome it. He regarded it—no doubt correctly—as a rival to his own efforts. Consequently, he fought it energetically. One of those who resisted his efforts to revive the Southern Baptist Association was J. H. Jenkins, of the United Baptists in Georgia. Nash said his enemies "sicced" Jenkins on him, and that Jenkins was "financially ruined trying to get out a paper, with an old hand press and worn out type" and "spent his last dollar" in the effort.

Indeed, Jenkins began publishing, in 1894, *The Harvest Gleaner*. We have located the first eight issues of volume III (Sept. 16 through Nov. 4, 1896), and the conflict between the two men is obvious. In one issue, Jenkins published a remark from Nash's *Baptist Review*: "We have fought the Jenkins movement

---

[123] Damon C. Dodd, *The Free Will Baptist Story* (Nashville, TN: Executive Department of the NAFWB, 1960). Dodd expressed hope that those of Kansas would also "unite with the Free Will Baptist movement." We are not aware that they did so. Thanks to Allen Mabra and Clarence Shepherd, ministers in the Union Association, for information to the effect that the Union Baptists in Oklahoma apparently obtained that identity from the ones who originally migrated to Kansas from North Carolina.

[124] Minutes, Oklahoma State FWB Association, 1954, 8, 12.

some over two years and if it is not dead it is lingering with an incurable disease." Jenkins replied, "We don't think that the Review's fighting has done our paper movement much harm."[125] Later on the same page he reported that Nash, in an apparent effort to revive his movement, was asking for a convention to be held at Macedonia Church in Lamar County, Alabama, in November of 1896. Jenkins said he "inferred" that the adoption of *The Harvest Gleaner* by the Mt. Moriah might have prompted this and added, with a wry pun on Nash's first name: "The Mt. Moriah was about the last rod our brother Bushrod had to lean on."[126]

Apparently, in 1899 Nash issued a circular letter in his own defense, saying,

> The Freewill Baptists of this State [NC] claim a membership of twelve thousand, and they are solid against the Williams plan of southern unity. The two Baptist Associations [Piny Grove and Mt. Zion] and the Pee Dee [FWB] Conference, of this State, the Ogeechee [UFWB] Association of Georgia, the South Eastern [UFWB] Association, of Alabama, and the Tupelo [FWB] Association of Miss., are opposed to it. They foot up[127] three thousand or about that, and are half the whole number of the Freewill Baptists in the South. Then we have five Associations left, aggregating thirty five hundred or four thousand, and the Williams plan will not carry a majority of these connections. So we must go up to Tennessee to look for southern unity. As for the signers they form no part of a church, but will be governed by the churches to which they belong.[128]

Writing later in 1905, Nash was making yet another effort, after Southern Unity had failed, to enlist support. Looking back, he referred to Williams as "the old renegade yankee, A. D. Williams," who was "noted as the friend and advocate of mixed schools and churches of white people and negroes in his early day." He added that Williams "took his position in Nashville" and "went to work on the Review and the Review went to work on him." He said this conflict lasted two years, and that Williams ("'old andy' as they called him," who

---

[125] *The Harvest Gleaner*, Sept. 16, 1896, 4.
[126] *The Harvest Gleaner*, Sept. 16, 1896, 4.
[127] "Foot up" was an idiomatic phrase meaning something like *total, add up to, count, tally*.
[128] Nash, B. W., "Circular Letter in Self Defense" (undated sheet). By the "signers" he was apparently referring to those who issued the call for a convention promoting southern unity in the fall of 1889, as reported below.

"referred to himself" as "Dr. A. D. Williams") "rallied our enemies against us from every point of the compass." Williams himself, Nash reported, defined the objective of the movement as "to merge all the Freewill Baptists in the South into one body."[129] Nash's scorn is obvious.

A. D. Williams

Alvin Dighton Williams was a well-known and widely-traveled minister among the Free Will Baptists of the North. (The picture of him is from the *Free Baptist Cyclopaedia*.) He had, indeed, relocated from Kenesaw, Nebraska, to the Nashville, Tennessee, area, in 1889, for the specific purpose of promoting southern unity. According to the *Free Baptist Cyclopaedia* article about him, and his obituary, Williams was born in Springfield, Pennsylvania, October 15, 1825, was converted at the age of thirteen, and began to preach not long thereafter. He completed Hamilton College in New York at the age of twenty-four.[130] Early in his ministry, he was pastor of a number of churches in Rhode Island, Massachusetts, Minnesota, Ohio, and West Virginia. He was actively involved in several educational roles and was often on the staff or publisher of one periodical or another. He, with his family, was the first permanent settler of the area in Kenesaw, Nebraska, in about 1872 or 1873, where he maintained a home thereafter. He was one of the organizers of the Nebraska Yearly Meeting. After his 1889-90 stint in Tennessee, apparently in 1891 or 1892, he moved to Oakland City, Indiana, where he headed up the efforts of the General Baptists in founding a college, turning what had seemed failure there into success. In declining health, he returned to his home in Nebraska at the end of the 1893-94 school term and died there on December 31, 1894.[131]

---

[129] Nash, B. W., "The Southern Baptist Association," *The Baptist Review*, January 30, 1905, 2-3.
[130] He typically listed himself as Rev. A. D. Williams, D. D., the doctoral degree apparently being honorary. In one place he listed himself as Rev. A. D. Williams, A. M., D. D., so he must have completed a Master of Arts; see A. D. Williams, *Benoni Stinson and the General Baptists* (Owensville, IN.: General Baptist Publishing House, 1892), 238-39.

Important for this chapter are Williams's efforts in behalf of Southern Unity. A Nebraska newspaper reported: "Rev. A. D. Williams of Kenesaw left last week [week of July 14, 1889] for Nashville, Tenn., where he will continue the publication of the *Baptist Herald*."[132] It is not clear that this publication "continued"; what is clear is that Williams almost immediately began publishing, in Tennessee, *The Christian Herald*. On August 18, a Nashville newspaper announced, "The Christian Herald, published in the interests of the Free Will and other Liberal Baptists of the South, has just made its appearance." The notice also indicated that Williams would preach at the North Nashville FWB Church (now Cofer's Chapel) on that morning and evening.[133]

What motivated Williams to become involved in promoting southern unity is not clear. It is possible that a General Baptist minister, who also labored some among Free Will Baptists—in West Virginia, at least—had some influence on Williams in this regard. His name was John E. Cox and according to his obituary he served churches in "Indiana, Ohio, Illinois, West Virginia, Kentucky, Michigan, South Carolina and Georgia."[134] He played little if any role in the story told here and would not be mentioned except for the fact that Nash included him as one involved in the push for southern unity, saying: "The Cox movement was thrust upon us in January 1887," and Nash had combatted it "with amalgamation and other arguments."[135] Later, he recounted the story of "the worst

---

[131] "Williams, Rev. Alvin Dighton, D. D.," *Free Baptist Cyclopaedia*, eds. G. A. Burgess and J. T. Ward (Free Baptist Cyclopaedia Co., 1889), 701-02. "Rev. Alvin D. Williams, D. D.," *The Morning Star*, March 7, 1895, 74. See also Betty Laverne Shirley, "A History of Oakland City College," (unpublished thesis, 1957), available at https://core.ac.uk/download/pdf/10688508.pdf.

[132] *Daily Nebraska State Journal*, July 23, 1889, 4.

[133] *The* (Nashville) *Daily American*, August 18, 1889, 2. In its issue for August 23, p. 2, this paper also carried this notice: "At an unusually full meeting of the First, or North Nashville Freewill Baptist Church, last Wednesday evening, Rev. A. D. Williams, D. D., was elected pastor, over Rev. J. L. Welsh [sic]. Dr. Williams is the local manager of the Christian Herald." This adds to our store of knowledge about Cofer's Chapel FWB Church, as does the following notice in the issue for October 20, 1891, p. 4: "The Freewill Baptist Church, a frame building on the Buena Vista pike near Belleville street was set on fire and burned up in a few minutes. The loss is about $1,100. The church was almost gone when the fire companies arrived. It was built about five years ago. No insurance."

[134] *The Indianapolis News*, December 7, 1932, 4. Cox certainly helped influence Williams to take on the work of establishing the General Baptist College; see Shirley, 59-60; it appears from Shirley's thesis that Williams was actually president of this (yet unopened) college even while he labored in Nashville for "Southern Unity."

[135] "Circular Letter in Self Defense."

conflict we have ever had with mortal man," saying that J. W. Lucas (before leaving North Carolina) had tried to take over *The Baptist Review* and, failing that, had relocated to East Tennessee where he "called to his assistance Rev. John E. Cox, of Ind., and Rev. A. D. Williams of some other seaport town, we know not where."[136] According to the *Free Baptist Cyclopaedia*, Cox published *The Free Baptist Herald* (1884-1888), which was "devoted especially to the interests of the denomination in the South"; this was while he was serving Free Will Baptist churches in West Virginia.[137]

Publications Promoting Southern Unity

No sooner had *The Christian Herald* appeared than *The Morning Star* in the North took notice, apparently (and not surprisingly, considering Williams's background) having received the very first issue. The editor recognized the new paper as promoting the latest effort toward bringing together the "scattered and separate Southern bodies [Baptists of the free will persuasion] into one compact and potent organization." He went on to quote *The Free Will Baptist* (of North Carolina) as opining that the effort was likely to fail, even though it offered a grand opportunity. He also quoted Nash's *The Baptist Review* as saying that "It is very clear to the minds of all" that the Williams movement "has not the least hopes of success" but had "developed a very strong tendency in favor of a general union"; and that any successful union must necessarily include the Original Free Will Baptists, of North Carolina, which was the largest of the Southern bodies. Finally, the *Morning Star* editor suggested that the Free Will Baptists of North Carolina and Tennessee seemed ready to unite, with three important provisions: (1) that no vested interests like names and structures would have to be sacrificed; (2) that only white liberal Baptist bodies were included; and (3) that the matter would have to be managed by Southern leaders themselves, free

---

[136] Nash, "The Baptist Review," in *The Baptist Review,* January 30, 1905, 3.
[137] The *Free Baptist Cyclopaedia*, 140 ("Cox, Rev. John E."); 205 ("Free Baptist Herald, The"). Interestingly, Cox was followed as pastor of the Free Will Baptist church in Hampton, West Virginia, by A. M. Stewart, founder of the white Free Will Baptist work in Texas and the subject of another chapter in this volume. Harrison and Barfield, 395, reported that Cox and C. B. Peckham, with H. H. Prater of South Carolina, made an unsuccessful but divisive effort to get the South Carolina FWB Conference to unite with the General Conference of the North.

from any unrequested aid on the part of the Free Will Baptists of the North.[138] (One wonders if this last was intended to be a not-so-subtle hint to Williams to be cautious in his efforts.)

Another new publication with similar aims had come into being at about the same time. This was the *Free Baptist Enterprise*, edited by the Rev. John L. Welch, Sr.[139] The first reference we have to this was in *The Morning Star* in July, 1889. The issue of July 18 said, "*The Free Will Baptist* of North Carolina is strongly in favor of a union of Southern Free-will Baptists into one organization. So also is the *Enterprise* of Tennessee. It is a movement in the right direction. Those scattered and feeble associations of open communion Baptists should come to the realization of the fact that 'in union there is strength.'"[140] A week later: "*The Free Baptist Enterprise*, published semi-monthly at Pleasant View, Tenn., the fourth number of which has just reached us, thinks that the proposed General Conference of Southern free Communion Baptist bodies may take place in November, at Nashville."[141] This appears to mean that there had been two issues in June and two in July, in which case the paper pre-dated *The Christian Herald* by about a month. The August issue of *The Morning Star* indicated, further, that this paper was the organ of "the churches and associations in Tennessee which are not connected with the Northern Freewill Baptists."[142]

Since we have no issues of either of these newspapers, it is not possible to tell whether they were working at cross purposes or in concert. Most of what we know about them comes from the pages of *The Morning Star*, which manifested strong interest in their efforts. It seems clear that they shared the vision for one large body of liberal Baptists of the South. It is possible that they differed, if at all, in the best way to proceed. *The Christian Herald* (a weekly) had just published (about the middle of August) a long list of ministers who "favor the idea of organizing a Southern general association of (white) Baptists who believe in free will, free salvation, and free communion, on the basis of uniting on points on which

---

[138] "Southern Unity," *The Morning Star*, August 22, 1889, 268.
[139] He was the father of the John L. Welch who became one of the founders of the National Association of Free Will Baptists.
[140] *The Morning Star*, July 18, 1889, 228.
[141] *The Morning Star*, July 25, 1889, 235.
[142] "Southern Unity," *The Morning Star*, August 22, 1889, 268.

we are agreed, and leaving points of difference to the several local bodies." The editor of *The Morning Star*, commenting on this, said that the latest proposal of *The Christian Herald* was for delegates from the other bodies to attend the annual session of the Original Free Will Baptists of North Carolina in November "and then begin the work of consolidation." *The Free Baptist Enterprise* (a bi-monthly), however, promoted a somewhat different approach: namely, for an assembly of delegates to meet in November at Nashville, organize the Tennessee bodies into a general association, and then "investigate the grand subject of consolidation of all Free Baptists in the South" into one General Conference.[143]

Apparently, the two men behind these publications soon realized that they must work together—if they had not realized this all along. Within a few weeks they merged the two publications into one, *The Christian Herald and Enterprise*. The October 17 issue of *The Morning Star* announced that *The Free Will Baptist* (of North Carolina) had reported on the merger of the two papers, adding that it was not clear whether Williams or Welch would edit the merged periodical.[144] Shortly thereafter *The Morning Star* published more information, naming *The Christian Herald and Enterprise* as the consolidation of two papers "that were for a short time published in the interests of Southern F. Baptists by Dr. A. D. Williams and Rev. J. L. Welch," with editorial management now in the hands of Williams, Welch, and J. W. Lucas of East Tennessee.[145] Furthermore, the paper had recently editorialized in answer to charges that the goal included mixing colored and white liberal Baptists:

> We know of no one connected with the Southern Unity movement who is in favor of mixed schools and churches—*not one!*—and the representation that the movement has any tendency whatever in this direction is an utter and inexcusable perversion of all the facts in the case. Every article written, every utterance made, in favor of Southern Unity, has declared positively, unequivocally, and emphatically, against mixed schools and churches, whenever the subject has been mentioned at all.[146]

---

[143] *The Morning Star*, August 29, 1889, 276.
[144] *The Morning Star*, October 17, 1889, 332.
[145] For more information about Lucas, see the chapter in this volume devoted to him and a school at Unicoi, Tennessee.
[146] *The Morning Star*, October 31, 1889, 348.

The 1889 Convention of the General Association

It appears that Williams was feeling the sting of accusations of "amalgamation" by Nash, and perhaps by others. *The Morning Star*, reflecting what it had read, added that a call for a convention in Nashville would probably soon be issued, perhaps to begin on Thursday before the second Sunday in December, to continue over Sunday.[147]

Sure enough, the call went out and was widely publicized. If the editors of the two papers had begun with two different plans of attack, they had apparently settled on a compromise. They would not first attend the annual session of the Original Free Will Baptists of North Carolina (as the *Herald* had suggested), and they would not first attempt to organize just the Tennessee associations into one (as the *Enterprise* had suggested). Instead, they called for a convention of all "Southern white Baptists who believe in free will, free salvation and free communion, on the basis of uniting on things in which we are agreed and of leaving points of difference to the several local bodies." The lengthy announcement appeared in a Nashville paper.[148]

---

[147] *The Morning Star*, October 31, 1889, 348.
[148] *The* (Nashville) *Daily American*, November 27, 1889, 8.

The convention would take place in Nashville, at the North Nashville FWB Church, December 5-8. The call invited "all Southern white Freewill or other, liberal Baptist Associations, conferences, Yearly Meetings, or other similar bodies, to send delegates." All delegates would be eligible to vote, but others were invited to come and offer advice "and thus enable Southern Freewill Baptists to become better acquainted with one another."

Most important was the broad combination of associations issuing this call. The following undersigned had been "appointed by their respective associations to call a convention to consider the question of Southern unity, as it is called, and, if thought best, to organize or take steps for organizing a general association." These were:

Union Assn. (TN): J. W. Lucas, A. H. Burgess;

Mt. Moriah Assn. (AL): W. H. McGee, Woods Springfield;

New American Assn. (TN): J. H. Ballard[149];

Tennessee River Assn. (TN/AL): G. W. Mitchell, S. C. Austin;

Cumberland Assn. (TN): G. R. Head, J. L. Welch, G. W. Binkley;

New Union Assn. (TN): M. Curtis;

Stone Assn. (TN): T. J. Clouse, Benjamin Clouse, M. Judd, J. L. Kinnard;

Clinch Valley Assn. (TN/VA): J. H. Ross, J. M. Rice (Bice?);

Ogeechee Assn. (GA): W. H. Hall.

In addition to these nine associations, where the individuals had apparently been officially named for this purpose, men from four other associations (which had not met in time to make this official) joined in issuing the call:

Chattahoochee Assn. (GA): D. J. Apperson;

Vernon Assn. (AL): T. W. Springfield;

Texas Assn. (TX): A. M. Stewart;

Old Mount Zion Assn. (AR): S. W. Blackburn.

---

[149] In an autobiographical pamphlet, *Life History of Rev. John H. Ballard* (Walnut, NC: [self-published], 1924), 8, Ballard said, "I also represented the French Broad Association, in a conference at Nashville, Tennessee, when we were making an effort to unite all our Southern churches into one body." Perhaps the New American Association became the French Broad; or else Ballard's memory confused the two.

All of these were Free Will Baptist associations except for the New Union Association of United Baptists in Tennessee.[150]

As noted, this call was widely publicized. In Nashville, the announcement reproduced above had already been preceded by a brief announcement on November 10.[151] On November 21, *The Morning Star* also made the announcement.[152] And on November 28 a similar announcement appeared on the front page of a Little Rock, Arkansas, newspaper.[153] No doubt there were other newspapers in the South that included an announcement of the convention. The Nashville paper, for the third time, announced the meeting on December 5, the day it began, but included this confusing sentence: "The name of the church, however, was changed to Free Baptist at the recent general convention at Harper's Ferry, Va."[154] (This shows that the Nashville editor was not able to distinguish between the northern denomination, to which his observation applied, and the southern, to which it did not.)

Not only was the convention widely publicized, the word about it was received among Free Will Baptists in different places, including those named above in the official call for the convention. Not all responded positively. Nash reported, for example, that "when southern unity came in 1889 he [T. W. Springfield] tried to carry the Vernon Association into it" but failed.[155] The Mount Moriah, on the other hand, led by Woods Springfield, son of T. W. Springfield in the Vernon, eagerly joined in with Southern Unity. The 1889 minutes record: "That we favor Southern Unity, as proposed in the Christian Herald

---

[150] Technically, the Ogeechee and Chattahoochee were "United Free Will Baptist" and the Stone was "Free Will Christian Baptist." The New Union Association of United Baptists was a small, apparently indigenous association in the vicinity of DeKalb and Coffee counties, Tennessee, organized in 1877 and at times exchanging corresponding delegates with the Stone Association of Free Will Christian Baptists and the Cumberland FWB Association. See the *Free Baptist Cyclopaedia*, 117 ("Christian Progress, The"); 145 ("Curtis, Rev. Matthew"); and 641 ("Tennessee"); the minutes of the Stone FWCB Association (Western Division) for 1879; and the minutes of the Cumberland FWB Association for 1886. Matthew Curtis is probably the M. Curtis mentioned in the (Nashville) *Daily American*, September 30, 1891, 5, as assisting in "a flourishing meeting" in progress at the North Nashville FWB Church. Interestingly, two of the churches in the New Union association had been Union Baptists, but whether connected with those in Virginia or North Carolina we do not know.
[151] *The* (Nashville) *Daily American*, November 10, 1889, 5.
[152] *The Morning Star*, November 21, 1889, 372.
[153] *The* (Little Rock) *Daily Arkansas Gazette*, November 28, 1889, 1.
[154] *The* (Nashville) *Daily American*, December 5, 1889, 2.
[155] Nash, "The Southern Baptist Association," in *The Baptist Review*, January 30, 1905, 2-3.

and Enterprise, and that we elect one or more delegates to attend the proposed Convention in propagating this consolidation." They also voted to have the minutes printed "at the office of the Christian Herald and Enterprise, Pleasant View, Tenn.," affirmed that they were not and never had been "a constituent member of the General Conference North," and arranged to send a copy of the recommendation for Southern Unity both to the *Free Baptist Enterprise* and to the *Baptist Review*.[156]

The Cape Fear FWB Conference in North Carolina, which had been so heavily influenced by Nash, was positive about Southern Unity. Their 1889 minutes record approval of a resolution indicating that they adopted Southern Unity and planned to represent, "either by letter or by delegation," at the convention scheduled to begin on December 5 in Nashville. Ultimately, they decided "to represent this body by letter."[157] The Martin Association in Georgia, however, considered a motion "to endorse the involvement of Southern Unity as set forth by A. D. Williams" with this outcome: "The subject was discussed and finally rejected."[158]

The convention was apparently a success. The same Arkansas paper just mentioned included a brief report that the Rev. Thomas Malloy had stopped in Little Rock on his way back from the convention to talk with the governor of the state, also a Baptist.[159] It said that the convention "had taken some action for the good of the denomination ... but had not effected permanent organization, leaving that for a future meeting to be held next month," and that Williams and Lucas had been appointed "to establish a Free Will Baptist journal" at Pleasant View "to teach the doctrine of the denomination."[160] But *The Morning Star* reported, on January 2, 1890, quoting *The Christian Herald*[161] to say that fourteen associations had voted for Southern Unity and that an organization had been formed, named "General Association of Baptists, believing in Free Will, Free

---

[156] Minutes, Mount Moriah FWB Association, 1889, 2-3, 7.
[157] Minutes, Cape Fear FWB Association, 1889, 6, 9.
[158] Minutes, Martin FWB Association, 1889, 2-3.
[159] Malloy (often Molloy) had been a minister in the Mount Moriah Association in Alabama and relocated to Arkansas.
[160] *The* (Little Rock) *Daily Gazette*, December 22, 1889, 2. If, indeed, there was something to be done "next month," it was probably to be the work of a committee.
[161] Apparently using a short name for the full *The Christian Herald and Enterprise*.

Salvation, and Free Communion," with the next session scheduled for December 1890. It is interesting to see, then, that the organization was *not* named "General Association of Free Will Baptists." (We could wish, of course, that we had minutes of the meetings of this organization. None are known to exist.)

The 1890 Session of the General Association

Williams continued his work of promotion, perhaps focusing on enlisting subscribers for the newspaper. In September of 1890, he was in Alabama: "Rev. A. D. Williams, D. D., of Ashland City, Tenn., editor Christian Herald, and one of the leading ministers of the Free-Will Baptist church of the South, was in town Tuesday."[162] In October a Nashville paper included this notice: "Rev. A. D. Williams, D. D., editor of the Christian Herald, returned yesterday from a successful trip as far south as southern Georgia and Alabama in the interest of his paper."[163] Indeed, he had been at the Chattahoochee FWB Association the week before, where he was recognized and preached. His other efforts there, however, had not been so successful, as witnessed by this entry in the Chattahoochee minutes: "The subject of the Southern Unity move was brought before the body, and Bro. A. D. Williams and others made some remarks, but the question was dropped without definite action."[164]

In the same month, the minutes of the Cumberland Association recorded that Williams was moderator and preached at the session. The body adopted a lengthy resolution presented by the Committee on Literature and Union, which "resolved" several closely-related things: (1) rejoicing in the success attained by the Herald and Enterprise, (2) commending "the ability and discretion" with which Williams had conducted it, (3) giving the paper "fullest confidence and heartiest support" and commending it to the General Association, (4) thanking God for the "increasing favor," in general, "toward the union of all white Liberal Baptists of the South in one unitary and coöperative association," (5) favoring the establishment of a denominational Publishing House to publish

---

[162] *The* (Hartselle) *Alabama Enquirer*, September 25, 1890, 3. His presence might have led to the notice about the upcoming General Association in Hartselle, which also appeared in the same issue.
[163] *The* (Nashville) *Daily American*, October 10, 1890, 2.
[164] Minutes, Chattahoochee FWB Association, 1890, 3.

the Herald and other literature under the oversight of the General Association, and (6) naming J. R. Gower, A. D. Williams, and J. E. Hudgens as delegates to the upcoming meeting of the General Association.[165] And in November this appeared: "Rev. Dr. Williams was in town [Nashville] yesterday, from Ashland City, making arrangements to move the Christian Herald, the organ of the Free-will Baptists, back to Nashville. A new press and other material will be added to the establishment."[166]

Indeed, the General Association met again in December of 1890, this time at Hartselle, Alabama, at a church in the Flint River FWB Association. The newspaper in that town ran several brief notices. On September 25, this appeared:

Free-Will Baptist Association

The General Association of the Free-Will Baptist Church of the South will convene in Hartselle on December 11th, 12th, 13th, and 14th. This body is composed of the leading members of the church, and it is a very influential body. Hartselle should feel complimented by being selected as the place for the Association to meet.[167]

On November 20, there was a notice about the "entertainment committee" for the convention.[168] Then another announcement, obviously more official, was published on November 27:

The General Association

The next meeting of the General Association of Baptists, believing in Free Will, Free Salvation and Free Communion, will be held at Hartselle, Alabama, within the Flint River Association, beginning on Thursday, December 11, 1890. Introductory sermon by Rev. W. H. McGee, at 2:30 p.m.

J. W. Lucas, Chairman of Associational Board[169]

---

[165] Minutes, Cumberland FWB Association, 1890, 2.

[166] *The* (Nashville) *Daily American*, November 4, 1890, 2. Our text has glossed over what apparently happened: namely, that Williams first published in Nashville, then when the two papers were combined published in Pleasant View, and then after the General Association was formed moved back to Nashville. One wonders whether the name had been changed back, simply, to *The Christian Herald*, or if the newspaper was merely shortening the title.

[167] *The* (Hartselle) *Alabama Enquirer*, September 25, 1890, 3. The nearby *Cullman Alabama Tribune*, October 16, 1890, 3, ran this in its "Locals" column: "The Free Will Baptist Association of the southern states, will convene in Hartselle on the first Thursday in December. A large number of distinguished preachers will be present."

[168] *The* (Hartselle) *Alabama Enquirer*, November 20, 1890, 1.

[169] *The* (Hartselle) *Alabama Enquirer*, November 27, 1890, 3.

Finally, the paper ran a brief report when the meeting was over:

Free-Will Baptist Association

The Free-Will Baptist Association of the Southern States convened in Hartselle on December 11th, 12th, 13th, and 14th. Rev. W. H. McGee, of Alabama was chairman, and Prof. J. W. Lucas, of Tenn., was Secretary. The meeting was very interesting, but a very small number was in attendance. Some able preaching was done and it is hoped that much good was accomplished.[170]

It is obvious from these notices that there was a difference between the organization's official and its popular name. Lucas, as an officer, gave the correct and official version: "General Association of Baptists, believing in. ..." Popularly, all participants were lumped together as "Free Will Baptists"—and no doubt that was almost entirely true. Even those associations (if there were any other than the New Union Association of United Baptists in Tennessee) were "free will" in sentiment.

The post-session report cited above indicates that "a very small number" attended. We have not found many minutes of associations that named delegates. As already indicated, the Chattahoochee in Georgia certainly did not. The Mount Moriah FWB Association in Alabama, however, did so. The 1890 minutes recorded, "That we elect one delegate to represent us in the General Association that is to convene at Hartselle, Ala., on Thursday before the second Sabbath in Dec., 1890, and that we contribute funds to defray his expenses."[171]

The Decline of the General Association

What is not entirely clear, now, is how long this organization lasted past 1890. Nor do we know when the last issue of *The Christian Herald and Enterprise* was published.[172] As already noted, A. D. Williams left Tennessee in late 1891 or early 1892 to devote his energies to another cause: the establishment of the General Baptists' Oakland City College in Indiana. It seems likely that at that

---

[170] *The* (Hartselle) *Alabama Enquirer*, December 18, 1890, 3.
[171] Minutes, Mount Moriah FWB Association, 1890, 3. The minutes were printed at the Freewill Baptist Publishing Co., Nashville, TN, where *The Christian Herald and Enterprise* was published.
[172] There is one indication that the paper lasted past Williams's relocation from Nashville. The 1893 edition of *Rowell's American Newspaper Directory* (New York, NY: Geo. P. Rowell & Co., 1893), 1035, listed it as published in Kenesaw, Nebraska.

point he would have viewed the General Association to be well planted and expected to flourish; but of course we cannot know that—and, if he thought that, he was overly optimistic.

The only other records we have found, of a session after 1890, are for 1896, in a Nashville newspaper, and 1897, in the minutes of the Cumberland FWB Association. An article published on October 22, 1896, reports that a session of the Cumberland Association was under way at the time at the North Nashville church, then adds this sentence: "The General Association, composed of representatives from all the States, will convene in the same church Monday, Oct. 26, for a three day's session."[173] Then, in its issue for October 27, a report of the activities on the 26th appears and includes interesting information.[174] For one thing, this was identified as "the fifth General Association of the Free Will Baptist Church." Had the organization met every year, 1896 would have been its eighth.[175] Apparently there had been, intentionally or not, some years when the General Association had not met.

Also of interest is the following: "The General Association is composed of the Western Stone Association, the Eastern Stone Association, the Cumberland Association, all in Middle Tennessee, and the Union Association of East Tennessee. The last named was admitted only yesterday and adds to the organization twenty-one churches and 1,072 members, making a total of 102 churches and 5,742 members." Obviously, the General Association had been reduced to members in the state of Tennessee, and Free Will Baptists only, which was a far cry from the original intention. (Perhaps, by this time, it really was a General Association of Free Will Baptists, as the newspaper termed it.)

Of equal interest is the fact that the names given (mostly on a list of committees) included at least two visitors from the Free Will Baptists of the North: G. A. Gordon, "Illinois Agent of the Free Will Baptist Church," who preached

---

[173] *The Nashville American*, October 22, 1896, 5. That was a busy month for Cofer's Chapel, entertaining the (Peden) triennial General Conference, the Cumberland Association, and the General Association! But see the appendix in this volume.

[174] *The* (Nashville) *Tennessean*, October 27, 1896, 3. All information about this session is from this article.

[175] Traditionally, many associations do not count the first, organizational, meeting as one of its "annual meetings." But even if we do not count the 1889 meeting, the 1896 one would have been its seventh, not its fifth, if it had met annually.

on the previous night; and H. M. Ford[176] of Hillsdale, Michigan, who was the Field Secretary for the Randallite General Conference. Ford had evidently attended the General Association before; in the 1898 minutes of the General Conference (North), his report included this: "I have visited the General Association of the South twice, and the Cumberland Association twice, and the Western Division of the Stone Association once. These white Freewill Baptists of the South spring from a different denominational ancestry than the Free Baptists of the north." One of those two visits, then, was in 1896. The other is not certain but might well have been 1897.[177]

At least an 1897 session of the General Association was scheduled, as the Cumberland Association minutes make clear. As early as 1890, the Cumberland's Committee on Literature and Union expressed interest in a "union of all white Liberal Baptists of the South" and named delegates to the coming session of the General Association (which met in Hartselle, Alabama, as seen above). In 1896 and 1897 also, the Cumberland had named delegates to the General Association, indicating that the latter session was scheduled to be "at Nashville, Tenn., Oct. 28, 1897." Representing the Union FWB Association in East Tennessee, J. W. Lucas attended this meeting and reported to the next session of the Union.[178] There were also delegates from the Georgia State Convention of Liberal Baptists.[179]

It seems likely that the General Association did not last very long beyond this. The only note we have found is in the 1899 minutes of the Union Association: "W. S. Barton and J. C. Stallard were appointed delegates to the General Association to be held with Liberty Church, beginning Thursday before the first

---

[176] Actually, the paper reads "H. U. Ford," but it is clear that this was the well-known and well-travelled H. M. Ford. Gordon and Ford also attended the Cumberland FWB Association in 1896, which met the week before the General Association; see *The Nashville American*, October 25, 1896, 5.

[177] Ford also visited the Cumberland in 1897; the Cumberland Association and General Association were apparently held close together. See Robert E. Picirilli, *History of Tennessee Free Will Baptists* ([Nashville]: Historical Commission of the Tennessee State Association of Free Will Baptists, 2012), 13-14.

[178] Minutes, Union FWB Association, 1898, 5.

[179] Minutes, Georgia State Convention of Liberal Baptists, 1897, 7, which also reported that J. W. Lucas had been named as a delegate to the next General Conference of the Free Baptists of the North.

Sunday in November 1899."[180] Whether this meeting actually occurred cannot be confirmed now.

For that matter, there is more than one possibility about the existence of this organization throughout the period 1889-99. Perhaps it had existed but had not met every year. Or perhaps it had fizzled out after its first few years and the Tennessee Free Will Baptists had co-opted its name and redirected it after, say, 1892. Regardless, it did not last long and it did not fulfill its purpose—as Nash had predicted. The fact that the Mount Moriah Association returned to the cause of Nash and the Southern Baptist Association in 1892 (only to leave him again in 1894) would at least seem to indicate that the General Association produced from the Southern Unity movement had lost its appeal to them.

Indeed, it may well be that the demise of the General Association was hastened by the birth of yet another unity movement, in the South, from an entirely different source. This was the (triennial) General Conference led by Thomas E. Peden of Ohio. Its first session was in 1895 in Ohio, followed by an adjourned session in 1896 scheduled for Nashville (at the North Nashville FWB Church).[181] Then there were regular sessions in 1898, 1901, 1904, 1907, and 1910.[182] The much broader success of that organization, though also relatively short-lived, would have tended to lessen interest in the General Association. The Cape Fear FWB Association in North Carolina, for example, expressed interest in this meeting before the 1901 session (in Nashville, at Cofer's Chapel again)[183] and named delegates to the session in 1904 (at Dunn, NC).[184]

For whatever reasons, then, the General Association, like Nash's Southern Baptist Association, did not survive.

Conclusions

One wonders how to evaluate these two extraordinary efforts toward the unity of liberal Baptists in the South. Apparently there was a strong desire for

---

[180] Minutes, Union FWB Association, 1899, 8.
[181] But see the appendix in this volume. The session met, instead, in Kentucky.
[182] The story of this organization has been told in Robert E. Picirilli, *Little Known Chapters in Free Will Baptist History* (Nashville, Randall House, 2015), 151-180 (chapter 5).
[183] Minutes, Cape Fear FWB Conference, 1900, 10.
[184] Minutes, Cape Fear FWB Conference, 1903, 12.

unification in the ecclesiastical "air." Some historians contend that such a desire was a fruit of the Second Great Awakening. We are willing to accept that but cannot explicate it at greater length.

Whatever the case, it is obvious that many of the Free Will Baptists in the South wanted to get together and would have been glad to include other Baptists of the free will persuasion in such an organization. But neither the effort of Nash nor the movement called Southern Unity succeeded beyond a decade, at best. Peden's General Conference did only a little better, lasting from 1895 to 1910.

It was not long, however, until similar efforts, involving Free Will Baptists exclusively, succeeded. The Cooperative General Association was formed in 1916, mostly (but not entirely) in the West. The General Conference was formed in 1921, mostly (but not entirely) in the East. And in 1935 those two broad bodies merged to form the National Association of Free Will Baptists—which has flourished to this day.[185]

---

[185] For more information about these bodies, see Picirilli, *Little Known Chapters*, chapter 6: "John H. Wolfe, the Lost Churches of Kansas and Nebraska, and the Co-operative General Association, 1910-1935, 181-244.

6

The Free Will Baptist School in Unicoi, Tennessee

A Story of J. W. Lucas and Free Will Baptists of the South and North, 1890-1910

There were educational efforts within Free Will Baptists that are not well known. We know about the Ayden Seminary (later Eureka College) in North Carolina and Tecumseh College in Oklahoma. We may even know a little about Woolsey College in East Tennessee or Zion Bible School in Southwest Georgia. And we are well aware of the significant institutions founded by those of the Randall movement, like Bates, Hillsdale, Rio Grande, and others. But almost nothing has been published about a school at Unicoi, Tennessee. Perhaps the reason is that it was short-lived, but the story is nonetheless interesting and has some lessons for us.

Unicoi was, and is, a small town in upper East Tennessee, about halfway between Erwin and Johnson City, a place that might seem unlikely for a denominational educational effort. It is part of Unicoi County—Erwin is the county seat—and even today has a population of only about 3,500, more or less. The educational effort first involved the Union Association of Free Will Baptists, whose churches were in that part of the state. In 1896, one of the Union ministers, J. W. Lucas, proposed that they raise $5,000 to build a school in the Midway vicinity. The story of this effort grows out from there in surprising ways.

To put this in context, while there were public elementary schools available almost everywhere in the United States at that time, public high schools were not so readily accessible. This was the very time when concern for more education was becoming widespread, but in Tennessee, at least, mandatory attendance through high school did not become law until shortly before 1915. Lucas was obviously on the cutting edge of the movement to raise the level of education among Free Will Baptists, especially for those going into the ministry.

J. W. Lucas: Life and Early Ministry in North Carolina

In 1896, when he made the proposal just mentioned, Lucas was principal of Midway High School, but his name is permanently linked to the school at Unicoi. It seems appropriate, then, to provide some background about the man. The *Free Baptist Cyclopaedia*, published in 1889 before he initiated the effort being described here, provides a brief summary, as follows. He was James Wilson Lucas, son of Alfred and Penelope (Giles) Lucas, born near Averysboro, North Carolina, on March 3, 1850.[1] At the age of twenty-five—July 21, 1875—he married Julia Creech and (at the time the *Cyclopaedia* was published) had two children.[2] He consecrated his life to God in 1863 and was licensed to preach in 1868, ordained in 1872. He served as pastor to various churches in the Union Association in Tennessee and was, for a time, clerk of the Bear Creek Q. M. of that body.[3] Apparently, he was especially active in education, and the *Cyclopaedia* said he was principal of

---

[1] Averysboro was evidently another way of writing Averasboro, NC, which is in Harnett County near Dunn, in the central part of the state. According to Lindsay Overby (who is married to Lucas's 1st cousin, 3x removed), as indicated in an email dated 12/30/16, the Lucas family were among the original settlers of this town.

[2] Ultimately, the Lucases had four daughters, according to the family tree on Ancestry.com. Thanks to my daughter, Jean Lewis, for unearthing this. The 1900 and 1910 censuses show that Julia was the mother of five, four living (Ada, Cora, Unella, and Zora); they must have lost a child before 1900; thanks to Robert Vaughn for this.

[3] He is listed in that capacity in the *Freewill Baptist Register and Year-Book* (Dover, NH: Morning Star Steam Job Printing House, 1884), 78.

the High School in Parrottsville, Tennessee, "where he is exerting an extended influence."[4]

His obituary, published in 1916, adds that he was converted at age 18 (this should be 13), graduated from Wake Forest College,[5] and died June 23, 1916.[6]

When I began research into the story of the school at Unicoi, I was aware that there was an active Free Will Baptist minister by the same name in Eastern North Carolina. I first assumed that they were two different persons but decided to check this out. To my surprise, I found they were the same, and this adds an interesting dimension to the story.[7]

Lucas's name first appears in the Cape Fear FWB Conference minutes for October 1868, when he was a delegate from the Pleasant Grove Church in Harnett County. Subsequently, he was named temporary clerk of a called session in December of the same year. If the information above is correct, that he was licensed in that year, the minutes do not confirm; but at the next biennial session in 1870, he was listed as a licensed minister and "appointed on a committee for the organization and supervision of Sabbath Schools throughout the Connexion."[8] The 1873 minutes report, "J. W. Lucas, having been examined in Conference, was commended to the Ordaining Council for ordination." This record was apparently confirming an ordination that had taken place in 1872 between the triennial 1870 and 1873 sessions when there was no regular meeting of the Conference.

---

[4] G. A. Burgess and J. T. Ward, eds., *Free Baptist Cyclopaedia: Historical and Biographical* (Free Baptist Cyclopaedia Co., 1886, 1889), 349-50.

[5] At Wake Forest he was a member of the Philomathesian Society. As such, he was on a committee that sent out a resolution of condolences in the death of a classmate; *The Wilmington* (NC) *Journal*, September 26, 1873, 3. Thanks to Robert L. Vaughn for sending this reference and others throughout this chapter identified with his initials (RLV) after the citations.

[6] See the 1916 minutes of the Union (TN) Association of Free Will Baptists, 22. Throughout this article I will not usually footnote references to associational minutes since all one needs to find the item is the name of the association and year of meeting. I will do so, however, for the minutes of the General Conference of Free Baptists, given that the size of that publication makes finding specific references much more difficult. Lucas's death certificate, located by Robert Vaughn, mistakenly shows Tennessee as his birthplace.

[7] A special thanks to Gary Barefoot, curator of the Free Will Baptist Historical Collection at the University of Mount Olive in North Carolina, for researching the manuscript minutes of the Cape Fear Conference and providing me with the information about his ministry with that Conference, summarized in the following paragraphs.

[8] Here, as often in that time, *connexion/connection* is another term for *denomination*.

Lucas was closely associated at the time with the Reverend B. B. Holder, whose address as a licensed minister in 1859 had been Averasboro. In 1868, Holder's address was Bushville, Alabama, and in 1870 two churches in southeastern Alabama (Judson and Bethsaida), "reared by Eld. B. B. Holder," were received into the Cape Fear. At the same meeting, Holder and Lucas "were sent as missionaries to those churches and for the promulgation of Christ's cause during the next biennial term." Indeed, the two men were granted certificates as missionaries to Alabama. In the 1873 minutes Lucas's address appears both as Lawrenceville, Alabama,[9] and Averysboro, North Carolina. So Lucas ministered for a time in Alabama, perhaps for the two-year stint mentioned in the minutes.

From 1874 on, the Cape Fear met annually and Lucas, along with Holder, was actively involved. Much of that time he was the clerk. He was interested in the temperance movement and addressed "the people of Averasboro," his hometown, on the subject in 1875.[10] His address in North Carolina changed about, from Elevation (1875) to DeVanes (1877) to Fremont (1878-79). He was pastor at Antioch and Laurel Chapel (1876), then at Colyer's (or Collier's) School House Church (1877). He was elected "to write out a revision of the old discipline and present the same," for which he would be remunerated. Indeed, the 1883 edition of the Cape Fear treatise includes, on the title page, "by J. W. Lucas."[11] He promoted "a union ... between the several branches of the Liberal Baptist churches[12] in the South and West" (1875) and, with Holder and R. A. Johnson, was named to a committee to represent the Cape Fear in a convention for this purpose if it were held.[13]

Lucas's interest in education shows up in the minutes for 1876, when he made a motion "to request the Moderator to appoint a committee to suggest

---

[9] Lawrenceville is in the southeastern corner of the state.

[10] *The* (Raleigh, NC) *Friend of Temperance*, January 6, 1875, 2 (RLV).

[11] *The Freewill Baptist Faith to which is added the Practices of Cape Fear Freewill Baptist Conference*, by J. W. Lucas, (Goldsboro, NC: Baptist Review Job Print, 1883.) *The Baptist Review* was a publication of B. W. Nash, who (as a Union Baptist) was promoting the unity of Southern Liberal Baptists referred to in the next sentence in the text.

[12] "Liberal Baptist" was a generic term for all Baptists of Arminian persuasion, regardless of denominational name.

[13] This would have been the movement spearheaded by B. W. Nash; the story appears in another chapter in this volume.

a plan for better education of indigent young men entering the ministry." An 1879 newspaper shows that Lucas was principal of Fremont (NC) Institute, "A Classical High School," at the time—apparently a school he established.[14] The same newspaper indicated that he would deliver a lecture in Fremont, on Sunday, entitled "Feet Washing as a Church Ordinance."[15] That newspaper had already indicated that Lucas, from the Cape Fear Association, had visited the 1879 session of the Neuse FWB Conference in November and preached.[16]

In the Cape Fear minutes for 1880, with Lucas still serving as clerk, he wrote a personal note beginning "To my successor." Apparently, he was giving up the job, and that was probably because he was planning to relocate. His name does not appear in the 1881 minutes at all, and the 1882 minutes refer to him as being in Tennessee. That fits precisely with what we know from sources in Tennessee.

Lucas in Tennessee. First Efforts Toward a School

The obituary of Lucas, mentioned above, includes the information that he "came to Woolsey College in 1881." This probably explains what brought him from the Cape Fear to East Tennessee.[17] This school—mostly a high school but with courses for ministerial training, including Biblical studies—had begun in 1873 or 1874 under the leadership of W. B. Woolsey.[18] This would have appealed to Lucas and fit well with his interests and abilities.

---

[14] *The Goldsboro Messenger*, December 4, 1879, 2, 3—which refers to the school as "Prof. J. Wilson Lucas's" (RLV). Perhaps the same school was involved in an announcement, headed "Princeton Items" (*The Goldsboro Messenger*, July 1, 1880, 3) to the effect that Lucas would open the fall session "about the 20th" of next month, and we bespeak for him a liberal patronage as he is a good teacher and is building up a good school." Princeton is about fifteen miles from Fremont (RLV).

[15] *The Goldsboro Messenger*, December 6, 1879, 1 (RLV).

[16] *The Goldsboro Messenger*, November 20, 1879, 3 (RLV). This was "the first session" of this conference, apparently being started, amiably, out of the Cape Fear. It evidently did not last long.

[17] B. W. Nash (see note 11), in *The Baptist Review* for Jan. 30, 1905, 3, claimed that Lucas, while still in NC, "wanted to be editor and laid his plans to capture the Review or get up an opposition paper, and failing in both cases, he quit the State, and went over to East Tennessee." Thanks to Gary Barefoot for providing a scan of this issue of *The Baptist Review*, the only issue we know to exist.

[18] The story of this institution is well told in Paul Woolsey, *God, a Hundred Years, and a Free Will Baptist Family*. I have given brief attention to it in my *History of Tennessee Free Will Baptists* (Nashville, TN: Historical Commission of the Tennessee State Association of Free Will Baptists, 2012), 24.

The obituary also indicates that he immediately devoted himself to the work of education and organization among the Free Will Baptists of the mountain area, which included East Tennessee, Western North Carolina, and Southwestern Virginia. The minutes of the Union Association show that he was at least as actively involved as he had been in the Cape Fear in North Carolina. He preached at the sessions several times, first in 1883, and was often clerk or moderator. His mailing address, in 1886, was Parrottsville. He was pastor of Mt. Zion church and appointed as a delegate to the (Randall) General Conference in Ohio in October 1886, but he did not go.

In 1889-90, he was involved in an effort to promote a General Association of Free Will Baptists that included Free Will Baptists of Tennessee and the South more broadly. An 1889 newspaper announcement included his name as among those issuing the call for the meeting. An 1890 announcement identified him as "Chairman of Associational Board." And a report of the meeting, at Hartselle, Alabama, December 11-14, 1890, indicated that he was elected its secretary.[19]

In 1891, he was pastor at Bear Creek, Clair Creek, Dawson's Grove, New Home, and St. Joseph's Chapel churches, and in 1893 at Midway and New Home. He would apparently continue at Midway from then until 1901. He often chaired the Union Association's Committee on Education, and the report of this committee in 1894 reveals one of his major concerns, emphasizing that religion and education are "twin sisters" and do not thrive alone. There are schools enough, he said, that "there is no excuse for ignorance," and parents who fail to ensure that their children obtain "the simple rudiments of education wrong the children, the state and the church." The following year's report for the same Committee, in 1895 (he was again chairman), added: "The Union Association ought to maintain one good high school at some central point where our children can have the advantages of higher education."

At the 1896 meeting of the Union Association, then, Lucas the pastor and educator proposed that the association begin a school. This was not new for

---

[19] "Freewill Baptists," the Nashville, TN *Daily American*, Nov. 27, 1889, 8 (RLV); "The General Association," Hartselle, AL, *Alabama Enquirer*, Nov. 27, 1890 (RLV); Dec. 18, 1890 (RLV). For more information in context, see the chapter in this volume devoted to unity movements in the South.

him. The 1916 obituary states, specifically, that Lucas established schools in Tennessee at Parrottsville, Midway, and Unicoi "for the express purpose of educating our poor Free Baptist children and ministers." During the 1894-95 term, at least, he was principal at McMinn Academy, a non-sectarian school in Rogersville, Tennessee.[20]

I have no information about the school at Parrottsville except that Lucas was there when the *Free Baptist Cyclopaedia* was published in 1889. Also, a Nashville newspaper, in 1886 published a letter about the school:

> Newport, Tenn., May 24.—[Special Letter]—We had the pleasure of witnessing the commencement exercises of Parrottsville high school May 20 and 21. This school has been conducted for some time by the able President, Prof. J. W. Lucas. He is an able educator and is really a "man of the times." He is doing a good work for Cooke County which she should appreciate. The exercises were successful, to say the least, and everyone went away pleased with the hospitality of the Professor and his school.[21]

About the school at Midway I can say more. He was principal there in 1896, when he made his pitch to the Union Association, and when he communicated with the General Conference in the North in 1898. He apparently continued in that capacity until he began the school in Unicoi. The one at Midway was not a Free Will Baptist school as such. Obviously, he desired to establish a school that would belong to the Free Will Baptists in the Union Association and the mountain region. And the 1896 minutes show the first concrete movement in that direction.

This came in the form of a report from the Committee on Education, which began by citing the example of the Free Baptists in the North and deploring the lack of interest in education among those of like faith in the South. After com-

---

[20] *Report of the Commissioner of Education for the Year 1894-95* (Washington, DC: Government Printing Office, 1896), 2100-01 (RLV). The school, for males only, was listed as one of the accredited secondary schools in Tennessee, meaning that its college preparatory graduates could be admitted to the University of Tennessee; see *University of Tennessee Register for 1894-'95* (Knoxville, TN: University of Tennessee, 1895), 13-14 (RLV). That he was also there in 1893 is indicated by an announcement in *The* (Jonesborough, TN) *Herald and Tribune*, August 30, 1893, 2 (RLV).

[21] *The* (Nashville, TN) *Daily American*, May 31, 1886. 1 (RLV).

mending "our worthy and beloved brother" Lucas for the school at Midway, and urging its support, the report continued,

> Let us co-operate with Bro. Lucas in his effort to establish a Southern F. B. School where our boys and girls may be trained under our own auspices to fight the battles of life and the F. B. cause. The school at Midway is not now a F. B. school. Therefore the following is submitted as supplementary to the above.
>
> A PROPOSITION FROM REV. J. W. LUCAS AS TO F. B. SCHOOL
>
> I propose to raise $5,000 for a Freewill Baptist school at Midway, or some other point on the main line of railroad on the following conditions: Ten dollars shall constitute a share and be entitled to one vote in the management of the property. No part of the amount subscribed shall be collected until $5,000 has been subscribed, then not more than one-fourth of stock shall be called for at one time.
>
> When subscriptions have been secured and first fourth part in, those who have paid in stock, shall name officers and managers of the funds and locate the school, etc., of this amount $1,000 is expected of Union Association. We recommend the above to the careful consideration of our people and ask them to act wisely in their own interest by acting at once.

The plan was bold and ambitious, but it was not destined to succeed. We do not possess Union Association minutes for the following year, but the minutes for 1898 make clear that they realized they could not fund such a school by themselves. The report of the Committee on Education included two main recommendations. First: "We are glad to know that Prof. Lucas is conducting a successful High School at Midway, near the center of the Association. We most heartily recommend this school to all our people, and urge them to patronize it." The second, prefaced by the recognition that "F. B. Training schools are a burning necessity," and "our small Association cannot successfully build and maintain such a school," was that the Union elect a committee of two to

> cooperate with similar committees from adjacent Associations in establishing and maintaining at some convenient point a first-class F. B. training school where our children may have educational advantages at the smallest possible cost under F. B. auspices, and where our young ministers may obtain better equipments [sic] to work for God and the F. B. cause.

But, in fact, the plan would progress no farther. Lucas would continue as principal of the high school at Midway—perhaps an independent or community-owned school—and as pastor of the Free Will Baptist church in the Midway community in Greene County.

Even so, the Free Will Baptists in that area continued to express interest in the cause of education. At the next year's session of the Union Association, in 1899, there was a report from a broader Educational Committee that had included representatives from Free Will Baptist associations in the Appalachian regions of Tennessee, North Carolina, and Virginia and had met at Midway on January 26 and 27:

> After a careful survey of the field and a full discussion of various propositions for a F. B. school central to associations here represented, the committee is of the opinion that we are not able at present to raise the funds necessary to establish and equip such school as we need, or to afford its proper support if established.
>
> Our most practical course is to endorse and patronize Midway High School under the management of Prof. J. W. Lucas, until, by co-operation and increased concern for education we are able to sustain a good school of our own. Midway is centrally located on the Southern railway, in a healthy Christian community. We have here an active church of more than one hundred members, with a live Sunday school, prayer meetings, etc.[22] School expenses are very low. No extravagant habits are encouraged. The course of instruction is that of a high school, strongly endorsed by the University of Tennessee. The instructors are practical educators. The principal is one of our own ministers, well and favorably known to most of our people, thoroughly qualified with a lifetime experience in the school. We cannot do better than entrust to him the training of our sons and daughters; and we would earnestly impress upon all our people the imperative duty of sustaining him in his effort and sacrifice to elevate our people and to prepare the way at an early date for a first-class F. B. training school.

In addition, the Union Association established a Ministerial Education Committee. In 1899, with Lucas as chairman, that committee reported:

> We recommend that all young men contemplating the work of the ministry give themselves the very best training possible at Midway or some oth-

---

[22] They were apparently referring to the Free Will Baptist church at Midway, where Lucas was pastor.

er good school. That the Educational Board render all necessary aid to such young men in Midway school under such restrictions as in its wisdom are best. We advise that no one be ordained to the ministry unless he has at least such education as may be obtained in the primary schools of Tennessee and familiarity with the Treatise and Butler-Dunn Theology, and consents to abstain from the use of tobacco and intoxicants, and devotes as much as possible of his time to the work of the ministry. We insist that those already in the ministry try to improve themselves that they may be more useful in the work. We, therefore, suggest that a course of reading be arranged for the ministry and that annual examinations be held on the same.

To this the Clerk added a note suggesting that the Butler-Dunn theology and Broadus's work on preparation and delivery of sermons constitute the course of reading for the next year. There are no further references to the "course of reading."

This Ministerial Education Committee undertook to collect funds and assist young ministers with their education at Midway. In 1900, Lucas reported, for this committee, that "three young ministers in Midway School have been aided to the amount of $25.12." Also: "Other young ministers are expected in Midway School and more funds are needed." Following the report, pledges toward this cause, totaling about $75.00, were made.

No doubt, Lucas was disappointed in the failure of his plan to begin a new and specifically Free Will Baptist high school, but his educational labors continued unabated.

The Northern General Conference Gets Involved

Indeed, Lucas had not abandoned his dream of a Free Will Baptist school in the mountains. He simply began to look elsewhere for the support needed, and that was to the General Conference of Free Baptists, the Randallites in the North. There was already some sense of relationship between the "freewillers" of the Union Association—and others in the mountain region—and those of the North, and I digress for a few paragraphs to fill in that background.

The Union Association was formed in 1872 by some of the Tennessee churches in the Toe (or Tow) River and American associations. Even earlier, in 1869, those two associations had written together to L. R. Burlingame of the General Conference and inquired about "amalgamation" with them. Subsequently, in 1874, the minutes of the General Conference include letters, seeking admission, from the American, Tow River, and Union Associations.[23] The letter from the Union, though typical of all three, is more detailed and interesting:

> Nearly forty years ago, two or three ministers in North Carolina[24] embraced the doctrines of free salvation and free communion, organized churches there, calling themselves Freewill Baptists, without knowledge of any others, and came into East Tennessee and did the same. We prospered till the terrible war came, and then, being all for the Union, we suffered in the extreme. We are all poor, hold our meetings in school-houses, and our ministers receive no salaries. We have adopted the articles of faith and the covenant, as published in your Treatise, and request to be received into your fellowship. The presence of your Home Mission secretary at our last meeting greatly encouraged us.

Admission was granted, even though the three associations represented only by letter and not in person.

The ease with which those in the mountains identified with the free-willers in the North is not all that surprising. There was considerable loyalty to the federal union in those parts, as indicated in the letter from the Union Association cited above. Distances, however, meant that representation by delegates from East Tennessee to triennial General Conference sessions in the North were not frequent. In 1886, Lucas was appointed as a delegate from the Union to the General Conference that would meet in Marion, Ohio, a location somewhat closer. He did not attend, however. For that matter, neither of the three associations in the mountains reported, even by letter, to the General Conference after they joined in 1874—not until the Union Association would again seek membership there in 1901.

Even so, the terminology used by the Union reflected the influence of the Randallites. At some point between 1888 and 1891, the Union substituted "Yearly Meeting" for "Association," but changed back in 1893. Between 1900 and 1903, they began to use "Free Baptist" instead of "Freewill Baptist," follow-

---

[23] Minutes of the General Conference of Freewill/Free Baptists, 1874, in I. D. Stewart, compiler, *Minutes of General Conference of the Freewill Baptist Connection*, vol. II (1859-1886), 277-80, 304.
[24] These were John Wheeler and Moses Peterson, joined by W. B. Woolsey.

ing the example of the General Conference in 1892.[25] "Freewill" was reinstated in 1920-21.

In 1898, according to the minutes of the General Conference, the report of H. M. Ford, its Field Secretary, indicated that from a "general" association in the South "Rev. and Prof. J. W. Lucas, of Midway Academy" (also a pastor Binkley of the Nashville Free Will Baptist Church[26]) had been named as a delegate to the General Conference.[27] But Lucas had written that he could not come, to his and Ford's regret. Ford spoke highly of him as "a ripe scholar and a rare man" who was endeavoring to make his academy [at Midway] especially helpful to Free Baptist young people preparing for the ministry, adding, "He labors under many difficulties and needs our moral support and sympathy."[28]

Interestingly, before continuing the account of the Union's participation in the General Conference of the North, I note that they apparently considered being part of Thomas Peden's breakaway, rival General Conference that met triennially from 1895 to 1910.[29] The Union minutes for 1896 include this resolution presented by Lucas:

> That Union Association is in hearty sympathy with all reasonable efforts to bring about union among all Freewill Baptist [sic], and that this body elect a representative to the General Conference of Freewill Baptists beginning Oct. 7th, 1896, in Nashville, Tenn., with instructions not to attend the same, if it becomes evident before Oct. 7th, that said Conference will not be general and representative.

Apparently, Lucas was aware of the nature of Peden's challenge to the General Conference of the North and realized that it might not succeed in supplanting that organization. But whether the Union decided not to attend this "adjourned"

---

[25] The reason for saying "between" certain years is that there are gaps in our holdings of minutes and I cannot determine the very year such a change was made.
[26] Subsequently named Cofer's Chapel FWB Church.
[27] The existence of this "General Association" has only recently come to light, and no minutes exist. It was *not* the "General Conference" founded by Thomas Peden. For more information about this association, see the chapter in this volume devoted to unity movements in the South. The minutes of the Georgia State Convention of Liberal Baptists for 1897, 7, confirm that Lucas was at this 1897 meeting in Nashville and named as a delegate to the General Conference (North).
[28] Minutes, General Conference of Free Baptists, 1898, 34.
[29] I have told the story of this organization in my *Little Known Chapters in Free Will Baptist History* (Randall House, 2015), chapter 5.

session or decided, after attending, not to participate further in that organization we cannot know. We do not have minutes for the 1896 meeting—which, shortly before it convened, was changed from Nashville to Kentucky.

In 1901, then, Lucas did succeed in attending the Randallite General Conference at Harper's Ferry, West Virginia, and in presenting his cause to that body—which brings me back to the account of Lucas's efforts to involve the General Conference in providing a school for Free Will Baptists in the mountains. (This makes clear that Lucas and the Union Association did not identify with Thomas Peden's rival General Conference.)

Even before the September session of the General Conference in 1901, Lucas had come to the attention of the Free Baptists of the North. In the issue of *The Morning Star* for January 24, 1901, a Reverend A. H. Whitaker of Michigan, writing from Chattanooga, Tennessee, described his visit to the South. In Midway, Tennessee, he had visited "Prof. J. W. Lucas and Prof. G. W. Lawrence and wife, faithfully toiling to establish a Freewill Baptist school." They were laboring, he said, at two great disadvantages: the people's indifference to education and the lack of endowment or buildings. Such buildings as they were using were "rude and uncomfortable," lacking paint or varnish or pictures on the walls, and with desks—"(where there are any)"—showing the keenness of knife blades. Whitaker made a passionate plea for the help of "kind hearted friends of means," asking, "Where are the men and women who will say to these needy mountaineers, We will furnish the teachers if you will furnish the buildings?"[30]

In August of 1901, an article by Lucas himself, dated July 22 in Midway, appeared in the same publication, appealing on behalf of the "bright boys and girls" of the Free Baptists of the mountain regions of Tennessee, Virginia, and North Carolina. A syndicate had offered 850 or 900 acres of land, "a beautiful town site" on the railroad, with a modern hotel building and several other buildings, and their desire was to move the school from Midway to this site. "Our idea," he said, "is to form here a settlement of progressive Free Baptists interested in educating their own children." To that end they would sell six or seven hundred acres for small farms, businesses, and residences. "The remainder with

---

[30] *The Morning Star* (Boston, Mass.), January 26, 1901, 4-5.

hotel, boarding house and office will be used for school purposes." They would need $30,000 to $35,000 for this project, part of which could be realized from sales and the rest by donations. Lucas asked for gifts and pledges to be paid, preferably, by January 1, 1902, promising, "Such amounts will be drawn only by parties legally authorized to receive and use the same for this purpose." He also invited inquiries from anyone desiring to be part of "the colony."[31]

This bold plan was therefore not only in Lucas's mind but before the Free Will Baptist public when the 1901 session of the General Conference convened in Harper's Ferry, West Virginia, September 4-10. At this session, the Union Association was formally admitted to the General Conference, with Lucas as its delegate.[32] (Apparently those involved were not aware that the Union had been admitted earlier.) He also served on more than one committee, gave an address entitled "The Work among the Mountain Whites," was nominated for (but not elected to) the General Board,[33] and was named a delegate to attend the National Anti-Saloon League later that year.[34]

More important for our purposes here, General Conference Field Secretary Ford's report to the session included this: "I wish to call attention to a school at Midway, Tenn., carried on by Profs Lucas and Lawrence for theological and academic purposes. Just now they are offered 9,000 acres of fine land and a fine building worth several thousand dollars, all for $25,000."[35]

Even more important, the minutes subsequently include the following "supplement" to the report of the General Conference Committee on Education:

> REPORT OF THE MOUNTAIN EDUCATIONAL COMMISSION
> Whereas our attention has been called to the very great need of educational facilities in the mountain regions of East Tennessee, Virginia, North Carolina, and the inability of the people themselves to provide these facilities; and

---

[31] *The Morning Star*, August 1, 1901, 4.
[32] *The Morning Star*, September 19, 1901, 1, in its report on the General Conference session, noted, "The Union Association of Tennessee ... [was] received. ... The president with felicitous remarks gave the hand of fellowship to Rev. J. W. Lucas." Lucas, in turn, "made a few remarks."
[33] Minutes, General Conference of Free Baptists, 1901, 17, 45, 47, 73, 78, 88, 100, 130.
[34] Minutes, General Conference of Free Baptists, 1901, 139. Frederick L. Wiley, *Free Baptists in Temperance Reform* (Boston, MA: Morning Star Publishing House, 1901), 30, reported that Lucas was named to attend this in December 1901, the Sixth National Anti-Saloon Convention in Washington, D. C., as a delegate from the General Conference.
[35] Minutes, General Conference of Free Baptists, 1901, 31. Secretary Ford got the acreage very wrong!

considering the great possibilities of these people if once educated, as shown by their loyalty during the Civil War, their independence of character, and their receptiveness to instruction; therefore,

Resolved, That we, the undersigned,[36] agree to enter into an organization under the name of the Mountain Educational Commission, which shall become a legal body, whose duties shall be to investigate the whole question of feasibility as to the need, location, and means for establishing an industrial school in that region under Christian influence. If found desirable and practicable and if a financial basis of at least $50,000 shall be guaranteed, this Commission shall proceed to locate and organize the school, and as soon as can reasonably be done commit its management to a board of trustees consisting of fifteen members named by this Commission, said trustees to be divided into three equal classes holding office respectively one, two, and three years. As the terms of these respective trustees shall expire their successors shall be elected for three years by the ballots of the remaining trustees from a list of ten persons nominated and presented by the Conference Board of the Free Baptist General Conference.[37]

The body adopted this report and so gave status to the Mountain Educational Commission. The Rev. George H. Ball was chairman and E. P. Metcalf the treasurer. J. W. Lucas was financial agent and secretary. Lucas appeared before the Conference Board at its next meeting on September 23, 1901, when he "presented the opening for educational work in the South, and asked for counsel of the Board."[38] It would seem that his dream of a Free Will Baptist high school in East Tennessee was about to be realized. Had this Commission followed its well-defined plan, much of the disappointment that ultimately followed might easily have been avoided.

Property at Unicoi and Early Success; the Role of the General Conference (North)

Meeting triennially, the General Conference would not have another session until 1904, but from the minutes for that year we learn that much had transpired since 1901. The Conference Board, which had been involved during the

---

[36] The names of "the undersigned" do not appear in the minutes. A subsequent article (*The Morning Star*, December 12, 1902, 4) lists eight men in addition to Ball, Metcalf, and Lucas, including G. W. Lawrence of Unicoi and the Hon. W. P. Brownlow of Jonesboro, Tennessee.

[37] Minutes, General Conference of Free Baptists, 1901, 123-24.

[38] *The Morning Star*, October 3, 1901, 4.

interim, reported that "It was the general purpose to establish a school for the mountaineers in Tennessee or North Carolina, if, after thorough investigation into the needs and conditions and location  and financial outlook, it seemed feasible."[39] One notes, however, that the new Commission acted more quickly than had been intended. Whether Lucas himself urged this is not indicated.

Regardless, in April 1902 the Mountain Education Commission agreed to purchase, from the Unicoi Development Company for $18,500, a tract of eight hundred acres at Unicoi,[40] "with a fine hotel [pictured above] and other buildings," reportedly valued at from $50,000 to $75,000.[41] The "grand hotel," with some thirty rooms, was "the central landmark of early Unicoi."[42] Apparently, the town had failed to develop as expected, largely because the railroad decided to locate its shop in Erwin instead of Unicoi, and so the large tract, with its empty hotel, became available for what appeared to be a bargain price.[43] Lucas was named the agent and empowered to sell lots. The Commission borrowed the money for the first payment from the General Conference.

Subsequently, a concerted effort was made to promote this project. *The Morning Star* published a three-part article in July 1902, by G. W. Lawrence, entitled "The Mountain Whites." This series focused on the impoverished and

---

[39] Minutes, General Conference of Free Baptists, 1904, 22-23.

illiterate state of those in Appalachia, and on the need for better education for the general population and for the ministry. The churches, said Lawrence, were guided by uneducated and uncompensated men and usually had preaching just once a month. There was need for a school that would provide education in books, values, life skills, and a useful trade. "The establishment of a school in these mountains having a good industrial department and giving opportunities for paying a part of the school expenses by labor will open the way for many poor boys and girls to gain an education," he said.[44] That same month an article by Lucas, entitled "Our Industrial School," announced the purchase of the property and stated that $4,000 was needed for a payment by September 1. He would "undertake to raise $1,000 of this among the mountaineers themselves," and if the poor people of the area could do that, at least $10,000 ought to come from other sources. He had recently been in New England, he said, to promote the cause.[45]

In September appeared a four-part report by the Reverend Z. A. Space entitled "A Visit to the South."[46] He had been to the area in and around Unicoi in early August to assist in "the property transaction." Like Lawrence, he emphasized the needs of the mountain whites; both men pointed out that these folk had been loyal to the Union and were as needy as the freed blacks in the South. He was pleased with "the mission of Profs. Lucas and Lawrence among these mountaineers" and spoke especially highly of Lucas, adding, "All honor to such a man." Lucas and Lawrence, he said, in response to the pleadings of the mountain people, had "espoused their cause and asked [Free Baptists] to co-operate." He noted, "We have probably less than a half dozen academic scholars in the five Associations of eastern Tennessee and western North Carolina." He concluded by observing that both Presbyterians and Baptists were giving their people proper care: "What are the Free Baptists going to do? Oh, we cannot put the question off any longer. *It must be answered.*"[47]

---

[44] *The Morning Star*, July 3, 1902, 4; July 24, 1902, 3; July 31, 1902, 3.
[45] *The Morning Star*, July 10, 1902, 4. Indeed, a report on the New Hampshire Y. M. (*The Morning Star*, July 3, 1902, 4) included this: "Rev. J. W. Lucas briefly presented his work among the Southern mountaineers, and received pledges amounting to seventy-six dollars."
[46] Space was a member of the General Conference Board.
[47] *The Morning Star*, September 11, 1902, 4; September 18, 1902, 4; September 28, 1902, 4; October 2, 1902, 4.

George Ball, chairman of the Commission, also wrote an article entitled "Our Opportunity." It appeared in December and expressed brimming optimism. He reviewed the terms of the purchase, emphasizing the ideal location and that the property was much more valuable than what had been paid. He spoke highly of Lucas and Lawrence. Lawrence and his wife, he said, had "become thoroughly identified with the people and are well qualified as college graduates to co-operate with Brother Lucas." Lucas had obviously made a great impression on him:

> Brother Lucas has sacrificed much in the cause of education for the mountain whites. He has thought over it, prayed over it, suffered for it, and worked for it for many years. The scheme of purchasing this property and the manipulation of it from first to last is due to him, and he now enters upon this vantage ground with a warmth and enthusiasm which no other person can possibly possess.

Indeed, said Ball, the Commission had only to secure payment for the property on loan, allow for the sale of enough building and farm lots to refund the money and pay off the loan, and hold title until the purchase money was refunded. Perhaps the Home Mission Society or the Women's Missionary Board would be called on to help with organizing or opening the school, but that was not the concern of the Commission. Ball was confident that the people in the area were "sure to rise in intelligence and strength and influence and prosperity if this educational enterprise materializes and is properly developed."[48]

Another article by Lucas appeared soon after Ball's, entitled "Our Work at Unicoi, Tenn." He, too, promoted the ideal location and "the purpose of establishing for the mountain youth a first-class school with Bible and industrial departments." The first payment had been made, but another, of $4,500, was due February 16, 1903. Although the sale of lots could be expected to provide much of the money needed, there was not time for this before the February payment, and for that matter a clear title to lots could not be given until after

---

[48] *The Morning Star*, December 12, 1902, 4.

the February payment was made. This payment "depends on voluntary contributions," he said.[49]

"The plan of the Commission," the Conference Board would say later, "was to interest prominent and influential people of Tennessee in the enterprise, and to raise the money substantially in the South, raising a part by the sale of a portion of the property. But this plan failed"[50]—even though "many families of [the Free Will Baptist] persuasion bought lots and built homes in order that their families could take advantage of the school."[51] The money was not forthcoming.

Consequently, the Commission voted in January 1903 to transfer "all its interests, rights and privileges, including title to the property" to the Free Baptist General Conference which would assume all the liabilities of the short-lived Commission. The transfer was made and the Conference Board, through its Executive Committee, had already begun to take over in December 1902. Of the $18,500 total, the Commission had received only $5,300, of which a little less than $500 had been raised by Lucas. Payments were due: about $4,500 in February 1903, $8,000 in August 1903, and $4,500 on October 16, 1904.[52]

The pages of *The Morning Star* continued to promote the project in 1903. In March, Mrs. Lawrence had a brief article reporting that a church had been organized in Unicoi with twenty-four charter members and that most of them had come to Unicoi since the property was purchased to participate in the school. A three-month school term had already been conducted, with many requesting that it be extended another month.[53] Just a week later, another article by her featured the elderly W. B. Woolsey and his wife, whose own Woolsey College had been very successful but was now closed. Woolsey was promoting the new educational effort at Unicoi.[54] In April, Lucas reported on the work of the new local church, which apparently met in the hotel building, and solicited the gift of "a second-hand chapel organ that does not creak too badly, and some good

---

[49] *The Morning Star*, December 25, 1902, 4.
[50] Minutes, General Conference of Free Baptists, 1904, 22-23.
[51] Adlerman, 12.
[52] Minutes, General Conference of Free Baptists, 1904, 22-23.
[53] *The Morning Star*, March 12, 1903, 4.
[54] *The Morning Star*, March 19, 1903, 4.

music books suited to our work." He indicated that about two dozen books, "shaped notes generally preferred," would do.[55]

Later in the same month, another article by Lucas focused on the sale of lots. His description of the situation adds interesting detail. The site for the town had been secured in 1890 by a syndicate that drew up plans for "a magnificent city." But the project failed and the property reverted to the original owner, then changed hands several times and wound up in the courts. It became a "stock farm," with "lambs reared in the hotel yard, the boarding-house turned into a hay barn, and repairs of fences and houses neglected." That was the condition when the Free Will Baptists took over, with no money for repairs or improvements. Lucas was charging rent to those cultivating the land and allowing them to pay by making repairs. He had sold enough lots to realize only "a few hundred dollars," and it was difficult to win the confidence of the people. "School must begin next fall," he said, "but if it is on a very small scale without [better] accommodations, it will not much improve conditions." He expressed appreciation for some gifts received: $42 from a donor in Minneapolis and a box of books from New York. A brother in New Hampshire and another in Indiana thought they could supply the organ and music books.[56]

In July 1903, a lengthy article by Lucas appeared, entitled "Our Work at Unicoi, Tenn." and a picture of the hotel building was included, captioned "A School for the Mountain Youth at Unicoi, Tenn." It was dated in March and reported on all aspects of the project. According to Lucas, their purpose was "to establish an institution where young men and women may receive, at the smallest possible cost, the best literary advantages with such Bible and industrial training as will fit them for the greatest usefulness, and especially as teachers and leaders for their people." Lots were available—"choice residence lots, 70 by 150 feet"—for $100, and good people were "urged to buy, build, and locate at Unicoi, help the work, and get the benefit of the climate and school." The school must open in the fall and there were many needs, including the opportunity for advanced studies that would attract the very best students. The hotel

---

[55] *The Morning Star*, April 9, 1903, 4.
[56] *The Morning Star*, April 30, 1903, 4.

and sixteen-room boarding-house must be extensively repaired as residences, respectively, for female and male boarding students, and a new building "with at least five recitation rooms, halls, and chapel" was a pressing need.[57] Immediately following the article was an announcement by Z. A. Space, for the Conference Board, that Mrs. C. C. H. Aldrich, of Buffalo, New York, wife of Rev. Schuyler Aldrich, had donated $5,000 for the school at Unicoi. Space urged others to follow her lead and praised Lucas.[58]

An August issue included a lengthy report which had been given by Lucas to a recent meeting of the Conference Board. Contracts for lots had been closed to the amount of $430, although only ten percent of the amount had actually been collected, with the balance owed. He was "disappointed" in the rate of sales. The new church, of twenty-six members, was sponsoring preaching at five different places and Sunday schools at three places in the vicinity. Two ministers from the Jack's Creek Free Will Baptist Association, E. W. Akard and D. L. Howell, had relocated to Unicoi and were assisting in that work. Many repairs on buildings and fences were needed. In the spring past, Lawrence had fitted out one room in the office building, "with furniture of his own make, and taught a small local school, charging regular tuition." But no school "of good grade" had been started and that had contributed to a general discouragement of the people. Even so, "a school this fall is an absolute necessity, and announcements should have been out a month ago." But he could make only temporary arrangements to accommodate perhaps a hundred students, most of them local, and he had not felt free to take action on his own before meeting with the Board. "Unless a fund can be provided [by the Board] from sources unknown to me, teachers must work for love, and take their pay on the other side of Jordan." The question, he said, was whether the Board would "take the matter in hand, select a faculty, look out for their support, and start a school which will meet demands and command respect." Or would they leave it to Lucas and others to do this on their own, in which case "the school must be on a very small scale" and disappointing. The report concluded with a full accounting of receipts and

---

[57] *The Morning Star*, July 30, 1903, 4-5.
[58] *The Morning Star*, July 30, 1903, 5.

disbursements from January 1, 1902, to February 1, 1903, when the work had been under the Commission, and from February 1 to July 7, 1903, when under the Conference Board. At the end of each period, more than $800 remained unpaid to agent Lucas, and for the period under the Board no compensation for his services had been paid or set.[59]

Apparently, in response to Lucas's appeal to the Conference Board, in July 1903 the Board appointed a committee of its own—Field Secretary H. M. Ford, Z. A. Space, and H. S. Myers—"to have charge of the school, devise plans for raising money, satisfy claims, and develop the enterprise and report to the Board." A September issue included a report by Ford, who had visited Unicoi in the middle of July "according to instructions." He reported that Unicoi "is not even a town, but a railroad station with scarcely twenty houses within a mile of the spot," a "country place, in a wide and delectable valley surrounded by majestic peaks. ... beautiful for situation, and the joy of the whole eastern end of Tennessee." He said that Lucas, the financial agent and principal of the school,

> for the past six weeks has been on horseback among the mountains of Tennessee and North Carolina visiting Yearly Meetings and Free Baptist homes, seeking students, and selling these lots to mountaineers. Brother Lucas is a hardy, large-boned, vigorous mountaineer himself, stands six feet three, a giant in stature, and is made to order for this special work now in hand. He is a man of strong character and educated in a Southern college.

Ford also spoke of G. W. Lawrence as "a worthy counterpart, a man of great faithfulness, great patience, a tireless worker with an eye to business, and a nature capable of large sacrifice for the cause." There would be a school this year, he said, which would be small but a beginning, and he urged donors to respond to the needs.[60]

This seems the appropriate place to insert a few words about George W. Lawrence, who would subsequently become an important figure in the developing story. His Find-A-Grave memorial includes a brief biographical sketch. He was born in England in 1854 and brought by his parents (John and Mary Hob-

---

[59] *The Morning Star*, August 6, 1903, 5, 9, 13.
[60] *The Morning Star*, September 10, 1903, 4-5.

gin; George and his brother, Richard, changed their last name while students at Hillsdale) to America when he was one year old. He completed an A. B. degree from Hillsdale College, in Michigan, in 1880, and was principal of a school at Jellico, Tennessee, from 1883-1888. Shot "by a drunken hireling for his temperance principles," he spent several years in recovery in Illinois, Michigan, and Iowa and then returned to Tennessee. Later, he taught mathematics at Lincoln Memorial University.[61] But nothing is said of his time at schools with Lucas, or of the conflict that developed between them.

On October 2, 1903, the Executive Committee of the Conference Board met at the *Morning Star* publishing house in Boston. The special committee for the Unicoi school reported. They had met and taken a number of actions, including paying Lucas's back salary up until February 1, 1903, and deferring "until further information is at hand" any salary from then until August 1. They would pay him $600 per year as principal, the money to come from the income from the farm. He himself could farm and turn in one third of the income to the denomination, but he must otherwise devote full time to the work of the school. He and Lawrence would have free rent and free gardens. They defined how lots should be sold and urged that this be done "as soon as possible." Meanwhile, Conference Treasurer Arthur Given was requested to make the August payment of $8,000, and a ministers' institute was scheduled at Unicoi for the week beginning November 17, 1903.[62]

The issue for November 12 included a set of six questions, asked by a subscriber to the paper, about the project. Lucas answered briefly. A fall session had begun on August 17 and some seventy-six students had enrolled to date. The two teachers were graduates of Hillsdale College—I assume the Lawrences. Grades being taught were from first to eighth, the first year of high school. There were both local and boarding students. He observed that there was little

---

[61] https://www.findagrave.com/memorial/57664745/george-w-lawrence (RLV). A notice about the shooting, in the Garden City, KS *Sentinel and Cultivator*, June 6, 1888, 6 (RLV), said "The attack is supposed to be in revenge for the aggressive temperance work of the missionaries," explaining that Lawrence was serving the American Missionary Association at the school at Jellico. The (Danville) *Kentucky Advocate* for November 2, 1888, 1 (RLV), named the shooter as J. M. Chandler and reported his release on a $1,000 bond after being "confined for several months in the Knoxville jail."

[62] *The Morning Star*, October 15, 1903, 4.

advertising and the accommodations were poor; furthermore, public schools were in session some of the time. Even so, some other families were expected in January, four homes were under construction, and a ministers' institute would be held November 17-23 under the supervision of Secretary Ford.[63] Indeed, Field Secretary Ford wrote his next "notes" for the paper from Unicoi on November 16, and in them he spoke of the General Conference's indebtedness, which had been increased by the payment of $6,000 more than had been received for the school property.[64]

A month later, Ford reported on his time at Unicoi for the institute. There was "a fair attendance of preachers and laymen" from four different associations and large, orderly crowds at night, listening intently. Father Woolsey and his wife and son T. H. Woolsey had been in attendance. On Monday, they had "wrestled with the problems of the school." Nine lots had been sold and other sales were expected, four houses had been built and another was in progress, there were thirty-four students at the time and others continually coming, Lawrence and wife were teaching and Lucas "looking after the affairs of the school." "The prospects are brightening and from the signs of the times there is a future for us. ... There is a growing interest in the school on the part of the people in the South." While he was there, one woman had ridden a mule fifty miles to arrange for the schooling of four young people from her area. It was time for Free Baptists to respond to the needs, he said: "This school year must surely see the school paid for."[65] Two weeks later, the paper carried a map of the immediate area, showing Unicoi surrounded by six associations of Free Will Baptist churches: the John Wheeler to the Northeast, Clinch Valley to the Northwest, the Union to

[65] *The Morning Star*, December 3, 1903, 4.

the West, the Toe River to the East, the Jack's Creek to the Southeast, and the French Broad to the Southwest. The caption indicated that the farthest church was just seventy-five miles from Unicoi "in a straight line."[66]

The 1904 minutes of the General Conference show that the Committee of the Conference Board had been active, each having visited Unicoi at least once and Ford three times. With Lucas in charge, managing but not teaching, the school at Unicoi had opened on August 15, 1903, with 65 students. It was expected to begin the 1904-05 term with 90 students.[67]

Lucas himself would say, later, that he had been reluctant to begin the school under the circumstances. Dr. Ball, he said, had "suggested that no school should be started until we could start one that would command respect and support." But G. W. Lawrence, who had been with Lucas in the school at Midway and was qualified to teach, was present and Lucas permitted him to teach a school for what he could realize, and it ran for about six years. However, it had been at the level of the lower public school grades and, by Lucas's implications, not what he had envisioned. He said that "the grade of the school was so low I could not ask for further aid [from the General Conference]."[68] It may be that there is something of "sour grapes" and self-justification in Lucas's observations, but we cannot know enough now to speak confidently about that.

At the time, however, Lucas continued to promote the project among the Free Will Baptists of the North. On January 20, 1904, he reported small gifts from Rhode Island and Massachusetts; and that the winter in Appalachia was the worst in ten years. He could not ride his horse over the mountains because the trails were "impassable on account of ice."[69]

At any rate, when the 1904 session of the General Conference convened, September 6-11 at Hillsdale, Michigan, the school had been in existence for one year. The outlook was cautious but optimistic. T. H. Woolsey, physician-layman

---

[66] *The Morning Star*, December 24, 1903, 5. Perhaps it did not matter that a person could not possibly travel there "in a straight line."

[67] Minutes, General Conference of Free Baptists, 1904, 22-23, 52. The figures do not differ significantly from what has been reported, above, from a different source. Apparently, students came and went, making enrollment fluid.

[68] J. W. Lucas, *Unicoi: Some Inside History* (Unicoi, TN: self-published, Sept. 24, 1915), 3-4.

[69] *The Morning Star*, January 28, 1904, 4.

son of Union Association father W. B. Woolsey, was the Union's delegate and Lucas was again present.[70] Field Secretary Ford's report had a lengthy section headed "Unicoi," which included this:

> The Unicoi school is yet in its infancy, in fact, it is hardly yet born. It is certainly in the experimental stage. It is not yet certain that a school such as we have hoped for can be made there. The people for whom the school is intended are not much given to the notion of an education; a few are, *a few*, and they are very much in earnest and are very serious about it, but the great bulk are satisfied to be exactly what their fathers were. ... Brother Lucas is fearful that northern people will get discouraged before the school makes any showing, for the making of the school is not the work of one year or two years; it is the work of ten or twenty years. We have not only to make a school, we must at the same time create a desire for a school and a thirst for education.[71]

I think I detect, in this description, something of the Northerners' condescending attitude toward their Southern, or at least their Appalachian, brethren, but that may not be fair. At any rate, Ford went on to describe more specifically the situation of the school itself.

> Professor Lucas is agent to sell the land and is our representative head at Unicoi. He has found no time to teach. ... On October 16 money must be forthcoming to make the last payment on the mortgage debt. We have hunted high and low, braved blizzards and waded through seas of snow to secure the money, but we have not secured it yet. ...
>
> The free school, which lasts from four to six months, is taught under the supervision of J. W. Lucas, our principal, and in conjunction with Unicoi, and last year we had about seventy students.[72]

There were already some signs of concern. The report of the Home Missions Department (under which the school was apparently operating) showed expenses of $2,000 more, for Unicoi, than had been received.[73] The Corresponding Secretary said, "At the close of the financial year the Unicoi account

---

[70] Minutes, General Conference of Free Baptists, 1904, 8, 22-23.
[71] Minutes, General Conference of Free Baptists, 1904, 56-57.
[72] Minutes, General Conference of Free Baptists, 1904, 56-57.
[73] Minutes, General Conference of Free Baptists, 1904, 31-34.

was overdrawn $7,929.11. ... The undertaking at Unicoi has called for a large expenditure."[74]

In particular, the final $4,500 payment on the property, due October 16, 1904, loomed large. The Finance Committee noted that the venture had no church behind it to take care of the payment, therefore "reliance is of necessity placed upon prompt contributions from the churches before the date of payment next month. Otherwise, money must be borrowed to meet the payment, and the home mission debt account be further increased." The Committee on Home Missions nonetheless recommended making the payment and "selling of the land not needed for school purposes as speedily as possible"; also that Field Secretary Ford proceed as soon as possible to secure gifts for this purpose before the note was due.[75]

Following the General Conference, at least three articles about the school at Unicoi appeared in the *Morning Star*. There were ninety students enrolled, "but mainly in the lower grades." Furthermore, provision had been made to support the school "this year," and pledges had been made to provide thirty-two desks for a classroom.[76]

By this time, it seems clear that Lucas was beginning to feel that the General Conference ought to be taking a more active role. His next article left no doubt. For one thing, he said he did not understand that any considerable part of the original goal to raise $50,000 "was to be raised in Tennessee or any other part of the South." Indeed, the inability of the people of the South to provide schools for themselves was the chief reason for involving the General Conference in the first place. The Mountain Educational Commission, he said, was "incorporated with a capital stock of a million good intentions—but no other available assets." He alone had been representing the Commission in attempting to raise the $50,000 in pledges—to be paid only when the whole amount had been pledged. ... He had not recently made excursions to raise funds beyond the Unicoi area, understanding that to be the responsibility of the Unicoi Committee [of

---

[74] Minutes, General Conference of Free Baptists, 1904, 39.
[75] Minutes, General Conference of Free Baptists, 1904, 126-27, 137.
[76] *The Morning Star*, September 29, 1904, 4.

the Conference Board]. He hoped, at another time, to be able to call attention to "what might have been done under certain other conditions."[77]

A week later, an article entitled "Mountaineers of the South" appeared, submitted by the Reverend J. C. Stallard of Midway, Tennessee. He began by saying that those of the North and East simply did not understand what life was like for those in Appalachia. There were fifteen or twenty thousand children in reach of Unicoi, he said, and something must be done for them now.[78]

The Outlook in the Region

Meanwhile, in Tennessee, the Union Association was pleased with the initial success. The minutes of the 1903 session include a report from its Committee on Education:

> This is the day of progress. The times demand education. The uneducated must be drawers of water and hewers of wood, from choice, as ample facilities are now given to all that will make proper effort to educate themselves. We are glad our people are becoming aroused to the importance of this subject. We note with pride the progress of the Unicoi enterprise. The General Conference has our sincere thanks for its interest in that school. As loyal Free Baptists we will talk, pray and work for that school and aid it with our means and patronage.

The 1904 report of the same committee included:

> We desire to call attention of our people, and all whom it may concern, to our Institution in Unicoi, and also tender our thanks to Rev. J. W. Lucas and brethren of the General Conference for such an institution at so great a cost ($18,500.00) for the purpose of educating our young people in this mountain country; and to say to all that such benevolence of the General Conference should not go by unheeded.

Again, in 1905:

> We would emphasize the importance to our mountain work of the efforts to build a first-class Free Baptist School at Unicoi. Let us pledge to that School

---

[77] *The Morning Star*, October 6, 1904, 4.
[78] *The Morning Star*, October 13, 1904, 4.

our prayers, sympathies and moral and financial support. Put your boys and girls into that school and help to make it the school we need.

One should remember that the school was intended for all Free Will Baptists in the Appalachian area. I have cited the Union Association minutes so much because we have more of those minutes, but the 1905 minutes of the Jack's Creek Association showed a similar attitude. The report on Education said, "We should use every faculty within our reach for the education of our children. The public schools should have our hearty support. The Unicoi school is peculiarly our own; let us pray and work for it, put our children there and encourage the management to make it the school we need." Lucas was present and named to draft a resolution of thanks to the General Conference.

Lucas apparently was still somewhat optimistic at this point. In *The Morning Star* for 1905, there are three different communications from him, two of them reporting on the school and the other on the situation at his church. In the issue for February 2, he reported the purchase of "thirty-two new patent double desks at a net cost of $94.67," made possible by friends, and expressed gratitude for "barrels and boxes" of books, toys, and clothing sent from New England, concluding, "Amid serious discouragements we are cheered by the interest and sympathy of distant friends."[79] In the fall, he reported that school opened on August 14, and forty-six pupils had entered. He had attended two annual meetings in Tennessee and three in North Carolina. All of them endorsed the school and promised to patronize it.[80]

His optimism was short lived.

Sliding Into Failure

It is hard to know, from our vantage point a century later, whether the school at Unicoi, which completed its second term in 1904-05, was doomed from the start or failed as a result of indifferent management or other problems.

---

[79] *The Morning Star*, February 2, 1905, 4.
[80] *The Morning Star*, October 5, 1905, 16.

Lucas himself would write later, looking back: "Possibly the ideal of the Educational Commission could not have been realized. It never had an opportunity."[81]

From the beginning, the leaders of the General Conference were essentially dependent, by long distance, on Lucas. Apparently, both they and he were unsuccessful in cultivating enough donations to cover the cost of the property or sustain the work. The most notable contribution obtained was from Mrs. C. C. H. Aldrich in New York, a gift of $5,000, apparently made in early 1903. Lucas, in his later defensive pamphlet, observed that the attempt to cultivate donors in the North, including further gifts from Mrs. Aldrich, was met by hesitation when the potential donors learned that the people in Appalachia were doing so little to help themselves.[82] For that matter, resources in the mountains were limited, even when considering the broader Free Will Baptist constituency in East Tennessee, Western North Carolina, and Southwestern Virginia.[83]

A number of lots of the original land were sold; Ulis Miller, writing in the 1990s, reported that he counted some forty-five deeds that had been issued by the General Conference, for tracts ranging from one to eight acres. One of these was for five acres, sold to E. W. Akard in 1906 for $350.[84] Akard would subsequently become one of the litigants involved. Apparently most of the proceeds went toward the debt for the original purchase price. But the prospects for more such sales must not have been all that bright, given that the General Conference soon arranged to sell much of the land to Lucas.

Furthermore, the effort at Unicoi soon suffered from serious division. Lucas would call this "the greatest hindrance to this work."[85] Perhaps this is what General Conference Field Secretary H. M. Ford meant in a terse and otherwise unexplained statement published in *The Morning Star* for March 8, 1906: "Unicoi too has claimed a little more attention than usual on account of complica-

---

[81] Lucas, 6.
[82] Lucas, 7.
[83] There were several of these associations during all or some of the time of the school, including the Toe River, John Wheeler, Jack's Creek, Unicoi, Watauga, and Clinch Valley. But we do not have minutes enough from most of these to contribute to the story.
[84] Ulis Miller, *History of the Jack's Creek Free Will Baptist Association* (Burnsville, NC: Yancey Graphics, 1994), 8.
[85] Lucas, 7.

tions."[86] Even so, Ford was soon to express some optimism; in the issue for July 5, 1906, he said, "Unicoi is going to have a good school next year. Prof. Lucas is stirring among the people and printed matter is to be scattered giving information about the school."[87] But perhaps he was simply "whistling past the graveyard." That all was not well was indicated shortly thereafter in the same publication in a statement issued by the committee for the school. Among other things, they said that in view of early expressions of desire for a school at Unicoi they had not felt "free to report for or against the wisdom of supporting a school." They recommended that the matter be referred to the Executive Committee, advising "that a personal conference with Mr. J. W. Lucas be had as soon as [they] could bring it about."[88] The committee consisted of Joseph W. Mauck, Alfred Williams Anthony, and Rivington D. Lord.

By this time Lucas apparently felt that the responsibility to administer and support a school was no longer primarily his. In June of 1907, a short and curious note from him, entitled "Thanks," appeared in *The Morning Star*. He thanked some contributors from New York and Boston for gifts of clothing and added, without explanation: "We have been waiting and hoping for some friend to tell through the paper that Unicoi is not dead but taking on new life."[89] Unless I overlooked it, there is no other report on the school at Unicoi in the 1907 issues of that denominational publication.

Whatever the circumstances, the initial success of the school was soon followed by a period of struggle and decline. When the triennial General Conference met again in 1907, the minutes also show that there had been a great deal of activity related to Unicoi since the 1904 session, much of it indicating problems and offering little in the way of explanation.

—Conference Board, July 1905: "Warrantee deeds were authorized for certain lots at Unicoi. The agent at Unicoi was directed not to promise warrantee deeds unless directed to do so by the Board."[90]

---

[86] *The Morning Star*, March 8, 1906, 2.
[87] *The Morning Star*, July 5, 1906, 12.
[88] *The Morning Star*, August 30, 1906, 12-13.
[89] *The Morning Star*, June 20, 1907, 12.
[90] Minutes, General Conference of Free Baptists, 1907, 20.

—Conference Board, July 1905: The Unicoi committee was retained and asked to investigate certain conditions at Unicoi.[91]

—Executive Committee, August 1905: N. C. Brackett asked to look into the situation at Unicoi.[92]

—Executive Committee, December 1905: Accepted Brackett's report on Unicoi.[93]

—Executive Committee, February 1906: "A proposition from Prof. Lucas concerning Unicoi property was read. The treasurer was authorized to go to Unicoi and to make arrangements for formation of a local organization for the school."[94]

—Executive Committee, March 1906: Treasurer reported a contract entered into with Prof. Lucas. Authority was given to execute warrantee deeds for certain lots at Unicoi.[95]

—Executive Committee, May 1906: Appropriated $200 for help at Unicoi. Voted to publish, in *The Morning Star*, facts concerning the so-called Unicoi Mission Board.[96]

—Executive Committee, September 1906: "Appropriated $400 to help maintain the School at Unicoi, not more than $200 this year and $200 next, with the understanding that General Conference will be under no further financial obligations to the school. The matter of employing teachers was left with Prof. Lucas consulting with President Mosher."[97]

Perhaps the most significant item appeared in the report of the General Conference Corresponding Secretary, Arthur Given:

> The Unicoi land, after reserving 150 acres with the buildings, was sold to Prof. J. W. Lucas on time. He has yet to pay on this deal $1,138.35. This will reduce the indebtedness incurred by the General Conference to $4,957.22. If it

---

[91] Minutes, General Conference of Free Baptists, 1907, 21-22.
[92] Minutes, General Conference of Free Baptists, 1907, 22.
[93] Minutes, General Conference of Free Baptists, 1907, 22.
[94] Minutes, General Conference of Free Baptists, 1907, 22.
[95] Minutes, General Conference of Free Baptists, 1907, 23.
[96] Minutes, General Conference of Free Baptists, 1907, 23. If anything about this was published in *The Morning Star* for 1906, I was not able to find it.
[97] Minutes, General Conference of Free Baptists, 1907, 25. George F. Mosher was First Vice President of the General Conference in 1907.

is thought best to accept the offer, Prof. Lucas agrees to pay the amount of this balance for the remaining land not including the hotel and some three or four acres of land. This will leave the hotel and a small campus for a school. This reserved property is well worth all that has been contributed for the school.[98]

This appears to mean, first, that all the original property that had not been sold as lots to individuals, except for 150 acres, was sold to Lucas and he still owed $1,138.35 for that. Second, he had the opportunity to purchase the remaining 150 acres—except for the hotel and its "three or four acres" that included a few other buildings—for $4,957.22, the amount that the General Conference still owed on the original purchase price. Third, the General Conference had not given up the idea of having a school on the property. To them, the sale of most of the property was for the purpose of repaying the original purchase price.

One tends to wonder about the motivation of Lucas. Was he taking an insider's advantage of the opportunity to increase his own holdings? Did the General Conference agree to this only to get out of the indebtedness for the property? In his own defense, Lucas would later write that he had just three choices: to let the property be sold to the highest bidder and run the risk of its going out of Free Will Baptist hands; to let his enemies—referring to G. W. Lawrence and associates—get the land; or to buy it himself. He chose the latter, he said, as "the least of the evils," after urging General Conference not to sell.[99] Whether Lucas was being entirely sincere or self-serving in this defense cannot now be determined.

By 1908, the school had ceased to function. The divisions became open and volatile.

Crisis: The First Lawsuit

Union Association minutes during this period also indicate that serious problems were developing. In 1906, a "Committee on the Unicoi High School" strongly urged support for it as "our own Institution." In 1908, the Committee on Education report referred to the effort of some to create division over the property, reminding: "The Gen'l Conf., has at Unicoi reserved for school pur-

---

[98] Minutes, General Conference of Free Baptists, 1907, 29-30.
[99] Lucas, 4-5.

poses about $10,000.00 worth of property which it is ready to turn over to us when we satisfy them that we can maintain a school." The 1909 report included: "Resolved that we request our people to take hold of the property according to the proposition of the General Conference."[100] In 1910, the Committee on Education professed to be "yet interested" in Unicoi and recommended that everyone hold ready "as soon as present litigation ceases to accept the very liberal proposition of General Conference in regard to that property and build a Free Baptist School at the earliest possible date."

The Union minutes, however, fall short of revealing the full measure of the storm that was rising in the crisis year of 1908, when—as far as I could find—the school was not even mentioned in the pages of *The Morning Star*. The minutes of the Jack's Creek Association are more helpful. There we find a pointed resolution in the report of its Committee on Education:

> Whereas during the years 1902-1908 the Mountain Educational Commission and its successor, the General Conference of Free Baptists did solicit and collect from many Free Baptists of North Carolina and Tennessee, certain sums of money for the alleged purpose of establishing an industrial school of high grade for the said Free Baptists and
>
> Whereas Mrs. C. C. H. Aldrich of Buffalo, N. Y., and many other people of the Northern States gave several thousand dollars to the General Conference of Free Baptists for the aforesaid purpose and
>
> Whereas said General Conference placed the control of said school enterprise and the lands purchased for the establishment of such a school completely in the hands of one person viz: J. W. Lucas whom years of trial prove to be both unable and unwilling to establish a school and
>
> Whereas said General Conference deeded Nov. 1907 all the aforesaid land not then sold, except about three acres to the said J. W. Lucas and has given him control of the hotel and Block 7, thus diverting all the money from the purpose for which it was given, and,
>
> Whereas we believe a radical change in the policy of our school enterprise is urgent, and
>
> Whereas a corporation, styled the Unicoi Collegiate Institute, consisting of D. L. Howell, E. W. Akard, G. W. Lawrence, W. P. Knowling and S. G.

---

[100] *The Morning Star*, November 4, 1909, 13, included a brief report of the 1909 session of the Union and included this resolution. No other references to the school at Unicoi occur in the 1909 issues of this publication. There is a brief report of the 1909 session of the Unicoi Association in the issue for October 21, 1909, 13, and nothing else about the work in Tennessee, except for a longer article entitled "Work in the South" (December 23, 1909, 12) by J. C. Stallard of Midway, Tennessee, of a more general nature.

Street was formed and duly registered at Erwin and Nashville, Tenn. January 2 and 4, 1908, whose sole purpose is to foster said school enterprise, therefore

Resolved, That we approve of the above corporation as our legal representative and sanction the efforts of said corporate body to secure possession of aforesaid property for school purposes as originally intended. We wish to place ourselves on record as being in favor of Christian Education and a better educated ministry. We earnestly urge our people to take forward steps in educational work.

Resolved, That we are thoroughly convinced from Professor Lucas' own statements and conduct that he did our cause an injustice in buying the Unicoi school property from the General Conference and thus diverting it from its original purpose,

Therefore we pledge our loyalty and support to the corporation at Unicoi, Tenn., styled the Unicoi Collegiate Institute, with the aforesaid persons as corporators [sic], in securing possession of said property and trying to carry out the original purpose.

Interestingly, Lucas was personally present for this session of the Jack's Creek Association but was not otherwise involved. This was in sharp contrast to the 1905 session of the same body three years earlier, when he was present, welcomed, and played an active role, including writing a resolution of appreciation to the General Conference.

This 1908 resolution refers to the forming of a corporation entitled the Unicoi Collegiate Institute. Indeed, such a corporation was registered on January 2, 1908, in Erwin, and on January 4, 1908, in Nashville. The charter indicates that the particular purposes of the corporation were "to organize, operate, maintain an institution of learning at or near Unicoi ... under the control and patronage of the Free Baptist Denomination." It provided for management of the institution by a Board of Trustees, three fourths of them members of the Free Baptist denomination in Unicoi County. They would have power "to prescribe the courses of study to be pursued," "to confer degrees," to provide for boarding students, and to exercise reasonable discipline of students.[101]

---

[101] A copy of the charter was obtained from the Tennessee State Library and Archives and is in the FWB Historical Collection.

The formation of this corporation appears to have followed directly from an action of the General Conference Board in October 1907, in the form of a resolution:

> That the proper officers of this General Conference be, and they are hereby authorized to execute in the name of General Conference a quit claim deed of Block 7, including the Hotel and some three and one-half acres of land connected with it, at Unicoi, Tennessee, to the Trustees of the Unicoi Collegiate Institute, when such a corporation has been legally organized for educational purposes, the deed to contain a condition that when said property shall not be used for educational purposes by a corporation controlled by members of the Free Baptist denomination, said deed shall be void and the property revert to General Conference.[102]

Interestingly, many of the incorporators were involved in the lawsuit that was to follow against Lucas and the General Conference. One of the incorporators, E. W. Akard, a minister in the Jack's Creek Association, was among those who had bought a parcel of the original property: five acres for $350.[103] Another, G. W. Lawrence, was the main leader of the opposition to Lucas, one whom Lucas referred to frequently as his enemy.

Another 1908 event was closely related: namely, the formation of the United Association of Mountain Free Will Baptists on October 29-31, 1908. The minutes claimed representation from the Jack's Creek, French Broad, Toe River, and Unicoi associations, the John Wheeler Yearly Meeting, and the Greene County Quarterly Meeting. Lucas would say that only three of the delegates were "legal" and implied that this organization came into existence to oppose him.[104] It does appear likely that it was organized because of the school issue. Its major item of business was to adopt a resolution similar to that which the Jack's Creek Association had already adopted in September, quoted above.[105]

---

[102] This action is not included in the report of the Conference Board for October 1907, as found in Minutes of the General Conference, 1907, 27-28; or 1910, 19-21. It is cited here from the Complainants' Brief and Assignment of Errors before the Court of Civil Appeals, May 1918, 10 (hereafter Complainants' Brief).
[103] Miller, 8.
[104] Lucas, 9.
[105] We have minutes for this association only for 1908 and 1909. The (Marshall, NC) French Broad News for October 26, 1911, 5 (RLV), carried a brief notice about the fourth annual session, beginning October 19, but included no information about business conducted.

G. W. Lawrence was clerk of this new formation and was probably the author of the resolution,[106] which was even more critical of Lucas. It said he had "betrayed the trust placed in him" and that there was "no further hope of doing anything in an educational or religious way under his leadership." He had "almost from the beginning sought to discourage [the school's] growth" and had desired only to "build himself up and secure the Unicoi property for himself for a mere pittance." Furthermore, the General Conference had consistently refused to investigate thoroughly and "shown itself unable through its agent to manage such an enterprise. In proof witness the facts that the decline in outside patronage from 1903-4 to 1907 was from 22 to zero, and at the present time, Oct. 1908, their agent controls all the property and there is no school."

In this way, those who organized the new association accomplished two things. They approved the formation of the Unicoi Collegiate Institute as their legal representative and sanctioned "the efforts of that corporate body to secure possession of the Unicoi property for school purposes as originally intended."

Most important, a lawsuit was filed as "State of Tennessee ex rel, et al, vs. J. W. Lucas et al."[107] The "ex rel" apparently indicates that the officers of the state were acting in behalf of other complainants, named in the court documents as W. P. Knowling, E. W. Akard, G. W. Lawrence, S. G. Street, C. C. Deyton, J. C. Stallard, William Stallard, John Campbell, and H. E. Horton.[108] Four of these were among the five who incorporated as the Unicoi Collegiate Institute, but the suit was not in the name of that corporation.

The suit was apparently filed in late 1907, and its primary object was to stop the sale of the final 150 acres to Lucas by the General Conference, the "et al" (which means "and others") who were defendants with Lucas.[109]

This lawsuit got attention in the 1910 minutes of the General Conference, which includes information about actions taken by the Conference Board or Executive Committee since the 1907 session. In October 1907, the Conference Board had authorized the execution of deeds involved in "carrying out the

---

[106] Lucas, 9, says Lawrence admitted as much under oath.
[107] A copy of the basic records of this suit is in the Free Will Baptist Historical Collection.
[108] Above Horton's initials, someone has written "(W. F.)," perhaps indicating that H. E. was not correct.
[109] Complainants' Brief, 2.

agreement with Mr. J. W. Lucas in reference to the property at Unicoi."[110] But in December of the same year the Executive Committee asked the president and the corresponding secretary "to carefully examine the condition of our interests in Unicoi, Tenn., and the treasurer to use caution in carrying out the action of the Board."[111] In April 1908, the Executive Committee instructed the recording secretary to call a special meeting of the Conference Board, among other things, to take action concerning "the disposition of property at Unicoi, Tenn."[112] In November 1908, the Executive Committee appointed President Mauck and Dr. Given "to represent General Conference in the suit concerning Unicoi property."[113] And in July 1909, the Conference Board instructed the president and the treasurer of General Conference "to employ counsel in the case of G. W. Lawrence and others relative to real estate at Unicoi."[114] If there was any reference to this legal action in the pages of *The Morning Star* in 1908 or 1909, I did not find it.

At each stage of the suit, first heard in the Chancery Court of Unicoi County at Erwin, the rulings were in favor of Lucas and the General Conference. This was the "present litigation" referred to in the 1910 minutes of the Union Association, cited above. The "Chancellor and Master" of the Court made his ruling on August 9, 1910. The complainants appealed to the State Supreme Court in Knoxville, which sent the case back to Erwin in September. The matter was not completely laid to rest until September 1, 1911. The complainants were required to pay all costs, and the actions of Lucas and the General Conference in selling the 150 acres to him were sustained. Among other things, the Court ruled that the remaining hotel building and three and a half acres were "sufficient upon which to conduct the school."[115]

A December 13, 1911, letter from Lucas to Joseph W. Mauck—president of Hillsdale College in Michigan and also president of the General Conference of Free Baptists—confirms the outcome of the suit. Although the merger with Northern Baptists had been consummated, the General Conference continued

---

[110] Minutes, General Conference of Free Baptists, 1910, 20.
[111] Minutes, General Conference of Free Baptists, 1910, 25.
[112] Minutes, General Conference of Free Baptists, 1910, 26.
[113] Minutes, General Conference of Free Baptists, 1910, 27.
[114] Minutes, General Conference of Free Baptists, 1910, 23.
[115] Complainants' Brief, 2.

to function as a legal entity and was involved with many of the matters that carried over after the merger, including the Unicoi situation. Among other things in the letter, Lucas said he was "sorry the mischief of Lawrence & Co. did not cease with the failure of their lawsuit." He concluded: "The outlook for a school in Unicoi is not flattering."[116]

Trouble in the Mountains

There was apparently no school at Unicoi from 1908 until 1913. Talmadge McNabb, in the 1985 article already cited, said that the local Unicoi people felt they had been gypped out of their money and school, adding that Lucas was "naturally but perhaps unfairly blamed for the whole affair." Some of McNabb's boyhood had been spent in Unicoi, and he had read the 1908 minutes of the United Mountain Association, which I have quoted above.

This fits generally with Lucas's later statement that the school ran "about six years," and his claim in the same place that sometimes he had taught classes "to one or two pupils."[117] Even if he were exaggerating the smallness for his own reasons, the picture was not bright and the end of the school must not have been unexpected.

Paul Woolsey regarded the merger of the General Conference with Northern Baptists, in 1910-11, as the final blow to this effort,[118] but there was much more to it than that. Bitter division had developed between Lucas and G. W. Lawrence, who had been associated with Lucas in the school at Midway and had come with him to Unicoi. No references indicate the *nature* of their differences; this might have been either cause or effect of the decline of the school—or some of both. Regardless, both men gathered others to their side of the affair and serious division developed.

There are other indications in the 1910 minutes of the General Conference that the trouble between Lucas and G. W. Lawrence had spilled over to interrupt the Free Will Baptist fellowship in East Tennessee. Earlier, perhaps in

---

[116] This and other letters to or from Mauck are in the "Mauck correspondence" (1911-1934) in the Free Will Baptist Historical Collection.

[117] Lucas, 5-6.

[118] Paul Woolsey, *God, A Hundred Years, and a Free Will Baptist Family* (Chuckey, TN: Union Free Will Baptist Association, 1949), 104.

1906, another association of churches had been formed, named the Unicoi Association of Free Baptists.[119] It was apparently organized without any objections by the Union Association, as indicated in the Union minutes for 1906. Lucas represented the Unicoi Association to the General Conference in 1907, but in 1910 Lawrence represented it—but was not seated, at first, because of protests received by the Executive Committee.

A Second Effort

The General Conference had not given up all hope of a school at Unicoi. The Mauck correspondence makes this clear—although it may indicate that they had given up on Lucas's management. In Lucas's December 1911 letter, cited above, he said he had sent a cut of the building to A. A. Myers, whom he knew had previously had some success in raising funds for schools. Perhaps Lucas had been asked by Myers or Mauck to do this. Myers had visited G. W. Lawrence in Unicoi. Lucas had shown Myers over the building. Furthermore, Lucas had heard a rumor that Myers, G. W. Lawrence (who "has been fighting our work"), and Lawrence's brother-in-law L. V. Dodge of Berea, Kentucky (who, he said, was moving into Lawrence's house in Unicoi), were going to try to start a school. He asked Mauck—sarcastically, no doubt—if he didn't think Myers would be in an awkward position trying to work in a school under the conditions.

Seven months later, July 10, 1912, Mauck wrote Lucas saying he chaired a committee charged to propose to the General Conference some disposition of the Unicoi property. He asked if Lucas had any plan to propose and said he had also written Myers for suggestions. Although he acknowledged that things were too divided for Myers or Lawrence to be successful, he allowed that if Myers could come up with a plan he thought the General Conference would convey the property (the building and the three and a half acres) to that organization. But he thought the three and a half acres were not enough and wondered if Lucas could donate or lease some acreage adjoining the part owned by General Conference. Whether Mauck was being serious or whimsical is hard to say.

---

[119] We have no minutes of this association before 1917.

Lucas answered, promptly, on July 12, 1912. He suggested three possibilities for the building: (1) some physicians might purchase it and establish a sanitarium; (2) the Presbyterians might trade another property where "we"—Free Will Baptists—are strong; (3) a school similar to that at Cairo might be established if funding could be found.[120] "There is no demand ... for an ordinary school at Unicoi," he said, observing that the small prospect for this, ten years earlier, had now been lost, and anyone trying to sell the idea of an ordinary school was deceived or deceiving. He knew the situation locally better than anyone advising Mauck and did not share Mauck's confidence in Myers. Should Lawrence, Myers, and Dodge start a school it would not be to Free Baptists' benefit or patronage. Lawrence just wanted the property, said Lucas, and the lawsuit should have settled that he was out. Interestingly, Lucas's family were using a few rooms of the house without any contract, and he expressed a willingness to lease it for making needed repairs.[121] He said nothing about Mauck's suggestion that he donate or lease some more of the land for a school.

On July 24, 1912, A. W. Anthony, Corresponding Secretary and Treasurer of the General Conference, wrote Mauck, perhaps in response to an inquiry from him, that Lucas still owed $750 of a $1,000 note due January 1, 1912; $1,000 due January 1, 1913; and $900 due January 1, 1914. (This was on the last 150 acres that Lucas had agreed to purchase.)

On August 15, 1912, Rivington D. Lord, a member of the General Conference Board, wrote Mauck to say that he approved his wise suggestion regarding affairs at Unicoi and had written the same to Anthony. He hoped Professor Dodge would take charge.

And so there appeared a flyer dated January 4, 1913, announcing that a school would begin on January 13 in the hotel building at Unicoi. The announcement was published by L. V. Dodge, and George G. Reeves would be the teacher. Among other things, the flyer said that a school should again be carried on in this property which "belongs to the General Conference of the Free Baptist denomination." Tuition was listed as: $1 per month for the first

---

[120] The General Conference sponsored a school for freed African-Americans at Cairo, Illinois.
[121] I *assume* this meant the hotel/school building, but it might refer to another house on the property. Miller, 7, has a picture of the "Lucas home," but it is not clear whether this is the building referred to here.

three grades; $1.25 for other common school grades, not including Algebra and Latin; and $1.50 for the higher grades.[122]

Mauck, then, on February 17, 1913, wrote to Anthony and Lord, enclosing copies of the flyer and observing that this struck him as "an excellent beginning."

On March 8, 1913, Lord wrote Mauck to commend him for his diplomatic handling of a "perplexing and delicate" situation. He agreed that Dodge's flyer represented a good beginning.

Not surprisingly, then, on March 19, 1913, Lucas wrote to Mauck in protest. He was "down and out" and Professor Dodge and the Lawrences were "in charge." He appeared to indicate that he did not so much oppose Dodge or Reeves the teacher but strenuously objected to the inclusion of the Lawrences as part of the work. They were the chief enemies of Lucas and the General Conference in earlier efforts and should have no place now, he said.

Nonetheless, the school at Unicoi was begun again, now led by L. V. Dodge who was the General Conference's new hope for success. In fact, the Conference was "lending" the property to G. W. Lawrence and his associates—the Unicoi Collegiate Institute—and was allowing them three years exactly, until January 1, 1916, to see if they could make a go of a school, with the understanding that if they did not succeed the General Conference would give up the project and make some other disposition of the building and its three and a half acres. If they did succeed, they would be able to take possession of the building and its small acreage for little or nothing.[123]

In the Union Association, as perhaps in other mountain associations, this news was welcomed. The Union minutes for 1913 include this report from a Committee on the Unicoi School, chaired by the new teacher himself:

> Whereas the Hotel building and 3 acres of land is still retained at Unicoi by the General Conference of Free Baptists and that said property is in the hands of the Mountain Free Baptists for a period of three years' to prove whether or not we want a school, therefore, be it resolved, that the membership of the Union Association use their money and influence to maintain the school enterprise begun at Unicoi.

---

[122] The Free Will Baptist Historical Collection has copies of this flyer.
[123] See the minutes of the General Conference of Free Baptists for 1917, 53.

> The outlook for the establishment of a denominational institution is intensely favorable and flattering. If after three years, we have shown, that we expect to support the school, the Hotel and grounds can be had for a very nominal sum, according to the statement of Pres. Jos. W Mauck of Hillsdale College, Chairman of the committee in charge; this statement being made to Prof L. V. Dodge, now custodian of the Unicoi property; otherwise it shall be dispensed of in any way the committee may deem wise. Geo. G. Reeves, Chairman.

The very same report was repeated in 1914 as the report of the Union's Education Committee. In 1915, however, with Lucas as chairman, the Education Committee report was somewhat different:

> We congratulate our people upon the excellent system of Public State Schools to which they have access. The poorest boy or girl in the land may now in these schools acquire a university or technical education. We do not know enough about the management, financial condition or work of the Unicoi school to return any suggestions in regard to it.

But in September 1916, although the three-year trial period had already expired on January 1—with little accomplished, apparently—the Union's Education Committee, now chaired by T. H. Woolsey, was more encouraging:

> We congratulate our people upon the excellent system of Public State Schools, to which they have access. We also recommend the school at Unicoi as being under good control by the teachers who are now in charge of the work at that place, and being more economical than it has in the past. Hoping its efforts may be crowned with success. We especially urge our people to support this work.

We do not have any records or reports that would indicate how Dodge and Reeves and those with them fared. What is clear is that they were not successful, at least not in the eyes of the General Conference—for whom "success" would have included a broad uniting behind the Unicoi Collegiate Institute and its efforts. Such unity did not develop. A brief filed by the attorneys for the General Conference in 1918 indicates the perspective of the Conference officials: "At the same time the Free Baptists at Unicoi were divided into factions, the school had been a failure, and it was clearly impossible to advance it or to build it up without funds, which could not be obtained in donations from others or gifts from the church."[124]

Consequently, at the end of the three-year trial, the General Conference decided to give up the project and sell the last of the property. The 1917 minutes of the Union Association include a very different Education Committee report:

> Since the Unicoi school is no longer a Free Baptist institution we recommend to all our people the new Baptist school recently opened at Tuscumseh [sic], Oklahoma, as a modern school that is strictly up-to-date.
> Furthermore, we recommend that our people exert their influence in securing Christian men and women in the Public School of the various communities in which they live.
> We desire to express our thanks to the Legislature of Tennessee for the enactment of a law requiring the reading of the Holy Bible in the Public Schools of our State.

I digress to add a note about one of those who came to help in the final effort at Unicoi. He was the Rev. Samra Smith, a North Carolina native who would afterward go from Unicoi to help with Tecumseh College in Oklahoma, a Free Will Baptist institution begun in 1917. I have told this story elsewhere.[125] In the Union Association minutes for 1913 his name appears: "On motion that every Free Baptist Church throw open their doors to Rev. Samra Smith as a soliciting agent for Unicoi School." In 1915, he and G. W. Lawrence were recognized as visitors to the Toe River Association from the Unicoi Association and they "gave talks ... about education and the school at Unicoi." The Toe River then endorsed the school. He was present there again in 1916. The 1917 minutes of the General Conference refer to him as "Prof. Samra Smith, recently of Unicoi, Tenn.," and as being on the faculty of Tecumseh College, "in charge of the departments of Chemistry and Biology."[126]

---

[124] Defendants' *Reply Brief for Free Baptists* in the Court of Civil Appeals, May term, 1918, 4 (hereafter *Reply Brief*).

[125] See Robert E. Picirilli, *Little Known Chapters in Free Will Baptist History* (Nashville, TN: Randall House, 2015), chapter 6.

[126] Minutes of the General Conference of Free Baptists, 1917, 53.

In 1917, then, the General Conference met again.[127] There is a concise summary of the Unicoi project included in the report of the Corresponding Secretary:

> The enterprise, which was launched at the session of General Conference at Harpers Ferry in 1901, for the establishment of a school for the Mountain Whites at Unicoi, Tennessee, has proved abortive. The local constituency, which should have been united in the support of the school, became hopelessly divided. Rev. J. W. Lucas, who awakened our confidence at various sessions of the General Conference, as he has reported the conditions of his own people, has died. Expert testimony, ... declares that the better way to help the people of those mountain sections is through improvement of the public schools, rather than by the establishment and maintenance of denominational schools. ... We have undertaken to withdraw from this work by selling the property, still remaining in our hands, to the authorities of the county, for the continuance of a school under state support, but we have been restrained by an injunction secured by one of the factions, under the leadership of Mr. G. W. Lawrence, to whom the property had been loaned for the testing of the possibilities of uniting the parties in a successful school. The time of the testing was limited to Jan. 1, 1916. Since that date we have been endeavoring to regain possession of the property; and the question of the dissolution of the injunction and all questions involved in the case have just been decided in favor of the General Conference. An appeal from this decision delays action.[128]

A Second Lawsuit

This report refers to the second lawsuit over the school at Unicoi. It was filed when the General Conference decided to sell the last piece of the property—the three and a half acres with the old hotel building—to Unicoi County for a public school. A tentative agreement to make this purchase was reached on January 3, 1916, when the Unicoi County Court passed a resolution to purchase the property for $3,000. On January 19, the Unicoi Collegiate Institute filed suit in an attempt to maintain the control of the property they had enjoyed since the beginning of 1913.[129]

---

[127] Once the merger was completed in 1910-11, the General Conference did not find it necessary to meet every three years. The next session after 1913 was in 1917.
[128] Minutes, General Conference of Free Baptists, 1917, 53.
[129] Complainants' Brief, 2; *Reply Brief*, 19

Their first step was to obtain a court order to stop the sale. A Writ of Injunction was issued by the Chancery Court at Erwin, accomplishing two things: (1) it prevented the General Conference from selling or otherwise disposing of the property, and Unicoi County from purchasing it; and (2) it enjoined both of them "from interfering with the complainant Unicoi Collegiate Institute in its possession and control of said property or further interfering with it in the conduct of said school, and in carrying out the trust for which said property was bought."[130]

This shows that the Unicoi Collegiate Institute was in fact occupying the building and conducting the school at the time, although we have no way of knowing how many students were enrolled. Whether L. V. Dodge was still managing the school is not indicated.

In filing suit, the Unicoi Collegiate Institute insisted that the funds for the property had been raised, and donations had been made—by Free Will Baptists of the mountain region and elsewhere—with the promise that it "would be perpetually used and maintained as a school, which would be conducted as a denominational school of the Free Will Baptist Church for the mountain people of the Appalachian region." They brought forward numerous persons, joining them in the suit, who had made donations and bore witness to what they had been given to understand.[131] For that reason, said the complainants, the manner in which the funds had been raised had created a "trust" that a "court of conscience" would recognize and enforce. Furthermore, the General Conference had "recognized the complainant Unicoi Collegiate Institute as a proper medium for carrying out the trust" by placing them in the position of conducting the school and putting them in possession of the property for that purpose. Consequently, the General Conference was acting in bad faith by attempting to oust the complainants from the property, in order to dispose of it and to divert the funds "from the purposes for which they were collected and invested."

---

[130] The court document quoted is actually dated in November 1915, in anticipation of the sale, but was apparently not filed until January 1916, after the Unicoi County Court resolved to purchase the property. A copy of this document is in the Free Will Baptist Historical Collection.

[131] *Reply Brief*, 4, states that there were twenty-six such donors added as co-complainants.

Indeed, the General Conference Board, in October 1907, had authorized its officers to deed the property to the Unicoi Collegiate Institute at such a time as it was "legally organized for educational purposes," which had no doubt spurred the incorporation of that body in January 1908. But, as Dr. A. W. Anthony would testify in the trial, they had failed to establish a strong school under denominational auspices, failed to unite opposing factions in Unicoi, and failed to secure adequate financial support. As a result, the Board had decided that the best course of action was to sell to Unicoi County for public school purposes.[132]

The case progressed along lines typical for such litigation, with various hearings, motions, deferrals, and the like. The decisive event was on August 8, 1917, when the Honorable Hal H. Haynes, Chancellor of the Chancery Court at Erwin, issued his decree in favor of the defendants, the General Conference of Free Baptists. His decree challenged all the contentions of "the Unicoi Collegiate Institute et al." The key parts of the ruling were as follows. The General Conference's deed to the property contained no stated conditions and neither an expressed nor an implied trust. It was not certain that any of the small sums contributed went into the purchase of the property; "they probably went to help canvass for, and to promote the church and educational venture, the unfortunate history of which, is portrayed in the record." And even if some of the gifts helped buy the property, there was no reason to assume the sort of trust the complainants were contending for. Even the substantial donation of Mrs. Aldrich (then deceased) was probably made to the General Conference and without expecting control over its use. Furthermore, the Court held that the General Conference might, indeed, be pursuing the wisest course in disposing of the property and terminating the effort for a school; "If it be 'a house divided against itself,' any sort of success is well nigh impossible."

The complainants gave immediate notice of intent to appeal the decree to the next term of the Tennessee State Supreme Court in Knoxville, in September 1917. Chancellor Haynes granted the appeal. The Supreme Court, in turn, sent the suit to the Court of Civil Appeals in Knoxville, where it was heard in May 1918 and again decided in favor of the General Conference and Unicoi County.

---

[132] *Reply Brief,* 9-10.

Finally, the case went back to the State Supreme Court later in 1918; again, the decision of the Chancery Court at Erwin was upheld.[133]

In the end, then, the General Conference abandoned the project, sold the final piece of the property to Unicoi County, and those who attempted to force the General Conference to maintain the school failed. In Miller's words, the Jack's Creek Association "was left with nothing but a sad experience, a lot of memories and all the court costs."[134] The disappointing story of the school at Unicoi was at an end—except that the Unicoi Board of Education converted the old hotel into a grammar school, and it continued to be used for such purposes until it burned on February 4, 1935.[135] Some, but not all, thought arson was involved.[136]

How do we evaluate this?

While any attempt to determine who was at fault in the failure of the Unicoi school project is almost entirely speculative at this point, I cannot help asking some questions and making some observations.

Of special interest is the fact that the General Conference of the Free Will Baptists of the North felt motivated to attempt to provide the means for a school for their southern brethren in Appalachia. On the surface, at least, that seems laudable. I assume they felt compassion, even if somewhat condescendingly, and sincerely wanted to help raise the educational level in the mountains, especially on behalf of those who would enter the ministry.

At the same time, their plans were not well made. They committed themselves to buy property before they had the means. They did not carefully explore the situation in Unicoi and the surrounding area. Perhaps they depended too much on one man. In some ways, then, the blame was partly theirs.

---

[133] Ulis Miller, 8, says that after the loss in Chancery Court in Erwin the complainants took the case to a "court of appeals" in Greeneville and after that to the Supreme Court in Knoxville. The voluminous records of the case before the Supreme Court (which I had copied in part) indicate, instead, the course I have described here. In Greeneville, I was told that there was never a court of appeals there.

[134] Miller, 8.

[135] Alderman, 13, said that the first two years of high school were also available there.

[136] McNabb, who had attended the public school in the hotel in his youth.

The complainants in the final lawsuit certainly considered that the General Conference had acted wrongly. They insisted that the Conference had recovered all its costs and had profited by as much as $11,000.[137] They based this—apparently overlooking the costs of operation between 1902 and 1916—on the fact that enough property had been sold to repay the original purchase price of $18,500 and the Conference had received in addition some $8,000 in donations for the project and expected to realize $3,000 from the sale. Furthermore, they said,

> The Conference has done virtually nothing towards maintaining the school, and yet it says it has not been a success. If it had taken the money which it now has, and which rightfully belongs to this school, and made an honest effort to conduct the character of school that was contemplated, then there would have been a much more successful venture than the school has thus far proven.[138]

Although the defendants would reply that the Conference itself had never intended to conduct a school themselves, there seems a measure of truth in the complainants' charges. Had there been better planning, better assessment of the situation, and a more direct hand in management, there might well have been a successful and lasting Free Will Baptist school in Unicoi. One cannot help but feel some sympathy for those who gave money and time toward establishing a school. As the litigants would say, if General Conference were allowed to sell the school and abandon the project, "It is quite clear that the mountain whites of the Appalachian section will never receive any benefit" from the funds donated for that purpose.[139]

What can we say about G. W. Lawrence and those, like E. W. Akard, who aligned themselves with him? There is simply not enough information available to provide an answer. We do not know the most important thing: namely, what drove Lawrence and Lucas apart. Perhaps he sincerely wanted to establish a good school and came to realize that Lucas was not going to do so and for selfish reasons. In that case, we can understand his campaign against him. If we

---

[137] Complainants' Brief, 11-12.
[138] Complainants' Brief, 12.
[139] Complainants' Brief, 23.

suppose that E. W. Akard, who bought a part of the land and moved his family there and expected a good school for his children, found that Lucas was not going to provide such a school, we can readily understand his disappointment and determination to overthrow Lucas.

But it is equally plausible that Lawrence and Akard and others were driven by selfish ambition and wanted to oust Lucas from his position as manager and take the property and the school for themselves. We all know that there have been such villains in the history of church-sponsored projects. At this date, Lawrence suffers from not having left any record of his actions and motives. There is not enough evidence to decide for or against him.

So, then, what can we say, in conclusion, about J. W. Lucas, with whom the idea of the school originated? Again, it is not possible, now, to answer this with confidence. As with Lawrence, there are two possibilities. It is possible that Lucas was at fault, that—as he was accused by Lawrence and his associates—he was motivated by selfish ambition and the failure of the school was a result.

To be sure, some blamed him, both at the time and later. Ulis Miller, in the 1990s, recorded some of their words and agreed with them. I have already included, above, the 1908 resolutions of the Jack's Creek Association and the United Association of Mountain Free Will Baptists. Miller reported that by 1907 and 1908 the Jack's Creek Free Will Baptists "began to lose faith in Mr. Lucas and his ability or willingness to establish a school. Mr. Lucas confessed to the Jack's Creek Free Baptist [sic] that he had done them an injustice by buying a part of the land." Miller went on to say that he had interviewed an elderly man who had attended the school and who said that Lucas "did very little to make a success of the school," being "more interested in buying the property than in establishing a school. He also allegedly gave false and discouraging reports to the General Conference."[140] While it seems precarious to put much stock in the memory of an elderly man in the 1990s who attended the school as a boy more than seventy years before, it remains possible that the failure was primarily that of J. W. Lucas.

---

[140] Miller, 6, 8.

But it is at least equally possible that he was not deserving of the blame. Certainly Lucas did not blame himself. Not long before his death he published a small, eleven page tract entitled *Unicoi: Some Inside History*. One of the things he said, about his purchase of the 150 acres, contradicts Miller's report: he said it "was the best that could be done under the circumstances," and he "owe[d] no man an apology for it."[141]

Among other things he said, "All I received from our mountain people went into the expense account and was fully accounted for in my itemized report of receipts and expenditures. This explains my oft repeated assertion that not a dollar received by me from our mountain people ever went into the Unicoi property."[142]

The greatest problem, he said, developed when those he had brought to Unicoi—referring to the Lawrences, primarily—purposed to poison minds against him and drive him out and take over for themselves. They had mounted a campaign to convince the people of the area that he had robbed them of their land. They had sent resolutions condemning him to the various associations and formed a broader association, with Lawrence as its clerk, to further their purposes—referring to the United Association of Mountain Free Will Baptists.[143]

His final paragraph bears quoting:

> It is very painful to me at this late date to be forced to make this defense. I fail to see how war on me will help build a school, or why anyone would try to build a school or church on bitter personal feeling. It has not been my purpose in this statement to wrong or misrepresent any one. I have tried to keep out of it any unkind feeling engendered by twelve years of unmerited and unrelenting persecution. But I am not willing to spend my declining days under a cloud, and go to the grave misunderstood, just to satisfy the spleen of one bitter character who after all can get out of it only very doubtful satisfaction.[144]

Those who knew Lucas best at the time, his fellow-ministers in the Union Association, apparently did not hold Lucas responsible.[145] After being identified with the new Unicoi Association for a couple of years, Lucas returned to the fellowship of the Union Association in 1908. According to the Union minutes for the annual meeting in September of that year, when the ministers' reports were given, his was deferred. There had been a called session in April because of some charges against him and a committee had been chosen to investigate further. When that committee reported, then, the minutes report, "On motion Bro. Lucas is exonerated and released from all censure. Report of Rev. J. W. Lucas received and character passed." No details are given. We can only guess that the charges came from Lawrence or his associates and related to his management of the school and the property.

From that point on he was active in the Union. From 1909 to 1912, he was President of the Union's Ministers' Conference and Moderator of the Association three of those years. In 1913, the problems surfaced again. After he was among those whose ministers' reports were received and their character passed, a motion was carried to rescind the action as it applied to him and refer the matter to a committee. Subsequently, however, the following was adopted: "On motion after a thorough investigation we find the charges against Rev. J. W. Lucas are frivolous, malicious, and unsustained; therefore he is exonerated from all former charges and this is never to be mentioned again as it is final." As before, one can only guess that Lawrence and his friends had made another effort to discredit him and had failed. Lucas would continue to be active in the Union. He was President of the Ministers' Conference again in 1915 and served on various committees and boards. He continued as pastor of the Unicoi church.

The 1916 minutes of the Union Association include his obituary, which shows further that his associates there did not hold him responsible for the failure of the school at Unicoi:

IN MEMORIAM.

Resolved, That we bow in humble submission to the will of the master in taking from our midst our beloved leader and wise counsellor, Rev. J. W. Lucas, who departed this life June 23rd, at Lincoln Memorial Hospital in Knoxville. ... He was a devoted Christian and suffered many unmerited persecutions which he took good naturedly, and yet amidst all this his wonderful brain power made him a great factor in every community in which he resided. ... He established schools at Parrottsville, Midway and Unicoi for the express purpose of educating our poor Free Baptist children and ministers under adverse and trying circumstances ..., but by no fault of his own he failed. His example before his people and his followers will be missed, but he has gone to receive the reward of the final faithful where there is no sorrow, no pain, no persecutions, no death.

T. H. Woolsey, J. L. Cagle, Wm. Stroup, Committee.

Such was the judgment of his peers, and a hundred years later we should probably leave it there.

The most important cause for the failure, as recognized both by the officers of the General Conference in the North and the judge on the scene, was the bitter division that developed between G. W. Lawrence and J. W. Lucas. There is simply not enough evidence, now, to determine their motives. Each accused the other of selfish ambition. The lesson is the very one that Judge Haynes assessed: a house divided against itself cannot stand. Perhaps both the men were wrong, in one way or another. Perhaps Lucas was out to enrich himself by obtaining the property. Perhaps Lawrence wanted to get some of the property cheaply and be the head of the school. Regardless, the animosity cursed the enterprise, even if it had been otherwise feasible.

In 1979, Talmadge McNabb wrote an earlier article for the Erwin newspaper entitled "Memories of Unicoi." In it he revealed that during its early history the old hotel that became the school gained the reputation as haunted. On his visit back to the site, where he had attended after it became a public elementary school, he was parked there one evening, indulging his memories, when he was sure he saw someone walking there in the moonlight and the misty haze, and he wondered to himself: "Was it the ghost of the Rev. J. W. Lucas, stalking the grounds, bemoaning the fate of his church school, and being blamed for its collapse?"[146]

We don't believe in ghosts, of course (and neither did McNabb), but if there are regrets in Heaven I suspect that Lucas and Lawrence have theirs. No doubt they understand the distressing history of the school at Unicoi much better now.

---

[146] *The Erwin* (Tennessee) *Record*, Jan. 17, 1979, 4-5 (RLV).

7

The Christian Workers Institutes, 1941-52

Forerunning the founding of Free Will Baptist Bible College was an enterprise not many remember or know much about. It was known collectively as the Christian Workers Institutes,[1] and it was apparently the brainchild of L. R. Ennis (pictured nearby) during his tenure as the first Executive Secretary of the National Association of Free Will Baptists (hereafter NAFWB).

Lonnie Reden Ennis was born in Harnett County, North Carolina, in 1895, the son of a Free Will Baptist minister. He attended the old Ayden Free Will Baptist Seminary and Moody Bible Institute, where he graduated in 1922. He would also graduate from Atlantic Christian College in 1947. Most of his ministry was as pastor of Free Will Baptist churches in his home state, but for a period of nine years he was a Southern Baptist pastor, returning to Free Will Baptists in 1940. He also taught and headed the work at Eureka College, was the first Executive Secretary of the NAFWB (1940-43), and served as president of Free Will Baptist Bible

---

[1] Often the middle word was *Workers'* or *Worker's*, but I have chosen to drop the apostrophe except when quoting another source that used it.

College (1944-47). The academic building at FWBBC (the original location) was named for him in 1967. He died August 17, 1977, and was buried in the Willow Dale Cemetery in Goldsboro, NC, where he and his wife of 54 years, Annie Lancaster Ennis, had maintained a home since about 1940.

L. C. Johnson, President of Free Will Baptist Bible College, in a series of articles in *Contact* magazine entitled "Over My Shoulder," discussed the early educational activities of the denomination. He wrote:

> Brother L. R. Ennis led in a movement to establish portable Bible institutes. These were conducted across our denomination and capitalized on the spirit of hopefulness brought about by the organization of the National Association in 1935. These institutes ... created a spirit of enthusiasm that would eventually lead to a formalized educational program.[2]

My purpose, here, is to tell the story of this work, which was from beginning to end linked with the executive office of the denomination, even though at first it was under the oversight of the Educational Board.

The Beginning of the Institutes

The 1940 minutes of the National Association of Free Will Baptists, meeting with the Paintsville Free Will Baptist Church in Kentucky, record that the Educational Board recommended "that the General Board of the National Association ... be advised to employ a national secretary whose duty it shall be to labor cooperatively with the Educational Board as well as with all other standing Boards."[3] This was immediately done, as the report of the General Board the next year (1941) shows:

> Upon the adjournment of the last session of the National Association the General Board, created in said session, convened in called session for the purpose of organizing for its duties and functions. After the election of the required officers of the Board, the Executive Committee was directed to secure and employ an Executive Secretary for the National Association. Due consideration having been given this duty by the Executive Committee, Rev. L. R. Ennis of Goldsboro, N. C. was employed at a salary of $50.00 per week,

---

[2] Johnson, L. C., "Over My Shoulder, Part II: Road to the Beginning," *Contact*, February 1979, 31.
[3] NAFWB minutes, 1940, 17. The Educational Board, at the time, consisted of J. R. Davidson, chairman, J. R. Bennett, Geo. D. Dunbar, Melvin Bingham, and Winford Davis.

it being understood that all compensation received from evangelistic meetings held, and pastorates served by the Executive Secretary should be credited on this salary. For the information of the Association, the Board wishes to state that from the funds made available by the Board of Education for the expenses of the Executive Secretary, there has been a total salary paid to date to him of $1,056.00, the remainder of his salary having been paid from the funds received for evangelistic and pastoral services.[4]

This makes clear that the original motivation and funding for the office of Executive Secretary came from the Educational Board and reflected their concerns for education. It is not surprising, then, that the General Board, apparently at Ennis's suggestion, immediately recommended, also in 1941, "That the Board of Education of the National Association be and is hereby requested to promote, plan, and direct, as may be found practical, Christian Workers' Institutes throughout the states of the National Association for the ensuing year."[5]

In this way, the work of the Christian Workers Institutes began. Indeed, in a sense, it was already under way. The report of the Educational Board, the same year, said that the Board, "in co-operation with our National Executive Secretary," had been conducting "training institutions and pastor's institutes in the various sections of our denomination" and desired "to promote and encourage and aid the establishing of these institutes in every state and section of the National Work." They added, "It is the opinion of this Board that possibly the Pastor's Institute is a logical beginning."[6]

Furthermore, they were eager to get the new program up and running. They provided for funding: "Be it Resolved, That the Education Board set apart $1000.00 for institute work." They also committed to an Institute in Georgia: "In view of the fact that the tri-state F. W. B. people of Georgia, Florida and Alabama have shown much interest in Christian Education that this Board approve the conducting of an institute in Jakin, Georgia."[7]

In fact, the first Institute had *already* been announced in the April 1941 issue of *The Free Will Baptist Gem* (hereafter *Gem*). Ennis had visited in Missouri for

---

[4] NAFWB minutes, 1941, 21.
[5] NAFWB minutes, 1941, 21.
[6] NAFWB minutes, 1941, 24.
[7] NAFWB minutes, 1941, 24-25.

two weeks during March and made plans for an Institute there. The *Gem* article was headed "Christian Institute" and began, "How would you like to attend a Christian Training Institute for two weeks, in the summer, in a good location, where the total expense for tuition and board would be only ten dollars or less?"

The announcement continued:

> Wouldn't you like to attend such an institute with such happy environment, which had a faculty of three of the most idealistic qualifications, including deep and sincere consecration to Christ, highly intelligent, with very lovable personalities so that each student would unhesitatingly drink deeply at the fountain of Instruction and Inspiration?
>
> If so, prepare yourself to come to Monett July 20th to August 1st. ...
>
> To give you an idea of the details of the plan of the Institute, we are arranging for the student body to take its meals together. School will begin at eight o'clock a.m. and remain in class sessions until twelve thirty p.m. ... The afternoon to be spent in directed recreation and fellowship. ... Early in the evening, say five thirty, we will meet for prayer and devotional meetings, closing the day with an evangelistic service, with the public attending.
>
> The major subject of this Institute will be soul-winning and, to be frank, we want *only those* to attend who have a burning passion to win lost souls.[8]

The June 1941 issue of the *Gem* gave further promotion to the upcoming Institute, devoting two whole pages to it.[9] The visiting faculty were to be Ennis (Goldsboro, NC), J. R. Davidson (Bryan, TX), Laura B. Barnard (Glennville, GA, home from India), and Agnes Frazier (Nashville, TN). The daily class schedule, July 21 to August 1, would be:

7:00 a.m., breakfast; morning devotions by Winford Davis

8:00 a.m., doctrine by Ennis: first week, salvation; second week, the Holy Spirit

9:00 a.m., by Davidson: first week, evangelism; second week, FWB League

10:00 a.m., missions by Barnard

11:00 a.m., Womans Auxiliary by Frazier

12:00 noon, by Ennis: first week, Sunday school administration; second week, homiletics

---

[8] *FWB Gem*, April 1941, 3. At this time the name of the program had not been settled.
[9] *FWB Gem*, June 1941, 12-13.

6:30 p.m., evening meal, followed by a time of prayer and praise led by Rollins

8:30 p.m., a sermon by someone to be selected.

Expenses for the Institute were $1 for registration and $7.50 for room and board, to be paid by July 21. The article requested that churches send offerings, which would be used to further reduce these costs to the students. The Institute was not just for Missouri students but for others across the denomination, especially the surrounding states of "Oklahoma, Arkansas, Texas, Kansas, Ohio, Illinois, Tennessee, etc."

Among other things, editor Rollins said, "Already, requests come pouring in for application blanks, which are being prepared and mailed out as quickly as the printers can release them. The fire is kindled, and we have great occasion to praise God." He characterized the faculty as "consecrated Christians" and anticipated that the students would likewise be consecrated ministers and Christian workers, warning that those who had "subversive motives, desiring a gay time as the worldly look for" should not come.[10]

Rollins's subsequent report about the Institute in the August issue was enthusiastic.[11] There were students from Missouri, Kansas, Arkansas, and Illinois, "and all of them speak with one voice in praise for the benefits derived." He called it "highly successful" and said that all involved were "elated" over this first Institute. Mentioning the examinations given at the end, he said that the students were "above average, intellectually."

The plan, he said, was that each student making passing grades would receive a certificate for the session, and that four such certificates would lead to a diploma. Furthermore, "the credits received in Institute work will be recognized in the Bible College the National Association shall establish." He emphasized the additional benefit of the fellowship experienced.

Rollins listed the thirty-four students enrolled, and in light of the fact that this was the very first of the Institutes,[12] I include their names. Twenty were

---

[10] At that time, of course, "gay" did not mean homosexual.
[11] *FWB Gem*, August 1941, 3. There were also brief references to this session in articles by J. R. Davidson and Ennis in *The Free Will Baptist*, October 15, 1941, 8, and October 22, 1941, 6.
[12] There had been at least one "Pastor's Institute" in Texas, conducted by Ennis, before this.

ordained ministers: O. T. Allred, B. F. Brown, Cecil Campbell, Winford Davis, Alice Dickey, Eunice Edwards,[13] Floy Hartley, Opal Hiltibidal, Harold Hoover, Lloyd Jeffreys, Paul Ketteman, Frank Linton, Mrs. Lowell Martin, Junetia Moore, Marie Thomas, Claude Timmons, Margaret Timmons, Kenneth Turner, W. K. Weston, and Melba White. The other fourteen were Jewell Campbell, Oleta Davis, Vera Dawdy, Evelyn Gates, Mammie Gates, Dorothy Lovell, Opal McClerren, Betty Lou Miller, Dr. Poole, Alta Powell, Betty Terry, Mrs. Kenneth Turner, Frances Weston, and Lonnie Weston.

A photograph taken during this first Institute in Monett, Missouri, appeared on the front page of the *Gem* for September 1941. It is not of sufficient quality to include here. But the photograph nearby shows the teachers, apparently in front of the home where they were staying while in Monett: L to R: Davidson, Ennis, Barnard, and Frazier.[14]

The Structure and Program of the Institutes

The pattern established at Monett proved to be fairly typical. The denominational publications often described the structure.[15]

Each session lasted about two weeks, beginning on a Monday, with classes for ten days or so. Most of the time there were five or six hours of classes each day and evangelistic or revival services in the evenings. Sometimes the classes were completed before a late lunch, as at Monett, and sometimes they extended into the afternoons. Later, the classes were in the evenings.

---

[14] The photograph was donated to the FWB Historical Collection by Helen Ketteman Smith, widow of Paul Ketteman, a student at the session where these four taught.

For the most part, the curriculum was similar throughout the history of the Institutes, with courses in Bible Doctrine, Biblical Survey, Evangelism, Public Speaking, Missions, Free Will Baptist Organization, Free Will Baptist League, Woman's Auxiliary, and Sunday School Administration. Later, at times, a course in Stewardship or Hymnology or Rural Church might be added.

The idea was to offer different content in four different two-week sessions. Thus, for example, the doctrine segments would vary from one session to another. A student completing a single two-week session successfully, which required attending two-thirds of the classes and passing a final examination, received a certificate. On completion of four different sessions, a diploma was awarded. The intention was to provide subsequent sessions in the same general area to make it possible for a student to do this, but a given student might have to travel to sessions in different places to complete sessions one, two, three, and four—as they were identified—and thus earn the diploma. They could be taken in any order and at the student's convenience.

Teachers were not always the same but usually included the Executive Secretary. Each teacher was paid an honorarium and travel expenses. At first, the honorarium was $25, but it was increased over time. Students were charged a small fee for registration: at first, $1.00, later $2.00. They were usually served meals together, and they paid a few dollars for that but were not charged for lodging in the homes of the members of the host church—or some of them might bed down in the host church's facilities.

Since the annual report of the Executive Secretary came during the summer session of the NAFWB, I will report each year's Institutes in those terms throughout this chapter. In that way, the Institutes for 1941-42, for example, are those that were conducted between the national conventions of 1941 and 1942. For each session listed, I will not repeat what has been said here but will note any significant items that are different for particular sessions. We have photographs of some of the sessions, and I will include those.

The First Year

During the very first year of operation, 1941-42, the Christian Workers Institutes enjoyed success. More sessions were scheduled and were announced and reported in one or both of the denominational publications, with Ennis quoted as saying that the program was "fraught with unlimited possibilities."[16] Additional potential faculty included Chester Pelt of Florida, L. C. Johnson of Georgia, Henry Melvin of North Carolina, and Mrs. John L. Welch of Tennessee.

Ennis's enthusiasm showed in his 1942 report to the National Association as Executive Secretary:

> Immediately following the 1941 session of the Association a new institution was inaugurated for the advancement of our great cause—The Christian Workers' Institute. For many years Free Will Baptists have realized the need of a medium of fellowship, education, and inspiration that would go beyond the possibilities of our great associational meetings. It is an accepted fact among those who have attended the Christian Workers' Institute that it is the answer to this need. During the year 4 sessions have been conducted at strategic points; namely, Monett, Missouri; Erwin, Tennessee; Flat River, Missouri; and Tulsa, Oklahoma. There have been 163 students from 9 states enrolled in these sessions, and 91 certificates awarded. Gifts from the faculty, students, and visitors of the Institute to our National work amounted to $576.18 for the year, and the salaries and expenses paid by the National Board of Education totaled $783.15. ... Undoubtedly the Christian Workers' Institute is one of the greatest unifying agencies among us. We need it. Let us keep it running.[17]

According to this report, four Institutes were completed during 1941-42. They were as follows:

- *Monett, Missouri, July 21-August 1, 1941* (First FWB Church). See information above.
- *Erwin, Tennessee, January 5-16, 1942* (Martin Chapel FWB Church). Teachers: Ennis, Barnard, Davidson, Pelt, and Fannie Polston (of Tennessee). Cost: $3 total, $1 registration and $2 room and board for the entire two weeks. Target audience: "the people of Tennessee, Western North Carolina, Virginia, West Virginia, Ohio, and Kentucky" (later sessions promised at strategic places within that broad territory). Thirty-one students registered; classes took three hours in the morning, two in the afternoon, and

---

[16] *FWB Gem*, December 1941, 5; January, 1942, 3-4; *The Free Will Baptist*, December 3, 1941, 6-7.
[17] NAFWB minutes, 1942, 21.

two in the evening. Enthusiastic student testimonials included "This work is destined to revolutionize the Free Will Baptist denomination."[18] Mrs. Eleanor Grindstaff would report later that the winter was officially called "Nineteen Hundred and Froze-to-Death"; that in the evenings Pelt would soak his feet in a basin of water in the living room where he stayed, that Ennis and Davidson slept in their socks where they stayed, and that Paul Woolsey (one of the students) sat in classes with his shoes off and his feet on the radiator.[19]

- *Flat River, Missouri, February 16-27, 1942.* Teachers: Ennis, Barnard, Polston, and Mrs. Pelt; the students showered the women with gifts at the end. Classes daily: three in the mornings, two in the afternoons, and two in the evenings. Forty students, the highest number yet. On Sunday, Flat River pastor Damon Dodd and his wife Sylvia had announced their commitment to go to the mission field in India and to pursue preparation in the Bible school that the Educational Board planned to begin. Ennis's report concluded: "God has manifested His approval in the work done in the Christian Workers' Institutes in some very special way in each of the sessions which has been held up to this time. ... A portable Bible school it is. Oh! How greatly it is needed."[20] (A set of questions for study, in preparation for the final examination, used in Flat River has been preserved and is reproduced in the Appendix to this chapter. Also, two photographs taken during this Institute are shown below.)

- *Tulsa, Oklahoma, June 1-11, 1942.* Teachers not named, but included Ennis, L. C. Johnson,[21] and apparently (from the photograph) Agnes Frazier and Laura B. Barnard. Sixty-nine students representing eight states; thirty-three earned certificates.[22] (The July issue of the *Gem* carried a picture of the Institute students and teachers on the front cover, reproduced below.

---

[18] *The Free Will Baptist*, December 24, 1941, 8-9; December 31, 1941, 8; January 21, 1942, 5-6.
[19] Letter from Eleanor Grindstaff to Miss Barnard, undated (c. Feb/Mar 1969), 1.
[20] *FWB Gem*, February 1942, 3-6; April 1942, 3-4; *The Free Will Baptist*, February 4, 1942, 6; March 11, 1942, 8. The Dodds would ultimately go to Cuba instead of India.
[21] Johnson, L. C., "Over My Shoulder, Part II: Road to the Beginning," *Contact*, February 1979, 31.
[22] *FWB Gem*, April 1942, 20; May 1942, 3-5, 9-11; July 1942, 3; *The Free Will Baptist*, July 1, 1942, 8.

The final examination administered at the end of this session appears in the Appendix to this chapter.)

During each of the last three of these sessions, the faculty, students, and others involved contributed $100 to fund one of the "Foundation Checks" for the Bible school that would begin in September of 1942. Here is a picture of the cancelled check from the Erwin, Tennessee, session. Each of the three has been preserved in a "book of memorials" that records the gifts made during that early period.[23]

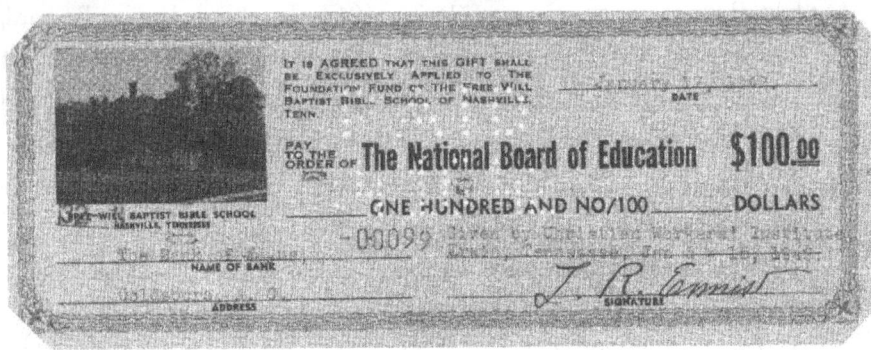

Judging from the personnel shown, this photograph was taken during the same Institute at Erwin, Tennessee, in January of 1942. Left to right are Ennis, Barnard, Polston, Davidson, and the two Pelts.

The two photographs that follow were taken during the Institute at Flat River, Missouri, in February of 1942. The first, of the smaller group, apparently represents the teachers and those officially enrolled, while the second, with the larger group, includes others in attendance. In the first photograph, Ennis can be seen,

Bible tucked in his left arm, immediately to the left of the church sign. Kneeling under the sign are C. J. Ketteman of Illinois, between (and behind) Alvin and Albert Halbrook. Standing in front to the right of the Halbrooks is Mrs.

242

Polston. On the right of the sign, in the back, are Damon and Sylvia Dodd (Dodd was pastor of the church) on either side of George Waggoner, also of Illinois.

The same people can be found in the second photograph.

The following photograph is from a scan of the cover of the *Gem*, showing the Institute in Tulsa, Oklahoma, in June of 1942. Ennis is at far left in coat and tie, Davidson to the right of the sign, Miss Barnard at far right with Bible tucked in her arm, and Mrs. Frazier on the front to the left of the sign and pastor Melvin Bingham. Johnson and Eunice Edwards are behind Mrs. Frazier, and Paul Ketteman (student) is on the back row, second from the right.

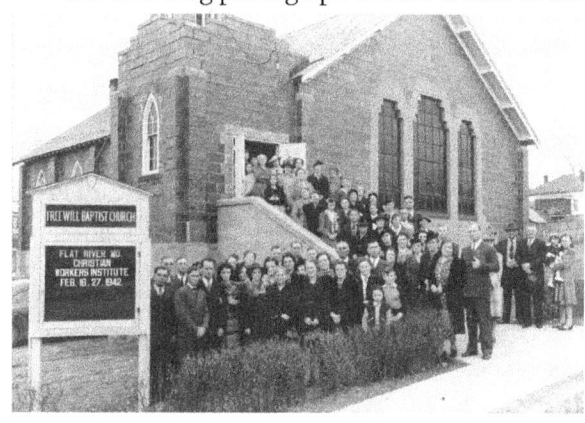

Transferring the Institutes to the Executive Secretary

After these successful Institutes, the 1942 report of the Educational Board to the NAFWB in Columbus, Mississippi, July 12-17, was understandably positive.

> There have been four Institutes conducted of two weeks duration each since the last session of the National Association. ... Quite a few are ... waiting for the opportunity to enlist for the completion of the fourth course and receive a normal diploma; which privilege shall be theirs immediately upon the close of this session.[24] ... One thousand dollars ($1,000.00) was appropriated a year ago for this cause, of which amount we have used $782.15. ... The greatest accomplishment educationally among our people for a period of many years has been realized. ... We have realized maximum results with minimum expenditures. The revival spirit which has prevailed in each session has served to stimulate support to our cause in general, and the vision of our people has been wonderfully broadened.[25]

Even so, it was the opinion of those involved that the responsibility for this particular ministry should be transferred from the Educational Board to the Executive Secretary. The report of the General Board included the following.

> Whereas, The Board of Education ... has made generous appropriations for the past two years toward the advancement of the entire work of the Association, and that recurrences of such temporary measures are no longer expedient or feasible—now that the Board of Education must look toward the opening of the Bible School, Therefore be it Resolved: 1. That the General Board of the National Association, in annual session this the 14th day of July, 1942, does hereby recommend that The Christian Workers' Institute be transferred from the Department of Christian Education to the Executive Department, and that it be conducted hereafter by the Executive Secretary as an extension and promotional service of the National Association.[26]

The General Board, together with this, recommended that the Executive Department have its own budget, from which the salary of the Executive Secretary would be paid, as well as "all salaries and expenses incident to the operation of the Christian Workers' Institute." These funds ($3,300 for the first year) would come from the Superannuation Board (10%), the Home Missions Board (20%), the Foreign Missions Board (30%), and the Educational Board (40%).[27]

The main reason for this seems compelling: the Educational Board was scheduled to open Free Will Baptist Bible College in September of 1942, and they would need to expend all their energies in that more demanding endeavor. Ennis, the Executive Secretary—frequently identified as the Dean of the Institutes—could shoulder the responsibility for the Institutes and free the Educational Board for its greater task. Perhaps he desired that role, but we have no way of knowing whether that was the case. For all practical purposes, he had done the work anyway.

The Second Year, 1942-43

As Ennis's sole responsibility, the Institutes continued to flourish. His report to the National Association, in July 1943, reflected optimism.

> Seven sessions of the Christian Workers' Institute have been held in five states of the National Association since our last national meeting. An enrollment of 185, with 135 receiving certificates or diplomas, attended these sessions as registered students. In addition to 420 hours spent in class work, evangelistic services were held, promotional itineraries and rallies conducted, and general meetings attended, collections for the work of the Association as a whole in the amount of $811.18 were received; and the actual cost, in salaries and expenses, of all institute work for the year amounted to $796.60. The Christian Workers' Institute is the most potent promotional factor in existence among Free Will Baptists.[28]

Regrettably, I have been able to identify only six of these seven sessions, as follows.

- *Monett, Missouri, July 20-32, 1942.* Session 4.[29] One new feature: Robert B. Crawford, an Alabama FWB minister and graduate student in the Van-

---

[27] NAFWB minutes, 1942, 17.

[28] NAFWB minutes, 1943, 4-5.

[29] This apparently means that of the four previous sessions two of them had provided the same content; I would guess that the session in Erwin, Tennessee, was a number 1 session like that in Monett, Missouri, in 1941.

derbilt School of Religion in Nashville, would teach a new course entitled "The Rural Church."[30]

- *Parrish, Alabama, August 24–September 4, 1942.* Session 1. Forty-one students (which included a D.V.B.S. taught at the same time). Teachers: Henry Melvin and Laura B. Barnard. Seventeen Institute certificates and one diploma awarded, but only two or three ministers enrolled; many students were high-schoolers. Interestingly, one of the students at this session was George Waggoner, who received his diploma (for completing all four sessions) as a result. He reported later that he was returning to his home in Illinois afterward when he stopped by Nashville to visit at the site of the new Bible school about to be opened there, where he planned to enroll.[31]

- *Rescue FWB Church, Whittington, Illinois, September 28–October 9, 1942.* Teachers: Ennis, Robert Crawford, Davidson, Pelt, and Agnes Frazier. Thirty-two students represented Illinois, Michigan, and North Carolina. The Rev. Elsie Curtis, expected to complete her Normal Diploma in the session, served with Pastor W. R. Burton to make arrangements. New features included evening promotional services in sixteen nearby local churches and a course in hymnology.[32] (Photographs of this Institute are below.)

- *Jakin, Georgia, November 23–December 3, 1942.* Session 1. Apparently the teachers were the two Pelts, with Chester heading the Institute in the absence of Ennis. The host local church made room and board available for $4.00. Mrs. Pelt, in her report of this session, indicated that it presented opportunities for those in Southwest Georgia, Southeast Alabama, and West Florida, but only nine regular students and one minister enrolled, all from Georgia.[33]

- *Highland Park FWB Church, Detroit, Michigan, March 1-11, 1943.* Session 2. Raymond Riggs, pastor. Room and board for $12. J. R. Davidson's report

---

[30] *FWB Gem*, July 1942, 3-6; *The Free Will Baptist*, July 1, 1942, 8.
[31] *FWB Gem*, August, 1942, 23; March 1943, 15; *The Free Will Baptist*, June 3, 1942, 7; July 29, 1942, 10; August 5, 1942, 13; September 23, 1942, 6-7; June 9, 1943, 9.
[32] *FWB Gem*, September, 1942, 3-5; November, 1942, 11-12; *The Free Will Baptist*, August 19, 1942, 6-7; October 28, 1942, 8.
[33] *The Free Will Baptist*, November 11, 1942, 6; December 30, 1942, 6.

of the session indicates that he and Damon Dodd conducted the session without Ennis. Twenty-eight "regular" students, of whom twenty-two received certificates.[34] (A photograph of this session appears below.)

- *Leeds, Alabama, June 7-18, 1943.* Session 2. Teachers: Damon Dodd (Bible Doctrine, History of Missions, Personal Evangelism), Sylvia Dodd (FWB League, Sunday School Administration); she also supervised a D.V.B.S. at the same time. Ten students, from Tennessee, Kentucky, and Alabama, all earning certificates. Estimated cost of board, $1 per day. A revival in the evenings led to the conversion of nineteen "and a great awakening among the church membership." In keeping with World War II circumstances, students were urged to bring their ration stamps, "in order that food may be pooled sufficient for the required meals."[35]

The two photographs following are from the session in Illinois.[36] The first is of the teachers and enrolled students at the Rescue Church. Ennis is in the center in the middle row. On the front, left to right, are Blanche Loftin, Elsie Curtis, Agnes Frazier, Robert Crawford, an unidentified lady, J. R. Davidson, Winona Riggs, and two other unidentified ladies. On the back row are C. J. Ketteman, Raymond Riggs, one unidentified, Howard Lyle, Dan Cronk, and two others unidentified. The second shows the much larger number present on "Rally Day" in Illinois, Sunday, October 4, in the afternoon—which Ennis called "the greatest denominational rally yet held during a session of the Christian Workers' Institute." The three men kneeling at front are (left to right) the Rev. W. R. Spurlock, Ennis, and the Rev. Riley Burton (pastor at Rescue). Standing behind the little boy on the left is D. E. Bain, C. J. Ketteman's father-in-law. George Waggoner stands behind Spurlock.

---

[34] *FWB Gem*, February 1943, 15-17; June 1943, 19-21; *The Free Will Baptist*, January 20, 1943, 8-9; May 12, 1943, 6-7.

[35] *FWB Gem*, March 1943, 15; May 1943, 8-9; *The Free Will Baptist*, February 3, 1943, 13; May 19, 1943, 6-7, 11; July 14, 1943, 9.

[36] Thanks to Jane Ketteman Jackson for donating the two photographs to the FWB Historical Collection and for some of the identifications. The Rev. C. J. Ketteman (also in the Flat River, MO, photographs above) was her father, who—according to Jane—"got up at 5 a.m., built a fire in the cook-stove, milked the cows, slopped the hogs, fed all the animals and chickens, finished his chores and was the first one at Rescue!" Jane, at the age of 10, appears in the photograph of the larger group, standing in front of J. R. Davidson near the center.

The following photograph is from the session in Michigan. Among those standing, from the left, are Pastor Raymond and Winona Riggs (third and fourth), Paul Ketteman (fifth), Damon and Sylvia Dodd (seventh and ninth), and Dan Cronk (twelfth); Mrs. Davidson is with her husband on the right.

1943-44: From L. R. Ennis to Robert Crawford

At the 1943 convention of the NAFWB, there were changes in the office of Executive Secretary that led to a change in personnel. The General Board recommended that the office be made full time and be located in Nashville.[37] Ennis had continued to be a pastor in North Carolina during his tenure. Perhaps he was not willing to give up that pastorate and move to Nashville, but we do not know that. Some published reports of the change say that Ennis resigned because of health problems. At any rate, the General Board recommended someone else for the position: namely, Henry Melvin.

There is a strange failure in the 1943 minutes. They do not show that Henry Melvin was elected; indeed, they do not report the election of *anyone* as Executive Secretary for 1943-44. Instead, the list of officers for 1943-44, in the front of the minutes, names Robert B. Crawford (pictured nearby), as Executive Secretary.[38] Perhaps he was elected and the minutes failed to report it, or perhaps the employment of a new Executive Secretary was assigned to the General Board

---

[38] NAFWB minutes, 1943, [2].

or Executive Committee (without being noted in the minutes) and they employed Crawford after the convention closed. Regardless, the next year's minutes show that Crawford was "re-elected" as Executive Secretary at an annual salary of $2,600 plus traveling expenses.[39]

Robert Barrett Crawford was a native of Alabama, born June 21, 1913. He graduated from the University of Alabama, after which he attended the Vanderbilt Divinity School in Nashville, Tennessee. He was converted at age 12, ordained to preach at age 21, and pastored churches in Alabama, Tennessee, North Carolina, and Florida. In addition to his service as Executive Secretary, succeeding Ennis, he represented Free Will Baptist Bible College for some twenty years later in life. He died August 9, 2001, and is buried near Ashland City, Tennessee.[40]

When Crawford took over as Executive Secretary, supervising the ministry of the Christian Workers Institutes, he issued a tri-fold brochure promoting the Institutes (pictured nearby).[41] It makes clear that Crawford's office was on the campus of the new Bible College on Richland Avenue in Nashville. Interestingly, Crawford was to serve on the faculty of Duke University's Summer Bible Institute in 1944, teaching about the rural church, a course he had also used in some of the Institutes previously.[42]

---

[39] NAFWB minutes, 1944, 18.
[40] Alton E. Loveless, compiler, *A Biographical Record of Free Will Baptist Ministers Burial Places*, vol. II (FWB Publications, 2016), 459-60.
[41] It is not dated, so we cannot be sure how soon he published this after he took office.
[42] *The Free Will Baptist*, May 10, 1944, 5.

In addition to Crawford, the brochure lists a ten-member faculty of the Institutes. They were Crawford, Laura B. Barnard, J. R. Davidson, Agnes Frazier, Henry Melvin, Mary Ann Welch, L. R. Ennis, Eunice Edwards, and two FWB-BC students, Damon and Sylvia Dodd.

The brochure also names and describes nine courses—to be offered in four groups, as before. The nine courses were: Bible Doctrine, Biblical Survey, Evangelism, Public Discourse, Missions, Free Will Baptist Organization, Free Will Baptist League, Woman's Auxiliary, and Sunday School Administration.

The registration fee for enrolling students was still $1.00. Room and board could also be arranged, for those traveling from a distance, at a reasonable cost or perhaps no cost at all.

One section of the brochure, entitled "Commendation," seems worth quoting in its entirety.

> This phase of the National Promotional Program is fraught with unlimited possibilities. It brings an opportunity of competent training for definite Christian service to the people where they are. It is virtually a portable Bible School. Please, local church workers, leaders in general organization, and ministers take advantage of your opportunity. Attend, by all means, those sessions of the Christian Workers' Institute which are held within your reach.

There is a taped interview with Crawford, by Harrold Harrison, recorded in November 1992, providing his recollections of the Institutes.[43] It does not give much information beyond that which is represented in this chapter, but it does add interesting observations about the books used in the classes, at least during part of Crawford's tenure. They included William Evans's books on Bible doctrines and personal evangelism as well as Agnes Frazier's manual for the woman's auxiliaries and Laura Barnard's book on missions, *His Name Among All Nations*.

Crawford's report to the NAFWB in 1944, at the end of his first year in office, showed continuing effectiveness:

---

[43] Robert Crawford, taped interview with Harrold Harrison, November 1992, in the FWB Historical Collection.

Four sessions of the Christian Worker's Institute have been held the past year with a total enrollment of 151 with 80 receiving certificates.[44] Along with the Institute evangelistic services were held, promotional services and rallies conducted and general meetings attended. There were 84 saved and reclaimed during Institutes, some dedicating their lives to the foreign fields. $429.69 was spent for all purposes in the Institutes. $869.00 was collected at the Institutes for all purposes. The Christian Workers Institute is proving to be of greater blessing and worth to our denomination all the time.[45]

The four sessions reported by Crawford were as follows, although for most of them we have no information except a mere listing earlier in the year in denominational publications.[46]

- *Kinston, North Carolina, January 17-28, 1944*, Bruce Barrow pastor. Session 1. Teachers: Crawford and the two Dodds. J. C. Griffin, in his well-known column "Notes and Quotes," included several testimonials from those who attended.[47]
- *Highland Park, Michigan, June 5-16, 1944*. Teachers: Crawford, Davidson, and Agnes Frazier. There is a photograph below that apparently was taken at this session.
- *Cordova, Alabama, June 5-16, 1944*. Teachers: Damon and Sylvia Dodd and Mrs. K. V. Shutes.
- *Camp Sawyer, Georgia, June 18-30, 1944*. Teachers: Crawford and George Waggoner.[48]

One notes that two Institutes were being scheduled at the same time, perhaps a first. It may be that summers had proved the best times for the Institutes.

The following photograph appears to show the 1944 session at Highland Park, Michigan. Robert Crawford is standing front, right; Pastor Raymond and Winona Riggs are in the center of the picture, with J. R. Davidson immediately

---

[44] The four sessions did not include the one in Mississippi *after* this report. I found no reports about any of these except for the January session in Kinston, NC.
[45] NAFWB minutes, 1944, 32.
[46] *FWB Gem*, May 1944, 12-13; *The Free Will Baptist*, April 26, 1944, 8; May 3, 1944, 8.
[47] *The Free Will Baptist*, December 15, 1943, 6; December 29, 1943, 8; January 5, 1944, 3, 8; January 12, 1944, 8; January 26, 1944, 6; February 2, 1944, 6.
[48] There is a passing reference to this session in *The Free Will Baptist*, November 9, 1949, 3.

behind Raymond; N. P. Gates (Mrs. Riggs's father) is on the left in the center. Agnes Frazier is in front in the dark sweater.

1944-45: Crawford's Second Year in Office

Crawford's 1945 report to the National Association was again glowing.

> Five sessions of Christian Workers Institutes have been held during the past year with a total enrollment of one hundred twenty-nine. Ninety-four have received certificates and four have received diplomas. Revivals have been held at night during each session of the Institutes. There have been thirty-eight additions to the Church, twenty-two reclaimed, and twenty-three who dedicated their lives for definite Christian service. Seven hundred and twenty-four dollars and eight cents have been expended for institute work. Five hundred and forty-eight dollars and fifty-seven cents were received for all purposes during Institutes. Figures do not estimate the worth of Christian Workers Institutes.[49]

These five sessions were as follows. Again, several of these are known only from a brief listing earlier in denominational publications.[50]

- *Pearce Chapel, Mississippi, July 17-28, 1944.* Teachers: Crawford and the Dodds.[51]
- *Core Creek FWB Church, Cove City, North Carolina, March 12-23, 1945.* Teachers: Crawford, Marie Thomas Hyatt of Missouri, and L. C. Johnson (now pastor in Mississippi). Registration still $1.00; room and board $6.00 per week or $9.00 for the entire term. J. C. Griffin encouraged all ministers to put this work before their congregations and "urge your young people at least to attend." R. B. Spencer, editor of the *Free Will Baptist*, observed that there were "several ministers who, no doubt, can make it convenient to attend the classes during the entire period of the Institute."[52]
- *Sylacauga, Alabama, May 7-18, 1945.* Teachers: Crawford, E. C. Morris, and Marie Hyatt.[53]
- *Flat River, Missouri, May 21–June 1, 1945.* Teachers: Crawford, Bruce Barrow, and one to be named.[54]
- *Nashville, Tennessee, June 4-15, 1945.*
- *Highland Park, Michigan, June 18-29, 1945.* Teachers: Crawford, E. C. Morris, Rebecca Stewart.[55]

I am conscious that this amounts to six rather than to five as reported by Crawford. In one of the later listings I have cited, the session announced for Nashville does not appear, so I suspect that it did not materialize.

1945-48: Crawford's Final Three Years

The report of the General Board in 1945 recommended that Crawford serve again during the 1945-46 year and at the same salary.[56] According to a listing found in the papers of Miss Laura B. Barnard, the following institutes were held in 1945-46:[57]

---

[51] *FWB Gem*, May 1944, 12-13; *The Free Will Baptist*, April 26, 1944, 8; May 3, 1944, 8; July 12, 1944, 9.
[52] *The Free Will Baptist*, February 7, 1945, 6; February 14, 1945, 6; February 28, 1945, 3.
[53] *The Free Will Baptist*, April 18, 1945, 6; April 25, 1945, 6.
[54] *The Free Will Baptist*, May 16, 1945, 3, made a point of introducing Barrow for this role. The issue for June 20, 1945, 7, included a testimonial that appears to mean that only Crawford and Barrow taught.
[55] Teachers' names from a list found in the papers of Laura B. Barnard. (But there are some inaccuracies in this list.)
[56] NAFWB minutes, 1945, 19.
[57] Miss Barnard had done some work toward recording the story of the Institutes, but I did not find it until after this chapter was completely written. Since there are some inaccuracies in the list referenced here, I

- *Phenix City, Alabama, August 1945.* Teachers: the Dodds and Crawford; 35 students, including some from Columbus, Georgia.
- *Flat River, Missouri, June 1946.*

At this point, the information provided in the minutes of the National Association ceased to be as full as before. Crawford continued to be Executive Secretary in 1946 and 1947, but his reports recorded in the minutes, each year, simply state that he had given detailed accounts of his activities to the General Board. No information about the Christian Workers Institutes appears.[58]

For that matter, unless I missed it, there is no mention of any Christian Workers Institute in the pages of the *Free Will Baptist* or the *Gem* in 1946.[59] The *Free Will Baptist*, at least, continued to provide a section for the ministries of the National Association, but apparently Crawford did not send the editor any announcements or reports of the Institutes. The National Association minutes for 1947 do show that, on the recommendation of the Executive Secretary, the General Board approved paying the teachers in the Institutes a total of $75 plus traveling expenses for one of the two-week sessions.[60]

Indeed, there were Institutes in 1947-48, as follows.
- *First FWB Church of Oklahoma City, March 3-14, 1947.* Session 2. Teachers: John L. Welch (Bible Doctrine, FWB Doctrine, Sermon Preparation); Crawford (Missions, Personal Soul Winning, Sunday School Administration); and Woman's Auxiliary and FWB League taught by someone yet to be named when this was published.[61]
- *Kilsyth, West Virginia, April 21–May 2, 1947.* Teachers: Crawford, Welch, and Mrs. Agnes Frazier.[62]
- *Niangua, Missouri, July 21–August 1, 1947.* Session 2. Teachers: Crawford, LaVerne Miley, and Miss Thora Arbogast; she would conduct a simultaneous D.V.B.S. Twenty-five enrolled, but only nine received certificates

---

cannot be sure of the information given, and I do not know who compiled the list.
[58] NAFWB minutes, 1946, 13; NAFWB minutes, 1947, 13.
[59] The *FWB Gem* was not published between April and December of 1946.
[60] NAFWB minutes, 1947, 12.
[61] *The Free Will Baptist*, January 15, 1947, 5; February 12, 1947, 13; February 26, 1947, 3, 11.
[62] *The Free Will Baptist*, March 12, 1947, 15. The list in Miss Barnard's papers names Mrs. Huey Gower instead of Mrs. Frazier.

(the others attended only one week). (This was in connection with the first annual youth camp there.)[63]

• *Huntington, West Virginia, May 1948.* Teachers: Crawford, J. L. Welch, perhaps Mrs. Gower.[64]

When the NAFWB convened in Pocahontas, Arkansas, in 1948, Crawford was still in office. His report, like those given in 1946 and 1947, included no details about the Christian Workers Institutes, although his report as treasurer of the NAFWB showed that LaVerne Miley had been paid as a teacher for an Institute in Missouri, and that Mrs. Huey Gower and John L. Welch had been paid as teachers for an Institute in West Virginia.[65] Perhaps Mrs. Gower had substituted for Mrs. Frazier, who had been announced.

1949-50: From Robert Crawford to Damon C. Dodd

The 1948 and 1949 minutes of the National Association raise a question that cannot now be resolved. In 1948, the record states that Ralph Lightsey was elected Executive Secretary and the Executive Committee was empowered to arrange a contract with him.[66] But there is no evidence that he served. Since there is no list of general officers for 1948-49 in the front of the 1948 minutes (as there usually was), his name is not there. Nor do the minutes for 1949 mention him or include a report from him. My conclusion is that Lightsey did not finally agree to serve and that the NAFWB was without an Executive Secretary during the year between the 1948 and 1949 sessions.[67] Perhaps he, like L. R. Ennis earlier, was not willing to relocate to Nashville, but that is speculation.

At least one change in the functioning of the Christian Workers Institutes was made at the 1948 session. The report of the General Board, adopting a recommendation from outgoing Executive Secretary Crawford, approved the idea that each Institute would be sponsored by the state where it was to be held, and

---

[63] *FWB Gem*, June 1947, 2; July 1947, 2, 11; August 1947, 15; *The Free Will Baptist*, June 18, 1947, 7. The list in Miss Barnard's papers names Marie Hyatt instead of Thora Arbogast.
[64] This institute appears only in the list in Miss Barnard's papers, and the one who prepared it was not sure that the woman teaching was Mrs. Gower.
[65] NAFWB minutes, 1948, 33-34.
[66] NAFWB minutes, 1948, 14.
[67] J. C. Griffin's report of the election of officers at the NAFWB in the *Free Will Baptist*, August 4, 1948, does not list an Executive Secretary.

that the state would pay the teaching staff.⁶⁸ It seems likely that this change did not work out.

In 1949, then, Damon C. Dodd (pictured nearby) was elected to the office and most certainly agreed to serve and relocate to Nashville. He and his wife Sylvia—both from Missouri—had been among the early students at Free Will Baptist Bible College, had taught in a number of the earlier Institutes, and had gone to Cuba as missionaries in October 1945, subsequently returning to the States in 1948 when he became pastor in Flat River, Missouri, again. Dodd was born February 14, 1916, and converted at the age of 15 under the preaching of the Reverend  Lizzie McAdams. He was ordained in 1936, and married Sylvia Wood in 1938. In addition to his service in this office, he was pastor of churches in Missouri, Tennessee, and Georgia, was Promotional Secretary for the Free Will Baptist Home Missions Department, and wrote numerous books and articles, including *The Free Will Baptist Story* and *Marching Through Georgia*. He died April 27, 2000, and is buried near Bellview, Georgia.⁶⁹

Upon his election, Dodd was asked to make a statement and responded, "I have one great desire: to see Free Will Baptists do what they can do."⁷⁰ At the same 1949 convention, the title of the office was changed from Executive Secretary to Promotional Secretary (often expressed as "Promotional Secretary-Treasurer").⁷¹ Perhaps this was Dodd's suggestion, but that is not certain. The 1949 minutes contain no information about Institutes during the 1948-49 year. Unless I missed it, there is no reference to Institutes in the *Free Will Baptist* for 1948 or 1949.

---

⁶⁹ Alton E. Loveless, compiler, *A Biographical Record of Free Will Baptist Ministers Burial Places*, vol. I (FWB Publications, 2016), 181-82.

The Christian Workers Institutes had all but died when Dodd took office in July 1949. For the year prior to that there had apparently been no Executive Secretary, and it seems likely that there had been few Institutes during Crawford's last couple of years in office. What seems clear is that Dodd set about to revive the program.

The 1950 minutes of the NAFWB indicate that Dodd's first report as Promotional Secretary was given and was intended to appear in the report section of the minutes.[72] For whatever reason, it was not included. One does learn, however, that a new course on stewardship had been prepared and was to be included in the curriculum of the Institutes.[73] And Dodd's report as treasurer included a disbursement for an Institute in West Virginia.[74]

Indeed, this session took place in 1950 prior to the July convention, as follows.

- *MacArthur, West Virginia, March 20(?)-29, 1950.* This was said to be "the first of the revived sessions of the Christian Worker's Institute Sessions." Teachers: Dodd, John L. Welch, and Ruby (Mrs. Harold) Dunlap. More than forty students enrolled, twenty receiving certificates. Courses: Bible Doctrine, Preaching, Sunday School Administration, Personal Soul-Winning, Stewardship, F. W. B. Doctrine, Woman's Auxiliary, Missions, and F. W. B. League.[75]

Like Crawford, Dodd soon issued a brochure promoting the ministry of the Christian Workers Institutes, a smaller, two-fold piece (pictured nearby).[76] His office, too, was at the college address, and he also represented the Institutes as "a well-rounded training program," "a portable Bible Institute."

He had changed the curriculum, incorporating some of the program of the Evangelical Teacher Training Association (ETTA). There would still be four two-week sessions, and the courses offered in each were stated. The Bible survey was an ETTA course in the fourth session. The doctrine segment was specific

---

[72] NAFWB minutes, 1950, 12.
[73] NAFWB minutes, 1950, 39.
[74] NAFWB minutes, 1950, 40.
[75] *FWB Gem*, June 1950, 11, 15; *The Free Will Baptist*, March 29, 1950, 6; May 10, 1950, 10, 15.
[76] The piece is not dated, so whether he published this before or after the West Virginia Institute is uncertain.

for each of the four sessions: salvation, the Holy Spirit, Christ, and the Church. Each session included Missions and Evangelism. There was a Sunday school segment in each session: administration, pedagogy, child study, and an ETTA course. The first and second sessions included FWB League and Woman's Auxiliary. The first session provided studies in NAFWB Administration and Stewardship. The second and third sessions included courses for ministers: Preparation and Delivery of Sermons and Pastoral Theology. And the third and fourth sessions included courses in Biblical Introduction. Obviously the program had become more ambitious and multiple courses were being offered at the same time in order to appeal to a broader variety of students with differing interests and responsibilities.

THE CHRISTIAN WORKER'S INSTITUTE—WHAT IS IT?

The National Association of Free Will Baptists through its Promotional Department is prepared to offer a well-rounded training program to any locality where as many as 25 people will come together for class instruction. This training course is offered through the Christian Worker's Institute and is so arranged that it can be set up in your church and use the facilities which you use. It is in reality a portable Bible Institute.

Furthermore, the cost had increased from $1.00 to $2.00 for registration for a session ($5.00 for a non-Free Will Baptist student), and anyone taking the Sunday school courses would have to purchase a book for 75¢. The awards structure apparently remained the same, but one could also earn a Teacher's Diploma—apparently from ETTA—by taking the Sunday school courses.

1950-51: Success Under Dodd

Dodd's efforts were apparently successful. His report to the NAFWB in 1951 included this:

1. Training Institutes
    Through the Promotional Department we have carried on an intensive program of training. This has been done through the Christian Workers In-

stitute and the Evangelical Teacher Training Association. Courses designed to present our church doctrines, organizations, National Association Administration, studies in Old and New Testament, Sunday School Management and Teaching, and Child Study have been offered to those who have enrolled. Eleven such sessions have been held with a total enrollment of 400. Of this number, 49 were ministers and 125 were Sunday School teachers and officers. 275 certificates and 7 diplomas have been awarded through the C. W. I. while 190 Sunday School certificates have been earned. Already more than a dozen Institutes have been scheduled for the coming year. Through our plan of $2.00 registration fee and a free will offering at the close of each session, these Christian Workers Institutes have been self-supporting.[77]

In Dodd's report as treasurer, he indicated that $1,100 had been received from the Christian Workers Institutes. There is no corresponding item under disbursements, but one is "honorariums," and this probably included the teachers in the Institutes.[78]

It is not possible to list the eleven Institutes that Dodd reported in July 1951. He probably meant to include the one in West Virginia that had taken place before the July 1950 convention. Here are four others that can be determined from announcements in denominational publications, but very little is known about some of them. It seems clear that the original format of the institutes had changed significantly.

- *Fairmount Park Church, Norfolk, Virginia, January 1-15, 1951.* Fifty-six enrolled, including the pastor, W. A. Hales. A new format: two forty-five minutes classes each evening for the entire two weeks. Courses: League, Sunday School, Auxiliary, Methods of Teaching, and Bible. Dodd urged that "anyone who takes this course and plans to attend a Bible college, may acquire credit toward an E. T. T. A. Certificate."[79]
- *Welcome Home Church, Hector, Arkansas, February 12-23, 1951.* Also in the evenings. Thirty-one students enrolled, thirty receiving certificates; twenty-five earned ETTA certificates. Five ministers were among those receiving awards.[80]

---

[77] NAFWB minutes, 1951, 52-53; *The Free Will Baptist,* July 5, 1951, 13; April 18, 1951, 6.
[78] NAFWB minutes, 1951, 55.
[79] *The Free Will Baptist,* November 29, 1950, 11; January 27, 1951, 11; *FWB Gem,* April 1951, 15.
[80] *FWB Gem,* March 1951, 8; April 1951, 11, 15; May 1951, 3; *The Free Will Baptist,* March 14, 1951, 3.

- *Oklahoma City, March 25–April 6, 1951.* Pastor Reford Wilson assisted in the teaching.[81]
- *East Nashville FWB Church, Tennessee, April, 1951.*[82]

1951-52: From the Promotional Office to the College

In his reports of Institute sessions, Dodd was consistent in mentioning the spirit of revival, with attendant conversions and rededications. It is also obvious that his personal schedule was crowded and demanding. His report as Promotional Secretary-Treasurer in 1952 was not printed in the NAFWB minutes, but a mimeographed copy, distributed at the convention, included the following.

> CHRISTIAN WORKERS' INSTITUTES
>
> We have been most active in the field of training through the Christian Workers' Institutes. Twelve sessions have been conducted in which 450 people have been enrolled. Of these, 280 have received C.W.I. certificates and 212 have qualified for the Sunday School certificates.
>
> The demand from our people for this type of program has become so great that it is impossible for the Promotional Department with its limited staff to meet it. Arrangements are being made for the Bible College to take over this phase of training and include it in an Extension department.

As with the eleven reported in the previous year, it is not possible to list the twelve reported in 1952. Here are the only three that can be identified, as found in denominational publications.

- *Fairmount Part FWB Church, Norfolk, Virginia, August 6-17, 1951.* Teachers: Joe Ange and Leroy Forlines.
- *Fairmount Part FWB Church, Norfolk, Virginia, August 20-31, 1951.* Teachers: Joe Ange and Leroy Forlines. (This represented yet another innovation in the Christian Workers Institutes program, with two sessions back to back.)[83]
- *Fairmount Part FWB Church, Norfolk, Virginia, January, 1952.* Pastor Hales, apparently eager that his workers be able to complete all four prescribed

---

[81] *FWB Gem*, May 1951, 3.
[82] *The Free Will Baptist*, March 7, 1951, 8.
[83] *The Free Will Baptist*, July 4, 1951, 16.

sessions for their diplomas, announced this not long after the dual August sessions.[84]

In accord with the arrangements Dodd had made, as he reported to the NAFWB in 1952, the General Board recommended "that the Christian Workers Institute be turned over to the Bible College."[85] The convention adopted this item and the responsibility for the Institutes returned to the agency that had sponsored them at first.[86]

It may be that Dodd conducted yet one more Institute in June 1953. The report of the "Florida Camp Meeting and Ministers' and Laymen's Institute" said that a Christian Workers' Institute took place during the period ending June 19, led by Dodd and W. B. Hughes. There were classes in Soul Winning, Doctrine, Christian Stewardship, and Sunday School Teaching.[87] But I am not certain that this was regarded as an official session of the Institute program.

Conclusion

The unintended effect of turning the program over to the college was to bring an end to the ministry of the Christian Workers Institutes. I say this was unintended because L. C. Johnson, president of FWBBC at the time, most certainly believed in this ministry and intended to pursue it, although with a somewhat different orientation: namely, as extension schools of the college. Indeed, in 1953 the college added Leroy Forlines to its staff for that very purpose: to teach in these extension schools. The *Free Will Baptist* announced, in its issue for June 5, 1953, that he had been "elected to the faculty of Free Will Baptist Bible College as extension teacher."

Forlines had graduated from the college in 1952 and served the Free Will Baptist Church in Newport News, Virginia, as pastor during 1952-53. He had already taught Institute sessions in nearby Norfolk, as noted above. He relocated to Nashville in August of 1953.

---

[84] *The Free Will Baptist*, December 19, 1951.
[85] NAFWB minutes, 1952, 27.
[86] NAFWB minutes, 1952, 16.
[87] *The Free Will Baptist*, July 15, 1953, 8, 14.

As intended, Forlines did indeed conduct some extension schools, but as a result of some changes in the college personnel, he was soon assigned other duties. Ralph Lightsey and Charles Thigpen, for different reasons, left the college. Forlines was given the responsibility of teaching Personal Evangelism and serving as Dean of Men. Furthermore, he would be expected, having only a bachelor's degree, to attend summer schools and work toward an advanced degree.

Still, he remembers conducting at least four of the extension schools. The first was at Eldridge, Alabama, at the Free Will Baptist Children's Home, November 16-27, 1953. The announcement indicated that it was especially for ministers and workers in the Sunday school, League, and Woman's Auxiliary.[88] The report of the session emphasized that the two subjects taught—Bible Doctrine and The Sunday School and Its Importance as an Auxiliary of the Church—were the same in content and requirements as similar courses in the college curriculum and would lead to an hour of college credit for each course.[89] Eleven students (of twelve enrolled) earned certificates and the credits. FWBBC President L. C. Johnson went down to deliver the commencement address.[90]

Of the extension schools that Forlines remembers, the second one was in Ina, Illinois, January 18-28, 1954, with five certificates awarded. It had been scheduled for the Free Will Baptist church there, but an unplanned revival had broken out and the sessions were held in the public school in Ina.[91] There were at least two others. One was at Wewoka, Oklahoma, during the first two weeks in May, 1954.[92] Another, at Fellowship FWB Church in Flat River, Missouri, where Rolla Smith was pastor, was the largest, with 45 students.[93] Each was at least two weeks in duration and focused primarily on Bible doctrines and Church auxiliaries. Probably all of these were during 1953 and 1954. A college report appearing in April 1955 showed that 101 students had been enrolled in extension schools.[94]

---

[88] *The Free Will Baptist*, October 28, 1953, 6; *FWB Gem*, November 1953, 5
[89] *The Free Will Baptist*, December 16, 1953, 7; *FWB Gem*, January 1954, 16.
[90] *The Free Will Baptist*, January 6, 1954, 6.
[91] *The Free Will Baptist*, March 10, 1954, 6.
[92] *The Free Will Baptist*, March 3, 1954, 6.
[93] *FWB Gem*, February 1955, 7; that this session was reported on this date would suggest that it probably took place near the end of 1954, but I have found no record of the dates.
[94] *The Free Will Baptist*, April 20, 1955, 5.

An extension school was scheduled for the Hazel Creek FWB Church in Northeast Missouri, on behalf of the Northeast Missouri Association, June 6-17, 1955.[95] Yet another was announced for the Colquitt, Georgia, area, sponsored by the Midway FWB Association, for August 20–September 9, 1955.[96] The announcement clarified that college credit would be awarded if the student subsequently decided to attend the college. It is obvious that no list of these extensions schools can be determined. I have not researched the matter past 1955 since the extension schools take me beyond my original purpose.

At any rate, the extension schools soon fell victim to Forlines's continuing education and duties at the college. Perhaps they and the Christian Workers Institutes had served their purpose in whetting the appetite of a denomination for more training. And the new college, now offering a full, four-year program of study,[97] had become the preferred way of obtaining that training.

For that matter, training for the laity was becoming more available by other means. I have already mentioned how those in Missouri began teaching courses during their annual youth encampment, for example. North Carolina established its own Sunday School Convention-Institute for training; the state also began offering institutes of various kinds in the summers at the Cragmont Assembly. Other states, including Michigan, began doing systematic teacher training.[98] And the Sunday School Convention of the National Association began promoting E.T.T.A. courses to train teachers at the local level.

Even so, Ennis, Crawford, and Dodd must be remembered and honored for their vision and hard work in providing the first systematic taste of Christian education offered by the newly-formed National Association of Free Will Baptists.

Appendix[99]

A set of questions given to the students at the Institute in Flat River, Missouri, in February 1942, to use in preparation for the examination at the end of the session.

1. Give age restrictions of a graded Sunday School, and name departments to which each group is assigned.
2. Name and explain the several parts of a Subject sermon.
3. Name the three forms of church music and tell at which service each should be used.
4. Name the officers of the Senior League.
5. Name the five committees of a League and tell which officer is chairman of each.
6. What is the relation of the Woman's Auxiliary to the church?
7. Name the officers which are provided for in the local Auxiliary constitution, and the duties of the chairman of each.
8. Tell how accuracy may be secured in reports of the officers.
9. Give an outline showing the Scriptural presentation of the condition of the "heathen," and our obligation to them.
10. Give the gist of the progress of the gospel from Pentecost to the Fall of Rome.
11. What does history reveal to us in the matter of: (1) God's obligation to the heathen; (2) the heathens' own responsibility; (3) our responsibility?
12. Give a brief outline showing the steps you would normally take in dealing with one who sincerely wants to be saved and is ready to meet the conditions.
13. How would you meet (from Scripture) the following difficulties: (1) I am a murderer; (2) God's Spirit has ceased to speak? Quote from memory 2 Tim. 3:16.
14. Give outline proof of the deity of Christ and one Scripture reference to substantiate each point.

---

[99] Thanks to George Waggoner for donating these documents to the FWB Historical Collection.

15. Explain Ransom, Propitiation, Reconciliation, and Substitution as applied to the death of Christ.
16. Give outline proof of the credibility of the resurrection.

The actual examination used in the Institute at Tulsa, Oklahoma, June 1-11, 1942.

1. Give proof of the personality of the Holy Spirit.
2. Explain the relationship of the Holy Spirit to the Lord Jesus Christ.
3. Give Dr. Scofield's explanation of the work of the Holy Spirit from Pentecost to the conversion of Cornelius.
4. Name and explain the parts of a sermon.
5. What important questions should be answered in the body of the sermon?
6. State the points in the Standard of Efficiency for Free Will Baptist Sunday Schools, which have been discussed in the class sessions.
7. Name the departments of a graded Sunday School, and give age restrictions for each.
8. By what four standards is a great book judged? How does the Bible compare when judged by those standards?
9. Name the dispensations and give the judgments that came during each.
10. Give the motto of the League and where found.
11. Give in your own words the purpose of the F.W.B.L.
12. Give four reasons why every Free Will Baptist church should have a Woman's Auxiliary.
13. Name four uses each Auxiliary member should make of the "Manual" and the "Year Book" in order that she may be a more efficient worker for Jesus' sake.
14. Write the three most important things learned in Auxiliary Course III.
15. Outline in six periods the history of the Christian Church, giving dates and events that mark the beginning and end of each period.

16. What do you think will be the future state of those in heathen lands who die without having heard the gospel? Give Scripture that clearly supports your view.
17. Define the following terms, and show how you would deal with any one of the groups: skeptic, agnostic, infidel, atheist.
18. Give the points discussed in class as suggested steps in dealing with Jewish individuals concerning their salvation.
19. Give any recommendations or criticism which to your mind might enable us to improve upon the Christian Workers' Institute.

Appendix
An Addition and Correction to Chapter Five of the volume, *Little Known Chapters in Free Will Baptist History*

That chapter was entitled "Thomas Peden and the 'National' that Might Have Been, 1892-1910." It dealt with a triennial General Conference led by Peden and intended to be the true replacement for the triennial General Conference of the Randall movement. On pages 295-96, under the heading "Sessions of the New General Conference," I listed an "adjourned session" for October 7, 1896, that met at Cofer's Chapel FWB Church in Nashville, Tennessee. The meeting had been announced in advance in the pages of *The Free Will Baptist* for May 27, 1896.

I can now report that, shortly before this meeting was scheduled to take place, Cofer's Chapel Church rescinded its permission for the session to be held there. The action took place on September 17 and cited "conflicting reports" that needed to be settled. These reports referred to confusing announcements of meetings of the Ohio River Yearly Meeting, on the same date, at two different places and to editorials about the confusion in *The Morning Star*. This action came just three weeks before the meeting was to take place and announcement of the cancellation appeared in the September 23 issue of *The Harvest Gleaner*.

As a result, Peden made last minute arrangements for the session to be held, instead, in Concord, Kentucky, just across the river from southern Ohio. *The Harvest Gleaner* for October 28 printed Peden's report of that meeting. I gather, from the report, that it dealt mostly, if not entirely, with routine events in Ohio. The executive committee was left to arrange for the next regular session in 1898—which, as we know, took place in Ayden, North Carolina.

This correction can be made because of the recent location of the first eight issues of volume III of *The Harvest Gleaner* in the archives at Auburn University in Southeast Alabama. We were able to make scans from the microfilm located there. In each issue, news is on page 4, and the first three pages are of broad interest, apparently provided by some sort of newspaper publication service. Only page 4 was typeset by the editor, J. H. Jenkins, a minister of the Chattahoochee United Free Will Baptist Association. The paper was published in Phoenix, Alabama, just across the Chattahoochee River from Columbus in Georgia, where Jenkins was serving as pastor of three UFWB churches.

It is the lot of historians, as more information is found, to correct themselves or to be corrected by others. Either way, we rejoice when information comes to light.

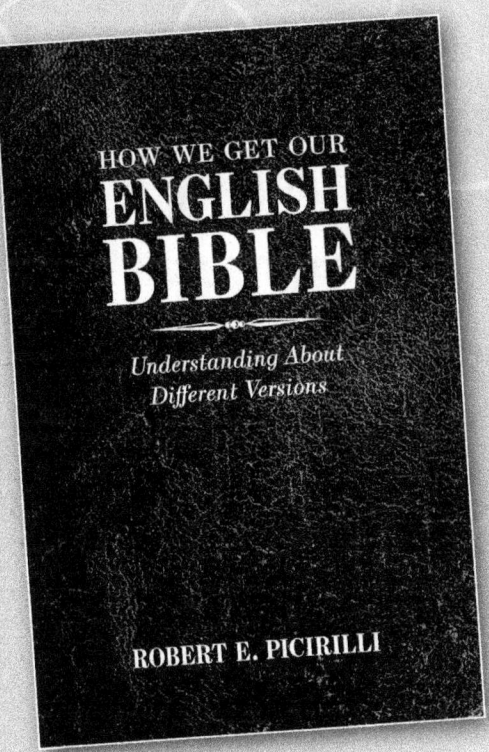

NEW!
from
ROBERT E. PICIRILLI

HOW DO WE GET THE ENGLISH BIBLE INTO OUR HANDS?
Dr. Picirilli provides useful insight to answer that question. This book is full of excellent information as the author explores how early versions of the Scripture were produced. He gives a thorough explanation of how the Word of God in written form has been preserved throughout generations while maintaining its authenticity and reliability.

PRICE: $15.99

AVAILABLE NOW AT
RANDALLHOUSE.COM

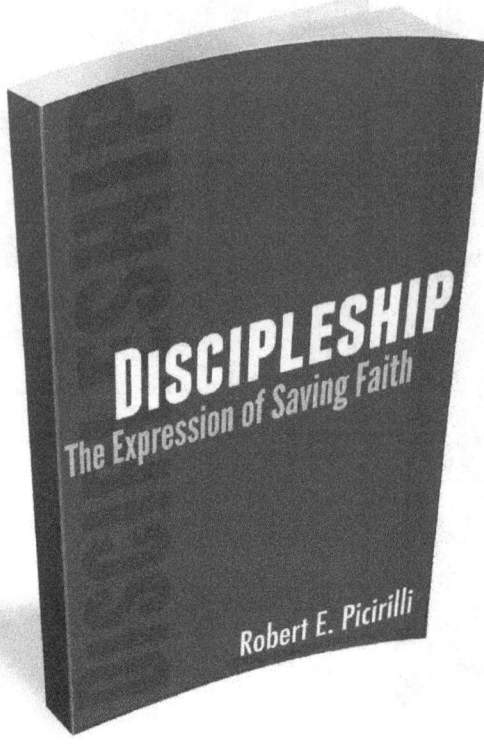

A New Testament study on salvation and what it means to be a disciple.

Discipleship is a great read for those who have grappled with questions like:

What does it mean to be a disciple of Jesus Christ?

Is being a disciple of Jesus the same thing as being a Christian?

What does a life of discipleship look like?

$14.99 • GROUP DISCOUNTS AVAILABLE

ORDER TODAY @ **RANDALLHOUSE.COM**
OR CALL **800.877.7030**

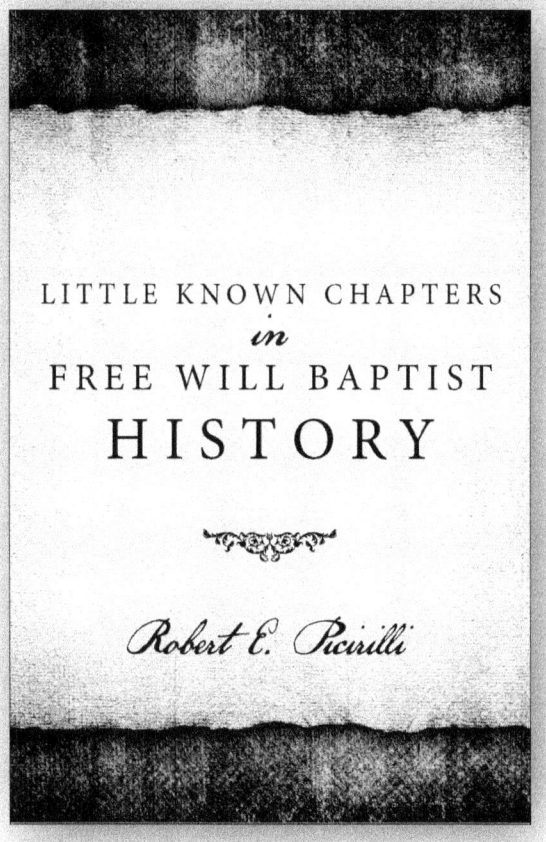

Interesting stories to be discovered and shared.

Little Known Chapters in FWB History
by Dr. Robert Picirilli

---

randall house
Available at randallhouse.com
1-800-877-7030

www.ingramcontent.com/pod-product-compliance
Lightning Source LLC
Chambersburg PA
CBHW050554170426
43201CB00011B/1692